Jacob's Story as Christian Scripture

Jacob's Story as Christian Scripture

Philip H. Kern

CASCADE *Books* · Eugene, Oregon

JACOB'S STORY AS CHRISTIAN SCRIPTURE

Cascade Books
An Imprint of Wipf and Stock Publishers
199 W. 8th Ave., Suite 3
Eugene, OR 97401

www.wipfandstock.com

PAPERBACK ISBN: 978-1-7252-5505-0
HARDCOVER ISBN: 978-1-7252-5506-7
EBOOK ISBN: 978-1-7252-5507-4

Cataloguing-in-Publication data:

Names: Kern, Philip H., author.

Title: Jacob's story as Christian scripture / by Philip H. Kern.

Description: Eugene, OR: Cascade Books, 2021 | Includes bibliographical references and index.

Identifiers: ISBN 978-1-7252-5505-0 (paperback) | ISBN 978-1-7252-5506-7 (hardcover) | ISBN 978-1-7252-5507-4 (ebook)

Subjects: LCSH: Jacob (Biblical patriarch). | Patriarchs (Bible).

Classification: BS573 K47 2021 (print) | BS573 (ebook)

01/04/21

Contents

Preface

GOD INTRODUCES HIMSELF TO his people through the Scriptures. This requires that there be at least a people, a writer, and a God who initiates a relationship. Genesis recounts the forming of a people by presenting from chapter 12 onward the story of those called Israel. They, like all humanity since the beginning, are called to live under God's rule, in his place, and in relationship with him. The Pentateuch presents the birth, development, and ordering of that people as well as the nature of their relationship with God as they experience his deliverance and live under his rule. It also introduces the land God will give them, though that becomes prominent only later.

The Jacob-cycle—a web of treachery and in-fighting, of theft, lies, and murder, of wrestling with friend and foe alike—is a significant part of the story of God's self-disclosure to his people. In it they discover the nature of their God, and also who they are. It teaches that their relationship is with a God who has chosen them not because they, any more than Jacob, are worthy, but because he keeps promises to Abraham and because he graciously exalts the humble and lowers the mighty.

So what is Jacob's story about? Central both literally and thematically is the story of reproduction. Jacob, despite significant obstacles, produces in short order a dozen children and vast flocks and herds. He thus becomes a distinct and powerful clan. This is consistent with Genesis's focus on identifying and establishing the line of promise, a story made complicated by God's selectivity. Divine preference bypasses the eldest, transferring the blessing from Abraham to Isaac (not Ishmael or the sons of Keturah) to Jacob (not Esau) to Judah and Joseph (not Reuben, Simeon, or Levi). This theme of establishing the "seed of Abraham" will inform much of what follows as the story recounts the growth of a people who eventually produce the one who undoes the effects of the curse, the blessed one who gives blessing. And if this is consistent with the purpose that Genesis served in the lives of God's people, then it should not surprise us when material from the Jacob-story informs the shape of messianic expectation in subsequent biblical literature. In this way then, to study the Jacob-story is, on the one hand, to pay close attention to Genesis 25–35, and on the other, to ask how subsequent Scripture uses this material to further develop the hopes of God's people. We will thus visit Micah, Obadiah, Malachi, John, and other texts that bear Jacob's imprint.

* * *

John Woodhouse, as principal of Moore College, invited me to deliver the 2010 Moore College Annual Lectures. Roughly half the material in this volume derives from that effort. When asking me to deliver them he remarked that Moore College's public events are limited in number, so it would be in everyone's interests for them to be accessible.

In the lectures I sought to use a voice appropriate to public speaking and preaching. Though it is at times painful to see it in print, I have nevertheless resisted wholesale changes. I have, however, reduced the Hebrew to a minimum. The NIV is used except where I supply my own translation or refer directly to other versions.

This book is not a commentary. It is my attempt to discover what I need to know about the Jacob story in order to preach it as Christian Scripture. So it is a prelude to that final step of bringing the text to bear on the life of one's hearers. While I might occasionally hint at application, that is more the reflex of one who preaches than an overt commitment.

Genesis 34 warrants separate comment. I overlooked it in the lectures, and have since discovered that virtually all biblical-theological explorations of Genesis and the Pentateuch do the same.[1] Over time, however, I discovered its importance to the themes of Genesis. It recounts horrific events and offers no comic relief, no light moments, or even shades of light and dark. All is black. That chapter took longer than any other, required more and wider reading, and exacted an emotional toll. I am glad to have done it, since it has allowed me to appreciate anew the

---

1. A notable exception is Parry, *Old Testament Story and Christian Ethics*.

blessings of what we might consider a normal family life and the laws and customs, fragile as they may be, of our society.

I am indebted to a host of accomplices. Paul Williamson, with his mastery of the Pentateuch's language and literature, has been not only a great friend but a willing sounding board. Brian Rosner, with whom I shared office space and musings on Scripture for many years, never failed to interrupt when it was most needed. He is missed, though his absence is softened by the knowledge that he is doing important work as principal of Ridley College. Peter Bolt, former head of New Testament at Moore College, always encouraged my research and provided support. Dave Thurston, Nate Kern, and David McDowell read drafts and made helpful comments. Emmaus Bible College in Dubuque, Iowa, was extraordinarily generous during a term in residence, providing me with an office and a place on the championship-winning intramural football team. Regular conversations with Dave MacLeod were the highlight of my time there. Librarians at Emmaus (John Rush) and Moore College (Julie Olsen and her fantastic staff) energetically responded to my interests. Churches that tolerated my experiments with material presented here include West Pennant Hills Community Church, Wauwatosa Bible Chapel, and North-mead Anglican. Thanks to the Freds and Ruth and to our spiritual home at Wauwatosa for many blessings. Without the generosity of the Moore College Council, including but not limited to a sabbatical, this volume would have never been written. It also wouldn't have been possible without the support, energy, and love of my wife, Amy. Finally, many thanks to Robin Parry and the crew at Wipf and Stock. I'm grateful for the way they overcame the unique challenges of 2020, working efficiently to bring this project to completion.

My father, as much as anyone I know, delighted in the stories of Genesis. He, along with my mother, taught them to us from our youth. My parents-by-marriage consistently bear witness to God's grace and have been a constant source of blessing. This book is dedicated to Linda Kern, Mike and Kim Miller, and to the memory of Ray and Ilse Kern.

Introduction

By GENESIS 47 ISAAC is dead. Even Rachel had died more than twenty years previous. Joseph was lost and is found. Jacob, standing where his grandfather had lied to save himself, answers Pharaoh's seemingly mundane queries about age (Gen 47:7–9). "My years have been few and difficult, and they do not equal the years of my fathers," he replies, still defining himself as the afflicted wanderer. And if we agree with Jacob's "difficult years" it is because Scripture presents him as the arch deceiver, the thief who by any means grasps the blessing, unconcerned with collateral damage. And so he was. But Moses paints new layers onto the portrait. Consider that immediately preceding this encounter, Pharaoh promises him and his sons "the best part of the land" (47:6). When they part, Jacob settles again in "the best part of the land" (47:11). He wanders no more.

Furthermore, and at the center of the event, Israel informs Pharaoh that "the years of my pilgrimage are a hundred and thirty" (47:9). One hundred and ten years, for the Egyptian Pharaohs who claimed immortality and were consumed with length of days, proved divine blessing.[1] Jacob, in answering, "A hundred and thirty . . . and they do not equal the years of . . . my fathers," tells Pharaoh, "I've lived long, and have some years left." This day differed from those that went before.

Finally, in the greatest court on earth, he shows none of the deference given, for example, to his brother Esau in Genesis 33. Instead, he gives his blessing (twice) to Pharaoh.

---

1. See, with evidence, McKenzie, "Jacob's Blessing on Pharaoh," 394–95.

xi

This vignette captures the essence of Israel: troublesome but favored by God. He who twice deceived his brother, clutching at blessing, now in the space of four verses twice gives blessing. Jacob is radically altered. But everyone changes over 130 years. We might be better served by focusing not on character development but on how Jacob's story relates to the main themes of Genesis, the Pentateuch, and the Bible as a whole. If the theme of the Pentateuch is the fulfilment of God's three-part promise concerning land, posterity, and a divine/human relationship, we read little in Genesis of the patriarchs acquiring land.[2] That remains to be explored in Numbers and Deuteronomy, and realized in Joshua. Furthermore, while the divine/human relationship is evident throughout Genesis, it remains "somewhat cryptic", with the "outworking variable and provisional."[3] Exodus, and with it, Leviticus, develop this major subtheme. But Genesis, especially Genesis 12–50, deals with posterity. It presents a clan that survives its own fratricidal tendencies and external crises often generated by internal failings.

With this narrowed focus we can ask the central question of Jacob's story: who will obtain the blessing? That is, who will inherit holy promises first spoken to Abraham but never intended as his alone? The first great narrative block, Genesis 12–24, deals with this question as it moves from a barren Sarah to Pharaoh's harem, then via the briefest of detours around Eliezer of Damascus (Gen 15:2) to Hagar and Ishmael (concerning whom God says, "I will make him into a great nation," Gen 21:18; see also 17:20), and finally to Isaac, returned from death.

The second major block, spanning Genesis 25 to 35, addresses the same question. It begins with Isaac's wife Rebekah (25:19). After twenty childless years, she will soon deliver twins. Turning convention on its head and enmeshed with sibling violence, God states that Esau will serve Jacob. The ensuing narrative tells of Jacob grasping the blessing and then, over many years, loosening his grip on it, until finally he can give blessing to others. Only then can those promises be handed down to the next genera-tion (and beyond). Along the way the text occasionally reveals the ratio-nale behind the elevation or demotion of Jacob's sons. It further reveals that—often despite our resistance—suffering, grief, and death accompany life lived under God's blessing.

---

2. My understanding of the shape of the promise, and its outworking within the Pen-tateuch, follows Alexander, *Paradise*, and Clines, *Theme*, 31–32, 45–60.

3. Clines, *Theme*, 46.

The story of Jacob's sons fills out the final grand narrative of Genesis, chapters 37–50. Despite lies, sexual abuse, still more violence among brothers, famine, enslavement, prison, and threats of death, God rescues his people and brings blessing to the nations through Joseph. The climax, however, Jacob's last testament (Gen 49), generates expectations that exalt neither Joseph nor Jacob's eldest son. It instead celebrates the ascendancy of Judah, the fourth son of an unloved wife.

As we read we can marvel at the God who makes promises to such people and therefore must constantly overcome obstacles to fulfilment. In what follows, we will explore the second great narrative block within Genesis 12–50, the story of Jacob, to hear its teachings concerning this giver of blessing. This is to do something unusual. The literature covering Jacob becomes thin, especially concerning the details of his children's birth and the breeding of his sheep and goats. This can be illustrated by considering two significant works, one classic, the other recent.

Gerhardus Vos, in his *Biblical Theology*, which to be fair focuses not on Genesis but the entire Bible, discusses the man who will be Israel over the space of six pages. Roughly the first third discusses the doctrine of election, a middle third the appearance of God at Bethel as Jacob flees the land (Gen 28), and the final third Jacob's wrestling with God upon his return (Gen 32).[4] In this Vos treats about 10 percent of the Jacob story.

Sidney Greidanus, in *Preaching Christ from Genesis*, leaps from 29:35 (at this point Jacob is twice married and has four of twelve sons) to 32:22–32, where Jacob wrestles with God.[5] From there the story of Joseph (beginning with Genesis 37) occupies the rest of the volume. That is, he investigates the Jacob material to about the middle, and then treats only eleven more verses before moving on.

This phenomenon can, I think, be explained. The broad pattern of Jacob's story is established early. Like Abraham, Isaac, Joseph, Moses, and the nation of Israel, he is born, travels from the land of his birth, and lives in light of promises from a gracious God. Each suffers, prospers, and produces children, but never finds rest. The similarities seemingly grant permission to rush past Jacob, since the truly important figures are Adam, Abraham, and Israel. The texture of each story, however, is unique. If Israel's self-understanding *vis-à-vis* both the cosmos and their God arises from Adam's story, then self-evidently the Jacob-who-is-Israel story

---

4. Vos, *Biblical Theology*, 93–99.

5. Greidanus, *Preaching Christ from Genesis*, 315–34.

also has much to teach them about God and about who they are. If the promises to Abraham provide the foundation for the nation's hopes, then Jacob's story explores those promises and the nature of their fulfilment. And if the nations, in Christ, inherit those same promises, then the Jacob story has much to teach us about both ourselves and the God of Abraham, Isaac, and the church of Jesus Christ.

Chapter 1

The Stolen Birthright

Genesis 25:27–34

IN THE BEGINNING GOD creates a harmonious kingdom where vice-regents rule. By Genesis 3 the crown is lost. The first husband and wife reject a God who is within himself relational and craves a relationship with them. Subsequent human relationships become a mirror of this rejection: husband and wife are estranged; brother kills brother; a townsman murders his neighbor; a father curses his son. Ever downward, encompassing all of humanity, until by Genesis 11 families, communities, nations, and language groups are divided.

Then into this story of fractious rebellion God speaks to Abraham (12:1–3). He engenders a hope in the reconciliation of all things through Abraham's seed, a coming one who will lift the curse, restore humanity's relationship with God, and turn the hearts of the fathers to their children. As Abraham's son appears, the promise ripens and hopes grow. But they don't advance much with Isaac, a passive character. Isaac presents scarcely more than a transitional figure who sets the stage for Jacob's exploits and for the God who will work in Jacob's life. In fact, the "Isaac story," the two chapters that move from Abraham to the birth of Jacob and Esau, contains only two verses that record Isaac's activity (24:63, 67). The rest, including even his marriage, recounts the deeds of others.[1] Beyond anything Isaac can offer, we need an active man with a healing hand. One who leaves reconciliation

---

1. While chapter 26 would seem to oppose this reading since it focuses on Isaac more directly, it does not present him as more active. If anything it is permeated with his passivity, on which see below.

in his wake. One who can wear the crown with dignity. One who can reunite families, restore communities and nations, and reconcile God with his children. Instead we get Jacob.

A Background Passage

Like Isaac, Jacob is a child of promise. The birth narrative begins and ends with references to Isaac's age: at forty he marries (25:20) and at sixty becomes a father (25:26). This emphasizes the divine initiative in Jacob's birth. Rebekah for twenty years does not conceive, but unlike his mother and daughters-in-law, Isaac turns to the LORD, not slave girls, and the LORD hears. Rebekah's joy is short-lived, however, for pregnancy threatens her life, the Hebrew referring to a crushing struggle within. She too goes to the LORD.[2]

Family Matters

God's response to her distress indicates in four brief statements that twins will come to term and eventually grow into two nations. They will, however, be neither equal nor follow custom: despite the older brother's chronological priority, God has decreed the superiority of the younger. This microcosm of international plotlines points to the earlier rise of Esau's kingdom, recounted already in Genesis 36 right down to the naming of kings (36:31–43), while Jacob must wait centuries for dominance.

The Struggle

Cain and Abel, Ishmael and Isaac, and Jacob's own sons are rivals.[3] However, unlike other brothers, and especially his passive father, Jacob fights

---

2. Sarna wonders whether her question is "why did I conceive if death is the outcome?" or the existential crisis, "why do I exist?" The Syriac supports the second possibility, which aligns with her reaction to Esau's marriage in Gen 27:46. In either case, the text clearly designates the source of the oracle. While the sparse account addresses neither location nor mediation, it leaves no doubt that the pronouncement is YHWH's word. His name appears twice, as both the consulted deity and the one who answers. Unlike various participants in the subsequent story, Rebekah is not associated with pagan activities (Sarna, *Genesis*, 179).

3. In Genesis, sisters get into the act as well: compare Leah and Rachel.

even before he is born. He wrestles in utero, and in childbirth itself holds on (25:26), unwilling to let go of the place allotted to another.

Esau, arriving first, is described passively: he emerges red and hairy, attributes that inform the following stories. Combined with subsequent characterization Esau is portrayed as unsophisticated.[4] Jacob, prenatally active, arrives grasping Esau's heel—another attribute that informs what follows. The names relate to these defining characteristics and so also play an ongoing role in the story.

An Improper Meal: A Hunt and a Pot of Stew

Infantile struggles continue into adulthood. In two brief verses (25:27–28) Genesis describes first Jacob and Esau's mature characters and then their parents' relationship with them. Esau was skilled in hunting, apparently thriving away from society. The biblical record consistently prefers domesticated over wild food: for example, while the Law allows the consumption of wild animals,[5] none are to be offered to the LORD. Furthermore, the only other designated hunter in the Bible is Nimrod (10:9). While surrounding nations often portray their kings as hunters, Israel does not.[6] Jewish kings do not hunt animals: they shepherd them. Esau's portrayal—especially when 27:40–42 ("You will live by the sword . . . . I will kill my brother Jacob . . . consoling himself with the thought of killing you") and 32:11 are taken into account—is of a fierce man who lives by his weapons.[7]

Jacob seems as much the opposite socially as physically, a man of peace happy to "stay at home among the tents" (25:27). The contrast is between the hunter and the farmer who prefers a settled existence.[8] The term used here to describe Jacob (*tam*), often rendered "quiet," means blameless, perfect, when applied to Job or Noah, and points to wholehearted commitment.[9]

4. See also Wenham, *Genesis 16–50*, 176, who notes that Judas in many paintings has red hair. Curiously, the only other use of this word, red, refers to David, the king who overcomes Edom (1 Sam 6:12; 7:14). So Walton, *Traveller*, 17, n. 20.

5. Lev 17:13.

6. So Sarna, *Genesis*, 181.

7. Walton (*Traveller*, 102) cites Gunkel (*Gensis*, 308), who argues that the characterization presented here opposes subsequent portrayals of Edom and Esau: Esau/Edom was famed for wisdom, and Israel for bravery—so Jer 49:7 and Baruch 3:22.

8. Already in Gen 4:20 tents and herds are drawn together.

9. The NRSV and earlier editions of the NIV render it "quiet." See also Job 1:1, 8 and 2:3; Gen 6:9.

Isaac prefers Esau, and not without reason: Esau provides his favorite meals (25:28). This foreshadows characteristics that lead to ruin. Rebekah's preference is unexplained. The text's silence presents her as more dignified than the man for whom food determines relationships.

Against this background, Esau is one day hunting while Jacob makes stew (25:29). Esau, arriving at camp hungry, commands, "Quick, let me have some of that red stew."[10] Doubtless he thinks the color derives from a choice piece of meat (25:30).[11] Red ('adom) and a similar word (dam) meaning blood are combined in several places in Scripture, offering a suggestive wordplay. The essence of life is in the blood: Esau sees in this stew that which will sustain him. He is a man in a hurry, and demands the red (hence his name Edom).

Jacob answers, "first sell me your birthright" (25:31). In our first adult encounter with Jacob, he is still trying to supplant the older brother, now not forcibly but opportunistically. At death's door the birthright holds no value for Esau. "I am about to die," he replies. The birthright's value is tied to faith as it promises future blessing. Myopic Esau cannot see its value if it holds no immediate benefit. After all, he is dying.

Birthright

Jacob uses four brief words to introduce the transaction. Esau's reply is expansive: "Look, I am about to die . . . . What good is the birthright to me?" (25:32). He isn't dying. Alongside his verbosity is the fact that the hunt, if it brings him near death at all, would generate a greater thirst than hunger. Yet he bargains for stew. Esau is not dying; but he is a man ruled by his belly. Like his father, his appetites determine his preferences.

The birthright elevates the eldest son, a social reality that stands despite its transfer several times in the biblical record.[12] The central notion is that

10. My translation. The nouns are, more precisely, ha' adom, this ha' adom.

11. This event most likely occurs in a shepherd camp. Otherwise servants, not Jacob, would be making meals, and Esau would not have appeared so desperate: surely at home he could have either turned to a parent to resolve the issue without trading his birthright or found a morsel sufficient for the crisis. Furthermore, despite being away from home, the boys probably bargained in the presence of others. If not, how could such a rash promise be binding? See Walton, *Genesis*, 550–51.

12. Compare Jacob's blessing of Judah over his elder brothers Reuben, Simeon and Levi in 49:3–12, and his grandson Ephraim over Manasseh in 48:13. This motif is treated in depth in Syrén, *Forsaken First-Born*. His treatment of the literary dimension of the text is of more interest to me than his discussion of the text's pre-history.

the eldest receives an extra portion of an otherwise equally divided material estate. Thus the more sons in a family, the less gained by the birthright; but for a family with only two, the birthright means an additional third of the inheritance. Esau does not trade away everything. And the exchange, in his mind at least, covers only material things. But in the Pentateuch the birthright means more: in Genesis 49:3, Jacob blesses Reuben with the words, "You are my firstborn, my might, the first sign of my strength, excelling in honor, excelling in power." And in Exodus 22:29b God says "You must give me the firstborn of your sons." The firstborn can thus be described as "quasi-holy," even functioning as priest before Levitical responsibilities became established.[13] To publicly despise this birthright is to show disrespect for the father, and ultimately God who is father. The story shows not only that Esau is impatient, impetuous. He is unworthy.

Esau Is Not Satisfied

Esau is not dying. Neither is he satisfied. Seeing red, he expects a rich stew. He probes the pot, searching for meat, realizing too late that he has sold his birthright for beans, lentils. Terse, desperate sounding words mark the end of the event: "he ate and drank and then got up and left" (25:34). He has been robbed.

The Bible's other "stew story" might indicate the value of the meal. In 2 Kings 4:38–41, under Elisha's watch, a pot of stew transforms from poisonous to edible. Unlike Elijah, who moved among kings, Elisha lives among and speaks to commoners. Furthermore, they eat this meal at a time of famine. Stew forms the diet of the poor during desperate times.[14] Esau sells his birthright for a meal. The author seems to add *"and it wasn't even a good one."*[15]

The narrator now informs, "so Esau despised his birthright" (25:34). Any sympathy for him in the face of Jacob's greed evaporates, as do the hopes we might have held for the favored younger son, the blameless

13. Walton, *Traveller*, 22.

14. Ryken et al., "Stew," 814.

15. The Bible frequently uses the belly as a metaphor for the passions. The world, the flesh, and the devil, often indistinguishable, cannot satisfy. The LORD, on the other hand, promises that "in that day" his people will "with joy . . . draw water from the wells of salvation" (Isa 12:3). He offers water, wine, milk, and bread that are without cost and able to satisfy (Isa 55:2–3). In John 7 (esp. 37–39), Jesus offers his Spirit as food and water, which alone gives life and satisfies the soul.

one. "Despised" does not mean that Esau hates his birthright, but that he thinks little of it. The birthright of Isaac's son includes a relationship with God and thus a role in the kingdom that he is establishing through this family. Hebrews 12:16 exhorts, let none of you be "sexually immoral or . . . godless like Esau who for a single meal sold his" birthright. The author of Hebrews thus explores the ethical dimension of the patriarchal family and finds in this event a warning for his congregation: they need to value the things of God more than this world. Esau lives in the moment, without regard for eternal realities.

The Christian participates in an end-times community, and therefore ought to be fully invested in the Lord's return.[16] John wonders whether people in his orbit will be ashamed "before him at [Jesus'] coming."[17] We might go further and ask, do we think lightly of his coming? Are we, like Esau, so taken with this world's offerings that we "despise" God's promises in Jesus? Churches hold out fulfilment, advancement, health, wealth, etc., while losing sight of God's solution to humanity's crisis: a cross to pay for sin so that believers might have eternal life.[18] If the church loses sight of eternal priorities, what hope for the world? Jesus pushes against the Esaus of his own day when he says, while discussing food and clothing, "Seek first his kingdom . . ." (Matt 6:25–34). Genesis 25 makes the same point as Jesus with a story about food. The next Jacob story will feature both food and clothing.

16. The church exists "in these last days" (Heb 1:2; 1 Pet 1:20) or in "the last hour" (1 John 2:18) as those "on whom the culmination of the ages has come" (1 Cor 10:11).

17. 1 John 2:28; see also Eph 5:11–14.

18. For NT discussion of salvation vis-à-vis inheritance, see Eph 1:13–14, 18–19; Col 1:12–14; 1 Pet 1:3–14.

Chapter 2

The Stolen Blessing

Genesis 27:1–24

GENESIS EMPLOYS VARIOUS MEANS to draw our attention backward and forward in chapter 27. One is to mimic features of the birthright episode. This creates, despite the rather lengthy insertion concerning Isaac, a unified birthright and blessing narrative. The intervening material more fully introduces Isaac as a character in his own right, showing him first in relationship with his father and now with his sons. He was not involved in the birthright events, but how can there be a blessing narrative without him? In chapter 26, his sins, wells, adversaries, and God are the same as his father's, but the author does little to indicate that he shares his father's priorities. Indeed, Genesis 26:5 and 24 explicitly state that Isaac is blessed because of his father's faith. Abraham is now off the stage, having lived until his grandsons' fifteenth year,[1] and his shadow grows shorter.

A Background Passage

Just as the story of the birthright builds upon information from a preceding event, so the story of the blessing grows out of 26:34–35. Here the book recounts another struggle within the family: where the first centered on birth, this one focuses on marriage to draw us into chapter 27.

---

1. 175 (Abraham's terminal age) − (100 [Abraham's age at Isaac's birth] + 40 [Isaac's marrying age] + 20 [the years between marriage and the twins' birth]) = 15.

Family Matters

Isaac was passive in his birth (not unusual, but noteworthy because Jacob was not), circumcision, relationship with Ishmael, sacrifice, and obtaining of a wife. Now it is time for action. Abraham had done everything to ensure that Isaac's bride was not a daughter of the land. Isaac, however, looks away as his firstborn marries not one but two Hittite women (26:34–35). Esau in this again appears unworthy to be the heir of Abraham's promise and father of a separate people. But what was Isaac thinking?[2]

The Struggle

In contrast to the comfort gained by Isaac's marriage (24:67)—the vigilant father sending a godly servant to procure a virtuous wife—Esau's marriages are toxic. Unusual terminology resembling the description of Job under the weight of calamity conveys the distress caused by Esau's marriages. The struggles that characterize the fraternal relationships now permeate the family.

An Improper Meal: A Hunt and a Platter of Food

Esau had associated hunger with impending death. Now Isaac apparently identifies blindness with death. His eyes are weak, though he has hardly been a man of vision to this point. He calls Esau, commissions a hunt, and makes plans to dine before dying, with a blessing sandwiched between.

Rebekah, overhearing, shares her own scheme with Jacob. She reports what Isaac said, adding to the blessing the words "in the presence of the LORD." Her words, "obey," "my word," and "command," usually associated with Torah and God, call for diligent obedience.[3] Jacob's role seems minimal: he merely obtains two goats and delivers them to Isaac. Rebekah will see to the flavor. Such is her plan, and as Jacob listens to the wife and mother of those he will soon betray, he quickly spots its weakness. Exhibiting neither

---

2. While the marriages are clearly troubling to Esau's parents, and while the record is structured so that they influence our reading of the subsequent story, they do not interfere with Isaac's preference for Esau over Jacob. So Walton, *Traveller*, 112.

3. Walton, *Traveller*, 115. He further reflects on vocabulary shared with the book of Proverbs, where meals connect with deception (23:3), and "smooth" (plus cognates, often translated as flattery) describes the deceiver: see Prov 2:16; 5:3; 6:24; 7:5; 7:21; 20:19; 26:28; 28:23; 29:5.

integrity nor concern that Isaac might distinguish goat from venison, he speaks of contrasting textures. Lost in translation is a wordplay on geographical terms: the words denoting "hairy" and "smooth" evoke Seir (see 25:25) and Mount Halak, which are paired in Joshua 11:17 and 12:7 to represent the southern border of Israel's conquest. Mount Halak sits at the edge of Seir, Esau's property (see Gen 32:3–4).[4] By means of these puns, Genesis indicates boundaries and reveals Jacob's fear of trespassing them.[5]

If Jacob is touched and uncovered, the result will not be blessing but curse. Rebekah replies without words of hope, saying only that she will bear the curse. Unless Isaac dies between blessing Jacob and Esau's appearance, the plan cannot but be discovered. Clothes and skins can hide the truth only during the moment of blessing. In this, it becomes clear that Rebekah believes the blessing is, once uttered, non-transferable. If the blessing cannot be transferred from Jacob to Esau in a story of deception and fraud, by what logic can the curse transfer from Jacob to Rebekah?[6] But curses, like leaven, do spread.

The plan, like the goats, is executed, reminding us again that Esau chases wild game while Jacob tends domesticated animals. Mother, knowing what father likes, quickly prepares the desired meal. Then she produces Esau's finest clothing. Is it strange that Esau's clothes are on hand? Had she already stolen them, or does he, with his two wives, four sons, and four daughters, share her dwelling?[7] If Esau lives with his parents, the proximity of the conspirators and victims makes her scheme even more startling. How can they maintain harmony after these deceptions? Whatever the case, she dresses her favorite, covers the exposed parts with hide, and hands

4. This attention to names informs the story-teller's strategy. The Jacob narratives continually play on the similarity of Rebekah, *bekorah* (birthright) and *berakah* (blessing). In 27:5–12 Rebekah and *barak* are repeated throughout, culminating in Jacob's final comment of v. 12: when Isaac discovers him, he will meet with curse, not blessing (*berakah*). This fixes our attention on names not merely as puns but as, at crucial points, revealers of truth. In what follows, the misuse of Esau's name carries the story. Subsequent events further build upon the use and abuse of names.

5. Sarna, *Genesis*, 191.

6. Wenham, *Genesis 16–50*, 207.

7. The alternative is to see the events of chapter 36 as taking place prior to the events recounted here. In that case, Esau with his family will have moved to Seir and is present because of his father's impending funeral. The hunt then would be an opportunistic request by Isaac for something he cannot normally get. The main drawback to this explanation is the weight of distress the marriages cause Rebekah: would she feel so strongly if Esau had long since moved away?

over the food. In the birthright narrative, the two sons are away from home, and Jacob acts on his own initiative. In this scene, and in this marriage, Rebekah is the active one, a point the book of Genesis stresses. She plans and then performs all that is within her power, to the very moment Jacob must engage with Isaac. She and Jacob form a pair in their active natures, just as Esau and Isaac share passivity.

Bearing the food, Jacob enters with a single word: "father" (27:18). Compared with Esau's confident approach a few minutes later (27:31), this suggests that the disguise fails to relieve Jacob's anxiety. Isaac's response, unless many in the community refer to him as "father" and he to them as "my son," indicates that Isaac knows it is either Jacob or Esau. He nevertheless enquires, "who are you, my son," apparently immediately suspicious. Jacob, in v. 19 asked for his name, now must speak. He lies, "I am Esau, your firstborn." I am here in obedience to your instructions. When asked by a doubtful Isaac how the meal took so little time he invokes the LORD's name, further modified as "your God" (27:20). Thus Rebekah in 27:7 and Jacob here name the God unmentioned by Isaac and Esau.

Genesis does not yet suggest that father's ears work better than his eyes, but suspicions rise to the point where Isaac summons a second witness: he touches the one who sounds like Jacob. Now Jacob stops talking, hoping that the clothes and the skins accomplish their task. Isaac feels the coarse hides on Jacob's hands and declares them to be the hands of Esau (27:22–23). How hairy was Esau?! Lacking in sight, unsure of hearing, and misled by touch, Isaac asks directly: are you indeed Esau? Jacob, learning quickly, answers only "I" (27:24).

So Isaac, suspicions but not stomach-satisfied, demands the food. Jacob obliges, and with few words the meal, and with it the blind taste test, is finished. Isaac invites Jacob to draw near and kiss him. Is it one last examination? If Isaac uncovers the truth now, he gets the pleasure of the meal without passing over his preferred son. But the clothes do their work as smell enters the story (27:27). With four lines, Isaac enlists heaven and earth as sources of blessing for his son.

The first element of the blessing relates the smell of Esau's clothes to the smell of a blessed field—a compliment in that culture if not ours. This advances to a call for the good things of heaven and earth, of grain and wine (27:28). He who adores fine dining desires that his son know the benefit of plentiful food. While this finds no direct parallel in God's blessing of Abraham in Genesis 12:2–3, when combined with what follows, it provides a wonderful exposition of divine promise. Note, however, that talk of grain and wine undercuts the aspect of Esau's character that appeals most to Isaac: it points to an agrarian existence, not the life of a hunter. Isaac, like Abraham, has been a restless wanderer, searching for water among hostile tribes. His blessing is that Esau, the bearer of the promise, will become a settled community. In this, he approaches the notion that God's blessing entails land and rest.

Isaac's next words relate to conflict among nations and within the family.[8] This at first glance imitates more closely the blessing of Genesis 12. But the resemblance has limits: God uses first person active verbs in every stanza, while Isaac must speak in a passive voice.[9] His words call for Esau to overcome, to be served. Isaac in this way telescopes national realities, for within Rebekah were two nations, the older the servant of the younger (Gen 25:23). In calling for nations and peoples to serve Esau, he seeks to overturn God's promise. The words "be lord over your brothers, and may the sons of your mother bow down to you" do not then subvert an until now legitimate blessing. They merely reiterate, albeit more explicitly, the content of the prior two clauses. Isaac undertakes to secure for his favorite plentiful food and drink, and superiority over Jacob.

Isaac's final stanza echoes Genesis 12:3 and God's promise to bless those who bless Abraham and curse those who curse Abraham. It omits, though, the promise of universal blessing, apparently not Isaac's concern. These words of blessing and curse drip with irony. First, plainly Isaac, though he blesses Jacob, will not thereby know blessing. His joy lasts no longer than the pleasure of the good meal. Second, Jacob will be immediately exposed: there is no hiding the deception. He has himself linked exposing the plot with a curse in 27:12–13, so Esau's subsequent vow to kill him is in effect the outworking of that curse. Third, and as a result, Esau, whom Isaac would bless, in cursing Jacob places himself under the curse: "may those who curse you be cursed." And Rebekah? Note that v. 13 does not say "if you are discovered let the curse fall on me." She says only: "Let the curse fall on me. Just do what I say." She, in advancing the recipient of the promise, calls down a curse on herself. Rebekah and both her sons are thus under a

8. Gen 27:29.

9. Much of the blessing Jacob pronounces on his children is in the passive too, but note two points: first, not all of it is (49:6–7 includes statements that are active and in the first person); and second, references to the LORD permeate the words, providing a foundation that Isaac's blessing lacks.

curse because of Isaac's plan to bless. Isaac too, already blessed of the LORD, in these events fares no better than the other three.

Everything is wrong with this sham blessing. It relates, to be sure, to land, superiority, and protection, yet differs from other blessings in Genesis. Isaac allows his passions to rule: he has a favored son, and despite the LORD's word, asserts his meager authority. Furthermore, Isaac speaks accurately if not truthfully when he claims not to know how much longer he will live: he lasts another forty years! Like Esau in the earlier story, the promise of a good meal is his undoing. To stress the "sensual" nature of Isaac's behavior, all five senses feature in the narrative, a rarity in Scripture. As Esau with respect to the birthright was "care-less," so Isaac concerning the blessing is "sense-less."[10]

Tension runs high, for Esau finishes second at the very moment Jacob comes out, repeating the verb but reversing the results of their birth-competition (25:25).[11] The food prepared, Esau enters into the presence of his father to deliver the main course. Isaac greets him with the words, "who are you?"[12] Who could it be but the one sent for the meal? Esau answers as Jacob had: "I am your son . . . your firstborn, Esau." At this Isaac goes into a rage, trembles violently, and—well—that's all. There is no other recorded response.[13] Esau wails, "Bless me—me too," but Isaac only speaks of the brother who "took *your* blessing"! Esau drags the name Jacob to the fore, for his brother truly is the grasper, and figuratively the deceiver. The grasper has twice deceived, taking the birthright and the blessing. Esau, to this point a willing participant in his father's plan to bless him alone, now asks if Isaac has any residual blessing. When the goal was to elevate Esau, the thought of an overflow never occurred to them, with the result that Jacob has everything.

The blessing, with few references to God, almost appears godly beside Isaac's answer to Esau (v. 37). With an abundance of first person pronouns, he declares that *he* has ordered the family relations and provided ample harvests, leaving nothing for *him* to do for Esau. This is extraordinary. He cannot manage his own family yet implies control over international affairs

---

10. Walton, *Genesis*, 555.

11. Hamilton, *Genesis 18–50*, 226. Both here and in 25:25, the term can be rendered "emerges." In chapter 34 the same verb will appear three times (34:1, 6, and 26), each at crucial moments. There too it meets with troubling results.

12. Gen 27:32.

13. Does he really need to ask who stole the blessing (27:33)?!

and the vicissitudes of harvest! Can such a "blessing" count for anything? Or is it merely the wishes of a supposedly dying man for his favorite son? But the poetic structure points away from Isaac to his central concern: he three times places the most important element before the verb. "*Lord* I have set him over you"; "all *brothers* I have given him as slaves"; "*with grain and wine* I have supported him."[14] What more has he to give?

Subsequent Scripture in fact locates fulfilment of these words at least in part not in Jacob's experience but Esau's. Thus Isaac's baser aspirations in small measure come to pass. But to this point in Genesis, genuine patriarchal blessings have been spoken not through an intermediary but by God himself (see 12:2–3).[15] God, not Abraham, blessed Isaac (26:2–5, 24).[16] And so it shall be with Jacob. But many miles will pass before God pronounces his blessing.[17]

Isaac, having digested the situation, now without fanfare pronounces words that in Hebrew practically repeat, and so parody, the blessing on Jacob. Esau thus literally receives the reverse of the first blessing. Where v. 28 spoke of heaven and earth, v. 39 speaks of earth and heaven. Verse 28's dew and richness become 39's richness and dew. And the preposition twice rendered "of" in 28 now means "away from." Esau will live not "of heaven's dew" but "away from the dew of heaven"; not "of earth's richness" but "away from earth's richness."[18] Rather than enjoying the rest provided by life in a settled community, Esau and Edom will "live by the sword." But Esau will grow restless and one day throw off the yoke of oppression.[19]

Like Esau with his overpriced lentils, Isaac's passions go unsatisfied. Events of his making spiral out of control to his great pain and anger. Unlike Esau, however, for his troubles Isaac gets two good meals.

---

14. Gen 27:37, my translation.

15. For reiterations of aspects of Abraham's blessing see 15:13–16; 17:5–8; 18:18. More precisely, however, these relate to the covenant rather than the blessing.

16. The nearest to an exception to this pattern is Melchizedek's blessing of Abraham (14:18), but, importantly, he does so as "priest of the most High God."

17. This does not mean that it will be long before God *blesses* Jacob, simply that the pronouncement is delayed. This raises questions concerning the events at Bethel, recounted in 28:10–15. Is this God's blessing, without being so-designated? Is the blessing distinct from what Bethel clearly provides, a covenant reiteration?

18. Waltke, *Genesis*, 381; Sarna, *Genesis*, 194.

19. 2 Kgs 8:20, 22 recount how, in the days of Jehoram, Edom gains independence.

Nobody Was Satisfied

With respect to the purity of Esau's bloodline, Isaac does nothing. But in advancing his favorite son, Isaac elevates his will over God's, resulting in a family on the verge of destruction. His wife has openly rebelled against his authority and wishes. How will that affect their relationship? Furthermore, his two sons virtually abandon him.

Rebekah, whose goals in this episode coincide with the word of the LORD, acquitted herself well in the birth story. But here she instigates the destruction of her family. She works only to advance her favorite, but Jacob's deceit finds its root in her plan. Her tragedy is not only that she plots against her husband and eldest son, but also that her favorite will leave and she will never see him again.

Esau held his birthright in light regard. The same does not seem true of the blessing. He seeks it with tears, but to no avail (Heb 12:17). The birthright and blessing are a unity: one cannot be sold for beans and the other held fast. His tears give way to anger as he vows to kill his brother. His parents were already overwhelmed by his bad marriages, and in 28:9 we read that he went and married the daughter of Isaac's rival Ishmael. Thus the story begins and ends with Esau's inability to pick wives.

Not surprisingly perhaps, Isaac's words to Esau resemble God's cursing of Cain.[20] Though God spares them, and they produce a fruitful lineage, both reside away from the land, strangers to agricultural abundance, their lives marked by violence. By such means we see again that Esau is alien to the promise.

But such interpretations of Esau, common as they are, do not tell the whole story. Esau, upon hearing that his parents want Jacob to marry a non-Canaanite, and that his own wives displease Isaac, himself marries a non-Canaanite. This marriage once more casts Isaac in a negative light. Abraham had resolved that Isaac would not marry a daughter of Canaan. Furthermore, though more easily overlooked, Genesis 21:21 tells us that Hagar obtained a wife for Ishmael from Egypt. Jacob in a few verses will be sent out of the land to obtain a wife. All around Esau, men are marrying non-Canaanites, but the favored son of Isaac appears to be without counsel in this matter. In the end then, Esau's attempts to marry within the extended family rather than take another Canaanite wife may suggest

20. Westermann, *Promises to the Fathers*, 78.

a desire to please his parents once he learns what they want. Sadly, Isaac has provided no help.

More importantly, Jacob is no more righteous than his brother. In the exchange of the birthright a meal figures prominently as events unfold away from home. The story of the blessing, however, invades the household. Jacob, by usurping the place of the eldest, undermining the wishes of the father, and perverting a meal, overthrows the conventions that defined family life. He lies, cheats, and destroys. If threats to God's promises permeate Genesis, can any be greater than the damage Jacob inflicts? He has torn the fabric of the people by which God will overturn the curse. How can he who now appears to have no God, family, or home be considered a suitable vehicle of blessing? He has no more virtue than Esau, and subsequent events sometimes suggest that he has less. But he possesses that one thing that gives us, as it does Israel's children, an unshakable hope. Despite his sins, God has chosen him.

God has promised great things for Jacob, but he attempts to grasp them by deception. First Esau's and then Isaac's fleshly indulgences provide Jacob's opportunity, but that never brings acquittal. He will suffer greatly during a lifetime of wrestling with God, receiving payment in kind as a reminder of his sins.[21] He differs from his brother in that his values extend beyond the mundane. But even if his interests tower over those of his father and brother, they are not determined by God.[22] Jacob dominates the center of his own world as much as Esau stands at the center of his own. Only slowly will Jacob discover who truly occupies the center of his world, his life, his hope.

The God of Abraham, Isaac, and . . .

Hebrews 11:20 somewhat surprisingly says that by faith Isaac blessed his two sons with respect to the future. The author of Hebrews, to be sure, sees righteousness where we struggle to find it, as in the stories of Lot and Sampson.

21. In Gen 27:23 Jacob's deception of Isaac with clothing and a goat is communicated with a stem that in Genesis relates to recognition and/or that which is foreign. Genesis 37:32 and 33 each use the same verb to communicate Jacob's deception at the hands of his sons, again with clothing and a goat, as he recognizes his son's garment. See also 38:25–26, where it relates to Tamar's deception of Judah involving yet again clothing and a goat (38:14–19).

22. Von Rad, referring to Lev 19:14 and Deut 27:18–20, sees in Jacob's deception of a blind man a sin against God's law (*Genesis*, 279–81).

But one must not over-read such comments. Hebrews neither sings their virtues nor forgives their sins. The writer, in urging his hearers to trust that God remains Lord despite their present distress, gives hope a particular shape by recalling a line of people who, whatever their shortcomings, grasped that God's purposes transcend their own timeframe and context. Thus, for all his faults, Isaac's future-orientation aligns him with those who trust in God. In this, one can speak of the God of Abraham and Isaac.

Yet the author speaks of four people directed by desire and ambition, building their own lives. They exist over against a God who, in the Pentateuch, is building houses. In Exodus, he calls the Israelites from building a house for a dead Pharaoh to build a house for the living God. In Genesis "the house of Israel and the house of Judah" is being established, but not with promising material. Indeed, at one level the story is bewildering: these are the roots of Christian faith? This is Israel, *our* story? We see plainly enough that Jacob isn't great. Thankfully for the Christian, the Jacob story is not about Jacob. It is the story of Jacob's God.

The God of Jacob

Each time the motif of Jacob as deceiver moves to the fore, references to Jacob's God as full of unrestrained mercy and grace accompany it. Thus, if Jacob's identity becomes the cause of judgment, God overcomes that obstacle to blessing by intervening with his gracious love. Paul develops this distinctly God-focused element of the story in Rom 9:10–13.

Romans 9 insists that, rather than physical descent, God's character and his nature as promise-maker alone guarantee the blessing for Jacob, apart from works. Indeed, the promise, given before birth, came before any righteous act could have been performed (Rom 9:11). A cynic might add that after birth Jacob seldom behaves better, noting that in the rare story where one of the twins performs well, Esau possesses the greater dignity (see below on Genesis 33).[23]

Thus, God's character shapes Christian hope. As he overcomes the effects of sin, ever portrayed in terms of estrangement, his patience is tested at every turn. Even those chosen to bless all too often become allies of the curse. But the LORD who places the younger before the older overturns the natural order to the advantage of his chosen one. In Christ,

---

23. See also Gen 27:41, where Esau vows to kill Jacob *after* Isaac's death. In this he shows greater respect for his father than Jacob does.

the eternally exalted one obeys his Father by becoming lower than a slave, humbling himself by bearing the curse in his body on the tree, with the dual results that he receives the highest name and we are restored to a relationship with him (Phil 2:5–11). First Corinthians 1 also speaks of how condescension to the cross opposes everything wise and powerful in this world (1 Cor 1:18–25; cf. Isa 29:14). As God acts in his Son he continues to overturn the natural order to the benefit of those who believe, covering sin with the blood of the cross so that sinners might be reconciled through that blood. One's sin is thus not one's fate in the face of God's grace.[24] And God's elevation of the sinner is not capricious. It is the outworking of his costly love. "Jacob have I loved . . ." (Mal 1:2).

Responding to Election

Election is the point at which Jacob most clearly identifies as Israel, and perhaps where Jacob most clearly resembles the church—sinners, alien to God's ways, and yet elect from before the foundations of the earth. We must therefore correctly identify Jacob's typological value: Jacob embodies the story of Israel, not of Jesus. The story of Jacob reveals the plotlines of his family both inside and beyond the boundaries of Genesis, but for the moment our attention can stay within. We learn from Genesis 31 that deceiving Jacob (the term appears there three times) loves a deceiving wife, who, if the *terafim* represent her father's and brother's inheritance, by stealing the family gods enacts the same theft that Jacob himself undertook. The first chapter concerning Jacob's family in the land, Genesis 34, details the use of religion as the opportunity to steal, murder, and destroy. Borrowing the term that described Jacob's deception of Esau in 27:35, the text reports, "Jacob's sons replied deceitfully" (34:13).[25] Like father, like son.

From Cain and Abel to Joseph and his brothers, every family in Genesis must face the divine choice of one brother over all others and the often violent reaction of the displaced. Equally unexplained and generative of plot is the exalted brother's response to his privileges. What should one make of Joseph trumpeting his dreams and flaunting his special coat? Do we find in the attitudes of Jacob and Joseph warnings given to the chosen ones? Will Israel, and do we, humbly marvel at God's grace as it reaches down to the lowly, or do we fall into a similar trap?

24. Brueggemann, *Genesis*, 215.
25. The form is identical.

There is another reaction to the doctrine of election, which accords well with our culture more generally and to which we who enjoy abundant blessing can naturally gravitate. Do we treat God with a sense of entitlement? Having settled comfortably into his grace, and having been transformed just enough by it and his Holy Spirit, have we come to believe that even the Living God should delight to have friends like us? To think so is to revert to the role of Jacob the deceiver. But we deceive only ourselves. In Genesis 42, Joseph's bewildered brothers face slavery and possible death. It is their moment of reckoning before the lord of Egypt for selling their brother, falsifying his death, and lying to their father. To accusations against them they twice reply, "we are honest men" (42:11, 31).

Like Jacob, and the sons of Israel, we must discern whether we are sinful recipients of grace, or honest and deserving men and women. To err is to face slavery and possible death.

Blessing in Genesis

Genesis's account of God's creating, choosing, and promising is interlaced with progressive stories of brotherly reconciliation. The first brother, Cain, upon learning of God's preferences, murders, and is therefore driven from the land. Isaac suffers at the hands of the older Ishmael (21:9), but ultimately Abraham sends the seven unchosen brothers, explicitly, "away from his son Isaac" and out of the land (25:6).[26] Jacob, prior to reconciliation, receives death threats from his older brother. They again live apart by Genesis 36, but where other brothers divide because of animosity or expulsion, these separate this time because their abundance overwhelms the land (36:7). Finally, by chapter 50 Joseph and his brothers not only live, but even live in the same country, saved and blessed of the LORD—though notably, and because of their prior relationship, not in the land.[27] Will Israel ever live both in harmony and in the land?

Our focus has been on the third of these accounts as we consider the man who wrestles with everybody, human and divine (32:28), destroys most of what he touches, and yet, because of God's unmerited favor, fulfils

---

26. Six sons of Keturah are named in Gen 25:2.

27. For a stimulating discussion of the four great stories of fraternal rivalry in Genesis, focusing on their narratological and theological implications, see Kaminsky, *Yet I Loved Jacob*, esp. section 1.

everything that God intends for him during his "few and evil years."[28] By the end, he is blessing foreign kings, his grandchildren (48:9–20), and ultimately the twelve tribes descended from him (49:28).

This raises questions about blessing. It is central to the Pentateuch, and provides the theme of Genesis. But what is blessing: pious wishes, prayers, an attempt to manipulate God? A previous generation of scholars linked blessings to pre-religious magic from Israel's early neighbors which Genesis "theologizes" by weaving in references to the LORD. Others, again based on comparison with prior Canaanite cultures, spoke of the transfer of life force in blessings as practiced by Melchizedek (14:19–20), Isaac, and Jacob.[29]

John Walton's explanation relies less on non-biblical precedents when he observes that some blessings are spoken by God and others by people, and that the former represent "an offer of [divine] favor," while the latter are "a wish for God's favor."[30] Underpinning biblical blessing is God's initial pronouncement in Genesis 1:28–30, where, as the climax of the creation account, God blessed the male and female, exhorting them, "Be fruitful and increase in number; fill the earth and subdue it," and then went on to speak of his lavish provision of food.[31] Already it contains the command, with the implied enabling, to bear children and to rule. After the fall, the curse impinges on the very heart of this blessing as it complicates childbearing (3:16), ruling (3:16, cf. 9:2) and food production (3:17–19; 4:12).

These tensions become the ongoing story of Scripture and of humanity, as the curses of a shattered world in Genesis 1–11 yield to re-emergent blessing in chapter 12, where God tells Abraham that his benevolence will be so great that the whole earth will participate in it.[32] As we will see, the unfolding iterations of this blessing relate to children, land, and authority. This trinity generates drama in the ensuing narrative, for each patriarch marries a wife who is unable to engage in the initial element of blessing: childbearing. Furthermore, each is landless except for small, scattered parcels, and lacking in power and influence to the point of requiring divine protection. Thus

28. Gen 47:9; my translation.

29. For the history of interpretation, see Mitchell, *The Meaning of Brk*, esp. chapter 2, but also the discussion of etymology on pp. 13–16.

30. Walton, *Genesis*, 53.

31. See Gen 9:1–3, where God reiterates the call to "Be fruitful and increase in number and fill the earth," as well as the provision of food, now including animals. The "fear and dread" of the animals relates to God's provision of food for humanity, but simultaneously makes their management more difficult.

32. Gen 12:2–3.

each element of blessing, the story repeats over and over, finds fulfilment not in human strength or skill, but in God who providentially chooses and distributes according to his own will.

But if we agree with Walton, should we conclude that Isaac's blessing is a mere wish? If so, why can he not recapture it and pass it to Esau? Walton maintains that the blessings are not prophecies, and extends this even to the detailed and extensive words Jacob pronounces over his sons and grandsons in Genesis 48–49. He does, however, concede that their inclusion in the canon indicates that, whatever they were in their original context, they are preserved and presented because God has ultimately worked in a way that corresponds with their content.[33] Thus they are not accorded the status of prophecy, but they function, we might say, as a prophetic word.

While this is helpful, it could be nuanced by differentiating between types of blessing, and for that matter, developing a taxonomy of terms that takes in covenant, prophecy, blessing, and promise. Unfortunately, we lack the space for such an undertaking. We must be content with a few observations.

When Jacob meets Pharaoh he blesses him (47:7), they discuss Jacob's age, Jacob blesses him again (47:10) and leaves. Is this to be understood as the pronouncement of a wish, or, as is more commonly accepted, does blessing here mean nothing more than a greeting?[34] That is, many think Jacob arrives, says his equivalent of "*Shalom.*" They talk. Jacob says "*Shalom,*" and departs. We do not know what Jacob says so can speak of neither intention nor reception. In other places, however, we do hear words of greeting. For example, in Ruth 2:4, Boaz greets a company of harvesters with, "The LORD be with you." They reply, "The LORD bless you." These words, one could justly argue, have no more religious content than does "God bless you" in reply to a sneeze.[35]

But the inclusion of Jacob before Pharaoh teaches more than that Jacob says hello and good-bye. It portrays Jacob, the bringer of blessing to the nations, at the end of his life twice uttering blessing over Egypt. Abraham

---

33. Walton, *Genesis*, 712–13.

34. Mitchell, *The Meaning of Brk*, 106–10. I am indebted to my colleague Paul Williamson both for the observation and for the reference. See also Scharbert, "Brk," 291; Waltke, *Genesis*, 587. Waltke further points to Gen 27:23 and 27, where it would be strange if 27:23 refers to actual "blessing" rather than a greeting (Waltke, *Genesis*, 379).

35. Consider also such terms as goodbye, *adios* and *adieu*, with their lost theological content.

had brought a curse on Pharaoh's household because of his family: Jacob now brings blessing because of his.[36]

Genesis 47:7–10 thus represents the smallest of blessing narratives. And blessing language can, at a linguistic level, be small or large. But at a narrative level, we must not miss an opportunity to see God's glorious promise bearing fruit in its season.

36. For a defense of the notion that Jacob blesses rather than merely greets, see McKenzie, "Jacob's Blessing," 393–94.

Chapter 3

Jacob at God's House

Genesis 27:41—28:22

How CAN A CURSED family, ruined by everything that marred the first family, including rejection of God's words, lies, betrayal, and ultimately murderous intent—how can this family be used of God? How can the curse be lifted? It starts as always with a word from the LORD.

Genesis 27:41—28:9 appears at first as little more than a transition. It wraps up preceding events, expresses the attitudes of the protagonists, and transfers Jacob from one scene to the next. And if it is treated as transitional, one might think that the remainder of chapter 28 is little more than a vehicle to move Jacob from Canaan to Paddan Aram. These verses, however, convey more than geography.

Opposing the Promised One

Thinking Isaac's demise imminent, Esau promises a second funeral (27:41).[1] This death sentence exposes the absurdity of Rebekah's offer to bear the curse even as it runs counter to Isaac's words of life and blessing. Rebekah, again taking control, hears of Esau's threat and for a second time schemes to thwart her elder son. She counsels flight, telling Jacob to stay with Laban in Harran for, literally, "a few days." After "a few days" she expects Esau to be "no longer angry," supposing that he'll "forget" what you have done to him" (27:43–45). She adds that she will then call him home.

---

1. Turner notes several similarities with the story of Cain and Abel (*Genesis*, 122).

So she says. But does she really think that a few days will pacify Esau? In fact, she never summons Jacob. Due to her own scheming, her favorite is lost to a far country and she never sees him again. Her final words to Jacob are ambiguous: "why should I lose both of you in one day?" (27:45). Does she mean Isaac's death and Esau's threat?[2] Or does "both of you" speak of her two sons: Esau is lost to her and she fears Jacob will be too?[3] By any reckoning, her loss is great.

Esau shrieks opposition to God's purposes.[4] Beyond mere bitterness, he threatens the vehicle by which God will lift the curse. In this, Esau is anti-Christ, for seed, land, descendants, and nations mean nothing without the bearer of the promise. Esau/Edom's threat never expires. Esau's grandson by his firstborn (Eliphaz), is Amalek.[5] As Israel enters the land of promise, the Amalekites attack the nation (Exod 17:8).[6] Divine victory achieved, the text reads, in words that recall (and reverse) the "blessing" Isaac gave Esau: "So Joshua overcame the Amalekite army with the sword" (Exod 17:13).

Edom's sword reappears throughout Israel's story. In 1 Samuel 22, Doeg the Edomite informs Saul that God's anointed, David, had visited the priestly village of Nob. When Saul's guards refuse to kill the priests (22:17) Doeg slaughters eighty-five priests and *puts to the sword* all the inhabitants of Nob, including infants.

Centuries later, as the Babylonians destroyed Jerusalem, Edom's voice was heard: "'Tear it down,' they cried, 'tear it down to its foundations!'" (Ps 137:7).[7]

2. So Youngblood, *Genesis*, 216.

3. Waltke (*Genesis*, 569–70, n.1) rejects the first view because Isaac "is not a near antecedent of 'you.'" This follows Hamilton ("Šhl," 106), who suggests that Esau's murder of Jacob would be a capital offense.

4. Blessings in Scripture point to relationship with the divine. God so closely identifies with the blessed one that to bless Jacob is to bless God. To be "hostile toward [Jacob] is tantamount to being hostile toward God." So Mitchell, *The Meaning of Brk*, 30.

5. Gen 36:11–12; see also 1 Chr 1:36.

6. So Num 20:21, where Edom meets Israel's request for passage "with a large and powerful army."

7. See also Ps 83:2–6.

Not even exile can satisfy Edom's bloodlust.[8] Esther 3 introduces Haman the Agagite.[9] Agag is the Amalekite king whose life Saul spared. Thus, while Saul grants clemency to Israel's historic enemy, he murders, through Doeg, those who mediate God to the nation. Now Edom, ascendant in Haman, again intends to destroy Israel, a plan thwarted only by divine intervention.[10]

At Jesus' birth, the murderous threat to the family of blessing, the nation out of Egypt, the monarchy under David, and Judah in exile, rises again in the Edomite, Herod the Great. His massacre of the infants of Bethlehem (Matt 2:16) corresponds to the story of the Bible and his own murderous character. Thirty years later, another Herod ridicules and degrades Jesus (Luke 23:8–12) prior to the cross, the ultimate diabolical scheme against the one whom nations will serve and to whom peoples will bow down (Gen 27:29). Thus the Herods work their evil at either end of Jesus' earthly ministry. And thus Esau's deadly promise echoes down the centuries.

Wedding-Bell Blues

Rebekah, without mentioning Esau's threats, raises with Isaac another issue. She bemoans Esau's wives and the pain they cause her (27:46). She thus touches on a shared concern, but also possibly suggests that Isaac's passivity stands behind her troubles. If only he had taken action in Esau's marriages! Lest heartache be multiplied, he must now find a suitable wife for Jacob. But the unfolding story reveals God to be the true matchmaker:

8. Later oracles against Edom dwell on this violent nature: "The terror you inspire and the pride of your heart have deceived you" (Jer 49:16). "Because you harbored an ancient hostility and delivered the Israelite over to the sword at the time of their calamity . . ." (Ezek 35:5). Amos similarly condemns Edom "because he pursued his brother with a sword . . . because his anger raged continually and his fury flamed unchecked" (Amos 1:11). Obadiah, writing nearly two centuries after Amos' age of luxury and stability gave way to bloodshed at the hands of the Babylonians, also focuses on Esau's sword: "Because of the violence against your brother Jacob, you will be covered with shame; you will be destroyed forever" (Obad 10).

9. "Agagite" is used in 3:10; 8:3, 5; 9:24; "Enemy of the Jews" in 3:10; 8:1; 9:10, 24. Josephus refers to Haman as "the Amalekite," and the Targums supplement "Agagite" with "descendent of Amalek." The LXX of 9:24 replaces "Agagite" with "Macedonian," thus contextualizing by identifying Haman as the Jews' bitter enemy. So Bush, *Esther*, 384.

10. God is further heard to say during this epoch, in words that echo Edom's humiliation of Israel, "He will punish your sin, daughter of Edom, and expose your wickedness" (Lam 4:22).

control is stripped one by one from each member of the family, beginning already with Isaac, who is again manipulated by his wife,[11] and extending ultimately even to Jacob himself.

Isaac, ever reacting, responds to Rebekah's request, itself a response to Esau's threats, by returning Jacob to his roots. He will leave the land of promise for Harran, where Abraham's servant had ninety-five years earlier found in Rebekah a wife suitable for Isaac. Isaac commands that Jacob shun the daughters of Canaan, instead marrying one of the daughters of his uncle Laban. But before sending Jacob, Isaac blesses him again.[12]

Irony runs in two directions. The first relates to marriage and will be touched upon in a moment. The second relates more directly to the content of the blessing.

Wedged between commands to marry properly is another blessing pronounced over Jacob. Esau had cried out, "do you have only one blessing, my father?" (27:38). We now learn Isaac has another, but it too goes to Jacob. With these words, Isaac finally acknowledges that Jacob is indeed God's chosen one. The content thus differs markedly from before, resembling more closely blessings found in Genesis 13:14–17 and 17:1–7. That is, unlike the hope intended for Esau of a fruitful land, God's promise to Abraham and this blessing speak of fruitful people in a possessed land.

And what an unlikely set of promises! Surely fathers have with less confidence advanced sons with better prospects. When Isaac invokes the LORD to produce "a community of peoples" and asks divine favor "so that you may take possession of *the land where you now reside* as a foreigner" (28:4), he seems to read from the wrong script. The enemy at home is known, but now he must face the unknown on a long and dangerous journey to a place he has never seen. When is the promise under greater threat than when Jacob flees the land, running from the family he has destroyed, toward only God knows what?

The spotlight now returns to Esau. His marrying, having set the scene and provided the transition into the next, is not yet finished. Learning that

---

11. Alter, *Genesis*, 46.

12. In the paragraph running from 28:1–5, the narrator refers first to the blessing, then to the command (28:1), but then, in the direct discourse that contains the content of both, he reverses the order (28:2–4). The paragraph then concludes by repeating the contents of the instructions (28:5) in order to indicate that Jacob went to the place and the family mentioned by his father. Thus the reader encounters in triplicate the instructions concerning place and descent of an appropriate wife, spoken by Rebekah (27:43), Isaac (28:1–2), and the narrator (28:5).

his father has blessed Jacob again(!) and sent him to Harran for the right sort of wife, and that Jacob was obedient to his parents in going there for a wife (28:7), it finally dawns on him: he should stop marrying Canaanite women. He therefore finds a new wife who meets this simple standard: Esau marries Ishmael's daughter. His journey as the rejected one thus "parodies Jacob's."[13] Both seek a wife. Both acquire several. But the rejected one, Esau, marries the daughter of the rejected one, Ishmael, while the chosen one returns blessed of the LORD.

Encountering the Unknown

Modern westerners embrace the future, defining the self in part by events unknown. The ancients adopted a different stance. Jacob exchanges all that has constructed his identity for a netherworld that challenges even the notion of existence. Departing alone raises questions of function and being, questions normally answered in terms of family, home, and the family gods he now leaves behind.[14] Since gods were associated with clans and land, Jacob's journey, like Abraham's, would generate a "divine void."[15] But Jacob reverses Abraham's journey. His grandfather had left Harran for a new country at seventy-five. Now Jacob leaves the promised land for Harran at roughly the same age. Abraham travelled in obedience and faith, escorted by God. To this point Jacob's only encounter with God's promise is through the father he has deceived, of a land he is now fleeing, of a family he has just destroyed.

The journey underway, he stops as darkness falls and fashions a bed with a rock pillow. We are told, in what at first seems extraneous, that he stops "because the sun had set."[16] But this sun will not be said to rise for twenty long years, until he reenters the land (32:31). He must face the long night of an exile of his own making.

Here Jacob dreams of a stairway rising to heaven (28:12). One cannot by human effort reach a God who is both personal and wholly other, as Genesis 11:1–9 teaches. But now the Lord of Heaven overturns that story of uprising by lowering himself into the human experience. Jacob's ladder

---

13. Waltke, *Genesis*, 383.

14. See esp. Walton for a discussion of Egyptian and Mesopotamian views of self, and how they intersect with communal realities (*Ancient Near East*, 148).

15. Walton, *Genesis*, 392.

16. Gen 28:11.

is a ziggurat,[17] a passageway through which the divine travels. Thus, "Jacob's ladder" is neither a ladder nor Jacob's: it shows God reaching into his world. "Angels of God . . . ascending and descending on it" further emphasize this bridging of heaven and earth. But why, if heaven is the angelic dwelling place, the curious order of first up, then down?

Identical language appears at a high point in John's Gospel. Jesus responds to Nathanael's exclamation that he is Son of God, and King of Israel—both royal titles—with the promise that he "will see heaven open, and the angels of God ascending and descending on the Son of Man" (John 1:49–51), for the king of heaven and earth has arrived. Thus Genesis provides the image by which Jesus claims to be the ladder of heaven, a bridge between the human and divine. The Christian Bethel therefore is his body given over to the cross on which he died and was glorified.

The salvation won by this king, and given expression in the apostolic writings, brings to full bloom seeds sown in Genesis. Jacob, as the LORD speaks to him, looks upon "ministering spirits" (Heb 1:14), who in one moment stand in God's presence and in another serve those earmarked for salvation. In light of the words to follow, their presence itself promises that God will help Jacob on his journey. The fact that they ascend first means that, unknown to Jacob, their presence and ministry to him were established before he ever learned of it.[18]

Beside this structure stands the LORD himself (28:13).[19] The sentences combine to focus attention. With shortening clauses the camera tightens from a stairway to angels (plural) that move on that stairway (arresting the eye) to, finally, the LORD (singular) standing beside it.[20] Every detail is important in itself, but each pulls the eye toward the LORD who dominates the scene.

17. The word appears only here in the Bible. The LXX offers *klimax*, pointing to a ladder or stairway. Houtman, "What Did Jacob See"; Cohen, *Biblical Hapax Legomena*, 34; Griffith ("The Celestial Ladder," 229–30) explains the text in terms of Egyptian rather than Mesopotamian backgrounds. Millard argues for Mesopotamian ("The Celestial Ladder," 86–87). So also von Rad (*Genesis*, 284). For a Freudian interpretation, see Couffignal, "Le Songe de Jacob."

18. Vos, *Biblical Theology*, 96.

19. "Beside" fits better than the NIV's "above" for three reasons. First, Jacob thinks that God shares the place with him (Waltke, *Genesis*, 390–91). Second, God does not *call* to Jacob, but simply "says." Third and most significant, in twenty-one other occurrences of this verb and preposition combination in the OT, it always means "stand beside," never "stand above" (Walton, *Genesis*, 571, n. 6).

20. Ross, *Creation and Blessing*, 488.

And God speaks, pronouncing himself "the LORD, the God of your father Abraham and the God of Isaac," attributing fatherhood not to Isaac, but to Jacob's grandfather.[21] Little in the text to this point suggests that Jacob has made God's acquaintance. But now God makes unilateral promises, reiterating aspects of the Abrahamic covenant and, notably, the second blessing Isaac pronounced.[22] He begins by promising that Jacob and his descendants would occupy "the land on which you are lying" (28:13). This resembles Isaac's departing words: may God bless "so that you may take possession of the land where you now reside" (28:4). God's promise then extends geographically beyond Isaac's as it speaks of descendants (lit. "seed," clearly a plural) who will occupy the four corners of the earth (28:14). The LORD adds, "All peoples on earth will be blessed through you and your offspring [lit. "seed," now less clearly a plural]." The Hebrew verb form used here is reflexive, suggesting that blessing (or curse) on the families and nations depends on how they treat Jacob's family.[23]

This must have floored Jacob. God and Isaac speak of possessing the land he is leaving, having sown disaster in his home. While he may have lived in the land yesterday and today, what are the odds he'll ever see it again? How will he last the night, much less the journey to distant lands and then home again? All three would have been fraught with peril. Furthermore, what good is a promise of descendants to an old man with no wife? And to speak of blessing coming to all *families* on earth! How can the destroyer of families and bringer of curse be the source of a blessed family, much less one that brings blessing to others?

---

21. Gen 28:13. The divine formula is unique in Scripture. Note too the language of 28:4—"the blessing given to Abraham." Together these references to Abraham likely indicate his vital role in Jacob's story. So Walton, *Traveller*, 48.

22. Dumbrell in his discussion of blessing in Genesis 12 correctly observes that the "sense of blessing is repeated in the experience of both Isaac (26:4), and Jacob"—citing Gen 28:4 and 14 (*Covenant and Creation*, 70). In fact, however, Genesis 12 plays virtually no role in this blessing. The name invoked by Isaac in 28:3, "God Almighty," repeats the holy name found in Gen 17:1; the call in 28:3 for abundant offspring resembles 17:2; and the reference to land (28:4), explicitly connected with the "blessing given to Abraham" (28:3), builds on 17:6–7. Turner discusses at length the relationship between the Abrahamic promises and those given to Jacob (*Announcements*, 135–41).

23. So also in Gen 12:3 and 18:8. See Walton (*Traveller*, 48), who further observes that the outworking of this promise is seen in Abraham in Egypt, Sodom and Gomorrah; Abraham and Abimelech; Isaac and Abimelech; Jacob and Laban (30:27–30 [on which see esp Mitchell, *The Meaning of Brk*, 70]); and Joseph in Egypt (see also Num 24:9; Ps 72:17).

Jacob sleeps on it, but stumbles toward answers. There may be no guarantees in life, but there are promises. God is disclosing something of himself to Jacob: "I am with you and will watch over you wherever you go" (28:15).[24] Like Jonah, Jacob can run, but not from God's presence. This God travels. Secondly, he "will bring [Jacob] back to this land." For this to occur, Jacob needs to survive the journeys ahead. Even as Abraham, as good as dead (Rom 4:19), believed the promise of a son, so Jacob, himself as good as dead, hears the promise of a safe return to Bethel. What can be accomplished by people for whom death holds no threat? Finally, God says, "I will not leave you until I have done what I have promised you." This means not that God *will* leave after fulfillment, but that they will surely be done.[25]

Jacob's character offers little hope. This is not a story of realized potential.[26] Instead, hope issues from God. No local deity, he even accompanies his people into exile. And he accomplishes what he promises.

The Fear of the Lord

Jacob's three responses are recorded.[27] First, he wakes with a dread surpassing his fear of Esau or the perils of the road. "Surely the Lord is in this place." In fear he says, "How awesome is this place! This is none other than the house of God; this is the gate of heaven" (28:16–17). This again recalls the account of Babel where Genesis ridicules human attempts to reach heaven with the words, "But the Lord *came down* to see the city and the tower the people were building" (11:5). The storyteller then adds that at Babylon God came down to enter into their experience and disrupt them (11:9).[28] For this moment, however, Bethel, not Babylon, is God's gate into this world.

---

24. Jacob is the first in the Bible to hear the words "I am with you," a formula that becomes a repeated word of hope to many of Israel's leaders. God makes this promise to Moses (Exod 3:12), Joshua (Josh 1:5), and Gideon (Judg 6:16). See Wenham, *Genesis 16–50*, 225. Moses, as he transfers leadership to Joshua, tells the nation: "The Lord himself goes with you; he will never leave you nor forsake you" (Deut 31:6). God's words to Jacob also recall Matthew's Gospel, which opens with the promise of Immanuel, God with us (Matt 1:23), and closes with Jesus telling his disciples, as he departs and disperses them among the nations, "surely I am with you always, to the very end of the age" (28:20).

25. Ross, *Creation and Blessing*, 491; Wenham, *Genesis 16–50*, 223.

26. On the relationship of hope, promise, and possibility, see Clines, *Themes*, 113–18.

27. See Waltke for the enumeration of Jacob's three responses (*Genesis*, 392–94).

28. Walton, *Ancient Near East*, 120–21. Waltke further notes that Babylon was understood to mean "gate of god", so that "gate of heaven" serves as a "counterpoint to Babylon" (*Genesis*, 392).

And whatever ungodly climbing Jacob's story reveals, it remains again for the LORD to come down to establish his presence.

Standing with God

Jacob, as a second response, establishes a "pillar" for a memorial with the rock that guarded his head (28:18). The word for "pillar" plays on the words used in 28:12, where the ladder is "standing," and v. 13, where God "stood." Even as the ladder "prefigured" the presence of God, the standing stone "postfigures" that same presence.[29]

The narration now moves back from actions to words: again the locale becomes prominent as Jacob "called that place Bethel" (28:18).[30] Why was the former name, Luz, withheld until this point? When will Jacob call that place Bethel? Is it only upon his return twenty years later that he uses that new name? The effect of withholding the old and introducing the new name—though the old has not yet passed away and the new has not yet arrived—is that God, in the narrative, finds Jacob in an apparently empty place, a random "somewhere."[31] A center for Canaanite rites is thus effectively blotted out of the story and subsequently from the map, for the place of false religion is rendered holy by his divine presence and becomes God's own house.

Bethel's role as the place of divine disclosure to Jacob—twice—is surprising given the ever narrower focus on Jerusalem as Israel's holy place. Sadly though, the story of Bethel ends not with worship of a self-disclosing God, but, after the tenth century, of calves.[32]

Jacob's declaration—"Bethel"—does not mean that he thought God restricted himself to this place.[33] The promise was that "I am with you and will watch over you wherever you go . . . I will not leave you."[34] Various stages of Israel's history find God's dwelling marked out with appropriate

29. Fokkelman, *Narrative Art*, 66. Also Waltke, *Genesis*, 393.

30. Referring to tithes and the house of God "hints" at subsequent developments in Jewish religious life. So Walton, *Traveller*, 55.

31. Fokkelman, *Narrative Art*, 74.

32. Wenham, *Genesis 16–50*, 224.

33. It is left to literary critics to explain why Bethel is given such an elevated status when the rest of the OT moves toward centralized religious life in the Jerusalem Temple: see Walton, *Traveller*, 41.

34. Gen 28:15.

materials. For now a simple rock will do. As the nation wanders, first through the desert and then through a land that they gradually occupy, the "house of God" is a tent that reflects glory but remains highly portable.[35] Once the wanderings end and David captures Jerusalem, David plans and Solomon constructs a dwelling of more permanent material—stone, wood, and precious metals—to house the ark of the covenant and mediate God's presence. When the people turn from God, confusing both the house with his presence and their selfish activities within that house with worship, God turns from them and the temple is destroyed.

In the NT, the temple takes on still better material. Stephen in Acts 7 argues, "The Most High does not live in houses made by human hands." He finds evidence in Isaiah 66:1–2, where the LORD says, "Heaven is my throne and earth is my footstool. What kind of house will you build for me? . . . Or where will my resting place be?"[36]

One cannot confine God to a house; but he himself builds temples. First, Jesus, the one true mediator and point of mediation between God and man, presents *himself* as the true temple (John 1:50; 2:19–22), for he becomes in his flesh the place of mediation.[37] Second, because of the Spirit poured out, Paul can enlist temple-language to exhort the church (1 Cor 3:10–14; Eph 2:19–22): "Don't you know that you yourselves are God's temple and that God's Spirit lives in you. If anyone destroys God's temple, God will destroy that person; for God's temple is sacred, and you together are that temple."[38] Here Paul warns the fractious that "you," the Spirit-indwelt community, are the building blocks of God's temple, and that judgment befalls those who attack the house of God from within. In chapter 6, Paul a second time speaks of the composition of the temple, this time referring not to the community as the dwelling place of the Holy Spirit, but to the individual: "Do you not know that your bodies are temples of the Holy Spirit, who is in you, whom you have received from God? You are not your own; you were bought at a price. Therefore honor God with your body."[39] The Christian's body, and the community of which he or she is part, are God's

---

35. Webb, in an assessment of the tabernacle's structure, describes it as "a kind of Jacob's ladder, linking heaven and earth" ("Heaven on Earth," 161), and "a kind of portable Sinai, a travelling holy mountain" ("Heaven on Earth", 163).

36. Acts 7:48–49.

37. So also Eph 2:18; 1 Tim 2:5; Heb 10:19–22.

38. 1 Cor 3:16–17.

39. 1 Cor 6:19–20.

temple, and thus sacred. Paul a third time challenges the Corinthians with this metaphor, now as a call to separation: "For we are the temple of the living God. As God has said: 'I will live with them and walk among them, and I will be their God, and they will be my people.'"[40]

Finally, in the eschaton "God's dwelling place is now among the people, and he will live with them. They will be his people, and God himself will be with them and be their God" (Rev 21:3). This thrice-stated assertion of God's presence combined with the promise to "be their God" pulls together the LORD's promise and Jacob's response in Genesis 28. Revelation in this way asserts that God so fulfils his word that the conditional element of Jacob's vow is fully realized: God has accompanied his people on their journey, provided for them, and brought them safely home. The fullness of this divine presence renders any temple redundant: "I did not see a temple in the city, because the LORD God Almighty and the Lamb are its temple."[41] Further, the gates of this temple-less city, unlike Nehemiah's, never close (21:25; cf. Neh 7:3), signifying the unending security of those who rest in God's presence.

God instructs Israel during the conquest to destroy the pillars in the land (Exod 23:24; 34:13; Deut 7:5; 12:3) and not to establish them (Deut 16:22; 1 Kgs 14:22–24). These commands sit alongside the erection of pillars by Jacob at crucial times: the LORD appearing to him (28:18 and 35:14), a treaty (31:45), and Rachel's death (35:20).[42] Moses sets up twelve, one per tribe, at the confirmation of the covenant (Exod 24:4). Joshua 4:20 speaks of twelve rocks taken from the Jordan to mark Israel's dry crossing. In fact, the book of Joshua records numerous occasions when rocks were set up as memorials.[43] Each consists of multiple rocks except the last, when Joshua himself erects a stone pillar as a witness to the covenant renewal that closes out his ministry (Josh 27:25–27).

The tension between prohibition and practice dissolves with the recognition that Canaanite pillars differ in every respect but material from Jewish pillars.[44] The former featured in cultic activities that included

---

40. 2 Cor 6:16; quoting Lev 26:12.

41. Rev 21:22.

42. Waltke, *Genesis*, 393.

43. Joshua 4:20; 7:26; 8:29; 10:27; 22:27—here they erect an altar rather than a pillar, but explicitly declare it to be not for sacrifice but a memorial; 24:27.

44. Wenham notes that non-conformity to the Law of Moses indicates "that this tradition does indeed go back to patriarchal times. . . . Indeed it is hard to envisage this episode being recorded at all after the late tenth century, when Bethel became a center for the Canaanite-style worship of bull calves" (*Genesis 16–50*, 224).

Asherah poles and altars, and were considered "the repositories of deities' spirits and perhaps functioned to symbolize their fertility."[45] Such relics have no place in a holy land from which mute idols must be removed. The pillars, on the other hand, recall God's activities or presence, or invoke his witness at the establishment of a treaty or covenant. In such cases, they testify to truth and thus appropriately stand before a God who speaks. The pillar Jacob establishes stands not as witness to a covenant (for the text relates the stone neither to Jacob's nor the LORD's words) but as a memorial to what Jacob has seen.[46]

Let's Make a Deal

Jacob's third response is the longest vow, indeed the only patriarchal vow, in Scripture.[47] His subsequent words reveal that he doesn't think he can domesticate or position God by constructing a shrine or memorial, for he speaks of God "be[ing] with me . . . on this journey" (28:20). Nevertheless, he lists the basic things he lacks (food, clothing, and safety) and vows that if God returns him safely, "then the LORD will be my God."[48]

The conditional elements in Jacob's words (28:20–21), some assert, do not indicate bargaining with God, for the vow constitutes a prayer in a ceremonial context.[49]

> . . . what tells against such a *hybris* is the biblical-theological argument that man in the O.T. is not in a superior position from which to choose Yhwh for a God as one of many possibilities, without himself being involved . . . . Moreover, it would here be in conflict with the tone of the narrative if Jacob in a matter-of-fact and presumptuous manner stipulated what conditions Yhwh would have to fulfil in order to be his God.[50]

45. Waltke, *Genesis*, 393, esp. n. 92.

46. Waltke, *Genesis*, 393. Compare Josh 22:26–27, where Reuben, Gad, and the half-tribe of Manasseh claim their "imposing altar" (so 22:10) serves only as a memorial: it is not for sacrifice.

47. Waltke, *Genesis*, 393.

48. Turner observes that Jacob responds less to the promise God makes here, to do with a nation, land, and universal blessing, than the stolen blessing, with its connection to more mundane needs. In this, Jacob appears "content with what he has wrested from Isaac's grasp, but appears somewhat distrustful of Yahweh" (*Genesis*, 125).

49. Calvin, *Genesis*, 2:121–22; Wenham, *Genesis 16–50*, 224.

50. Fokkelman, *Narrative Art*, 75–76.

Is Bethel thus the place of Jacob's "conversion"? He has, to be sure, given to God all he possesses: a rock, some oil, and the promise that when he receives more he will give a tenth.[51] But the fact remains that Jacob, though not in a superior position with respect to Esau, grasped with some success that which was above him. And much of that success, both before and after this night, came through rough negotiation. The biblical-theological truth that "man . . . is not in a superior position" has not throughout history stopped people from "stipulat[ing] what conditions" God "would have to fulfil."

Even the event itself doesn't present Jacob as having arrived. Generally in the OT prophets receive visions, while false prophets dream dreams.[52] Since in a dream the individual's consciousness "is more or less loosened from his personality," God granted dreams to those whose "spiritual state was ill-adapted" for divine communication.[53] Genesis recounts ten dream narratives, involving Abimelech (20:3), Jacob twice (28:12; 31:10), though by chapter 46 he has progressed to a vision, Laban (31:24), youthful Joseph (37:5), but not later, Pharaoh's butler and baker (40:5, 16), and Pharaoh (41:1).[54] In this company, Jacob dreams as "outsider,"[55] but at last he moves in the right direction.

Nevertheless, Jacob "still sounds like a bargain-hunter."[56] The man who bought the birthright with lentils, and stole the blessing with goat and garments, now bargains with God for food and clothes.[57] He has not to this point exhibited faith, and in subsequent events does not claim the LORD as his God until he returns to Bethel. Only then will Jacob cleanse his tent of idols (Gen 35:2). In between, superstition abounds. Abraham and Isaac have a God (28:13). Jacob will not, at least in the same way, for some time. But even if Jacob does not yet own him, the LORD nevertheless owns Jacob.

So this passage, at first glance a geographical transition, becomes the next step in Jacob's spiritual life. Many miles lie ahead, none more important than the one that locates the LORD God beside him. The efforts and dangers

---

51. Wenham, *Genesis 16–50*, 226.

52. Vos, *Biblical Theology*, 71–72.

53. Vos, *Biblical Theology*, 71.

54. For a catalogue of dreams in Genesis, see Lipton, *Revisions*, 9.

55. Walton, *Genesis*, 574; see also his discussion in *Ancient Near East*, 243.

56. Brueggemann, who adds, "Even in this solemn moment . . . [he still adds an 'if'] (v. 20)" (*Genesis*, 248). Also Cartledge, *Vows*, 168; Alter, *Genesis*, 150.

57. Turner, *Announcements*, 141.

of a trip from Beersheba to Harran never appear in the story.[58] For only this night matters, and Jacob does not act this night; he observes. He does not go to God; he finds God beside him. And he is not given commands or warnings, only gracious promises from God to an undeserving sinner.

---

58. The distance is approximately six hundred miles or one thousand kilometers.

Chapter 4

Jacob Finds a Wife (or Two)

Genesis 29:1–30

ENERGIZED BY GOD'S PROMISES, Jacob "continued on his journey," expressed more idiomatically in Hebrew as he "lifted up his feet." Usually when meeting the LORD, one lifts the eyes, but that would hardly be relevant here. He leaves in full stride, but alone and without possessions. He will not return that way.

Without ado we are told he arrives, ominously, at "the land of the Eastern peoples."[1] But the scene he encounters is languid, pastoral, painted with sun-bleached hues. Below an unbroken blue sky is a watered land dotted with sheep. At the center of the picture is a well sufficient for several flocks, surrounded by shepherds enjoying their siesta. The details present a scene tailor-made for Jacob: he is clever, urbane, a shepherd who will surely thrive in such a place. On the periphery of this still-life we now detect movement: a woman of rare beauty approaches with her sheep. From all this, Genesis fixes our attention on a stone, referring to it three times in 29:2–3 (see also 29:10). This stone, covering the well, is so big that it hinders the shepherds' work, generating a serenity that will soon be shattered.[2]

---

1. Waltke, *Genesis*, 400; see also 85, where he writes: "But movement to the east in Genesis is usually negative, in the context of judgment (3:24; 4:16), vainglory and greed (11:2; 13:11), and alienation (25:6)" (Waltke, *Genesis*, 85).

2. What are we to make of Genesis' fixation with the rock? Does it recall God's presence at Bethel? Does it indicate God's presence in Harran (similar to 1 Cor 10:4, "The spiritual rock that accompanied them, and that rock was Jesus"), demonstrating that the God who promised to accompany him has indeed gone with him? Or does it, even as that previous rock symbolized God's presence and protective power, here testify to

Wells and Brides

Jacob trades the periphery for center stage, arriving from nowhere to disturb the peace. Approaching the shepherds he asks, "Where are you from?"

"From Harran," they reply (29:4).

"Do you know," Jacob inquires against all odds, "Laban, Nahor's grandson?" Laban was introduced already in Genesis 24 as greedy, reluctant to release a servant, and willing to detain a married (or at least engaged) female relative.

With a second affirmation Jacob discovers himself to be in the right place: "Yes, we know him" (29:5). References to emotion are withheld, but coming in the wake of so much fear, this reply would have calmed troubled waters. He asks those who know his uncle, "Is Laban *shalom*?"[3]

The answer comes back, "Yes, *shalom*, and here is his daughter Rachel" (29:6). Laban, Laban's family, and his village are all "*shalom*." Having sparked a conflagration at home, Jacob hopes to one day "return safely" (i.e., "in *shalom*," 28:21). Now he finds another household at peace. The reader knows Jacob well enough by this point, to hear, "Yes, *shalom*, . . . but not for long."

With this, another facet of Jacob's character surfaces. The single-minded deceiver is equally focused on work and knowledgeable around sheep. He transforms the quiet scene to one of activity, commanding his new acquaintances, "water the sheep and take them back to pasture," for the sun is still high.[4] The shepherds resist, the stone again coming to the fore, because "until all the flocks are gathered" they cannot water the sheep (29:8). Since sheep offer little help moving heavy objects, the point may be that only when the shepherds team together can they move the stone. Or, as some have proposed, the community has agreed to forego water until all the shepherds gather. If this is the case, then from the outset Jacob defies local custom.

But here comes Rachel. Like Jacob, she tends sheep.[5] Indeed, she alone in Scripture is called a shepherdess.[6] In other ways too, we will discover, she

---

Jacob's power? It will in a moment define his presence and illustrate his strength. Waltke, *Genesis*, 399. Maybe Jacob, shrewd and strong, can go it alone.

3. My translation.

4. Even the reference to the sun, notably, is conveyed with an imperative (29:7).

5. Note too that she arrives after several other shepherds. She, like Jacob, is a conscientious worker.

6. Duguid, *Relentless Grace*, 66. This stands despite the fact that others perform at

is a suitable match for Jacob. Upon seeing her, Jacob single-handedly moves the stone, and waters Laban's sheep. He has the strength, and does the work, of a team. If we assumed that this man of the tents, overtaken by Esau at birth, beloved of his mother, and smooth of skin, was for these reasons not physically robust, we find ourselves mistaken. The shepherds of this village are no match for him—at least with respect to shepherding. One glimpse of his cousin makes him stronger than three of them (Gen 29:2).

His feat of strength complete, Jacob kisses Rachel and begins to weep. Verse 12 suggests that this is a kiss of greeting, for we now learn that Jacob has introduced himself as a close relative. But surely his tears express the relief of surviving the journey and the joy of discovering the woman he has left his father and mother to marry.[7]

As Rachel runs home, we must remain at the well for a moment. Much is made of the contrast between Abraham's servant, who found a wife for Isaac at a well, and Jacob, who similarly locates his fiancé. The former account establishes a narrative form found several times in Scripture and structured as follows: the protagonist (or in the first instance, his representative) travels to a far-off place; after he arrives at a well, the future bride approaches; either the prospective bride or groom draws water; the woman goes home to report the meeting; the traveler is brought to the woman's house; the traveler (or his master) and the girl are wed.[8]

These plotlines shaped Genesis 24 and now Genesis 29. At least two more encounters fit the form. In Exodus 2:15, Moses while fleeing from Pharaoh arrives at a well. Here he finds the seven daughters of Reuel, set upon by shepherds. He rescues them and waters their flock (2:17). The grateful father invites him to dinner (2:20), after which the marriage to Zipporah seems inevitable. The account is stripped down to a man on a journey who finds a woman harassed at a well, comes to her aid, is invited to stay, and marries her. It unfolds much like the story of Abraham's servant and Jacob.[9]

---

least part of the task, e.g., the seven daughters of Reuel, who draw water for sheep. The narrative, however, distinguishes the daughters from the shepherds (Exod 2:16–17). See also Song of Solomon 1:8.

7. Bar-Efrat correctly observes that Jacob's energy and emotion spring from finding the relative he was to marry (*Narrative Art*, 119). It is easy to overlook Isaac's command to marry one of Laban's daughters (28:2): that is, Jacob was not sent on a quest to find a wife but to marry a cousin; Wenham, *Genesis 16–50*, 213–14. Rachel's beauty is mentioned later, and then only to explain his preference for Rachel over Leah.

8. Alter, *Art*, 51–57.

9. Turner notes that well-stories in Genesis can point in another direction (*Genesis*,

This formal analysis helps answer a question generated within John's Gospel. In John 2, Jesus turns water into wine at a wedding. In the ensuing discussion, the master of the banquet confuses Jesus with the groom (John 2:9–10). In chapter 3, the Baptist's disciples express frustration when the crowds forsake him. John reminds them that he himself had distinguished between the Christ and the forerunner (3:28). Then he adds, "The bride belongs to the bridegroom. The friend who attends the bridegroom waits and listens for him, and is full of joy when he hears the bridegroom's voice. That joy is mine, and is now complete" (3:29).

So in consecutive chapters, John identifies Jesus with, and then as, the groom. The question naturally arises, who is the bride? At this very point Jesus goes on a journey, arrives at a well in Samaria (indeed Jacob's well) to find a woman there at the wrong time, and offers her water that springs up to salvation. Interwoven with talk of water and the Holy Spirit is her marital history. She has had five husbands, and now lives with man number six. What she needs—plainly—is man number seven—the groom who stands before her holding out words of life. The account closes with the woman and her village responding in faith and celebration.[10]

So John, via this story form, exploits the image of the wedding banquet[11] to teach that Jesus is the Messiah and that the bride of Christ expands,[12] against hope, to include a Samaritan woman and a village of men and women rejected by Israel but welcomed into the fold by Jesus (also John 10:16). Distasteful as the notion of Jesus marrying such a person may be, to resist is to align with those who reject Jesus and the forgiveness that permeates the gospel.

---

127). In chapters 16, 21, and 26, such stories include conflict. Perhaps here too, conflict is certain.

10. On the literary form in the context of John 4, see Eslinger, "Wooing," 167–70; Staley, *Print's First Kiss*, 98–103. For a fuller but perhaps not always convincing development of the details in the context of Jesus and the woman, see Brant, "Husband Hunting," 211–16.

11. The wedding appears again in Rev 19:7–9, 22:17, on which see below. Marriage also informs Eph 5:25–27. God is portrayed as a husband in Isa 54:5–7; Hos 2:19.

12. Note that each reference to Jesus as the groom sits in an eschatological setting: Matt 25:1–13; Mark 2:19–20; Luke 5:33–35.

Life with Laban

Echoes of Genesis 24 abound, for within the same plotline, the same Laban who greeted Abraham's servant now welcomes Jacob. Alongside common features, however, are equally important differences. Abraham's servant prayed that the LORD would guide him (24:12), and then established a means to assess the woman's character (24:13–14). Praise then poured forth when Rebekah passed the test (24:26–27).[13] Jacob, on the other hand, doesn't pray for a wife; he doesn't even acknowledge God's presence. Upon seeing her, he (rather than Rachel) waters the animals, her character remaining veiled, beauty her only stated qualification. Finally, Jacob offers no praise. If the problem with being an atheist is not knowing who to thank, then Jacob lives like an atheist.

Jacob now provides a fixed point of reference as events move toward or away from him. Rachel runs home to announce his arrival, the narrator following her from Jacob crying at the well to Laban running to meet him. The main characters in this story and this family are runners. Laban embraces Jacob and kisses him (29:13). No doubt the embrace includes a pat-down, for the last time Laban heard from one of his relatives, the messenger led ten camels loaded with "all kinds of good things" (24:10). Laban takes him home, where Jacob tells him "all these things" (29:13). The contrast between "all kinds of things" and "all these things" (literally "words"), reminds us that Jacob arrives empty handed. The former represented the estate of the groom just as Jacob's words indicate his net worth. All he can offer is himself, his bloodline, and a recounting of how he got here. Genesis will not let us forget why Jacob is in Paddan Aram.

Having heard "all these things" Laban replies, "you are my own flesh and blood" (29:14). What words elicit this response? Levels of story collide: surely the principal answer lies in Jacob informing Laban of family connections, with the possible addition of his parent's desire that he marry Laban's daughter (28:2) and the success of his journey. Informed of Jacob's close relationship, Laban's reply fits perfectly. But we know what Laban does not. Had Jacob revealed his true character, Laban could still rightly reply, "you are my own flesh and blood." Storm clouds are gathering.

13. Waltke, *Genesis*, 399.

Bargaining for Brides

After a month of providing for Jacob and learning of both his impoverished state and capacity for work, Laban offers Jacob the chance to earn an honest wage. The shift is subtle and undramatic: quietly Laban reveals that flesh and blood mean little to him, that he will pay Jacob for Jacob's work, which is another way of saying that he will pay Jacob *if* Jacob works. Thus, he exchanges familial bonds for a master-servant relationship. Wage negotiations will inevitably yield to labor disputes.[14]

Before Jacob responds, the narrator intrudes to speak of Laban's two daughters. This is a surprise. We've met Rachel, but only now learn of Leah (29:16). At least in the story so far, the younger sibling has again supplanted the older. Furthermore, the only description of Leah relates to her weak eyes (29:17).[15] The words thus recall Isaac and his weak eyes in 27:1. Former events cannot escape our consciousness, even if Jacob's sins are far from *his* mind. While the forced recollection is appropriate, "weak" may not be the best translation: options include "lovely," "tender," and "delicate."[16] "Tender" or "delicate" come closest to the point. It's not that she needed glasses or had a vacant expression, but that she had attractive eyes. Her beauty was focused.[17] Rachel, on the other hand, was steeped in it. Jacob, after only a month, loves Rachel. The text suggests that beauty had won Jacob's affections,[18] casting him for the first time in a similar light to his father, letting his appetites determine his preferences. But the text never implies that he chooses wrongly, that she isn't his proper wife.

Having learned of Leah, we hear Jacob's answer: he will work seven years for Rachel's hand. This is a high-priced wife. The hard bargainer has gone soft, as desperate for Rachel as Esau had once been for food.[19] Will this story end more happily? The standard shepherd's annual wage was ten

14 Fokkelman, *Narrative Art*, 127.

15. So NAS, RSV.

16. Walton, *Genesis*, 586. For early Jewish reflection, see Zucker and Reiss, *Matriarchs*, 174–75.

17. Her appearance is understood variously. Wenham asks if she is unmarried and likely to remain unmarried because she is ugly (*Genesis 16–50*, 235–37). Fokkelman speaks of her plainness (*Narrative Art*, 127).

18. Bar-Efrat, *Narrative Art*, 49. Also described as beautiful are Bathsheba (2 Sam 11:2), Tamar (2 Sam 13:1), and Abishag (1 Kgs 1:4). David is said to have beautiful eyes (1 Sam 16:12) and his son Absalom was praised above all others for his unblemished beauty (2 Sam 14:25). So Bar-Efrat, *Narrative Art*, 49–50.

19. Turner, *Genesis*, 127.

shekels, while the standard bride-price—paid to provide for the bride in the event of death or divorce—was thirty to forty shekels, with a maximum set at fifty (Deut 22:29).[20] But lacking resources, Jacob has no leverage. Besides, the bride-price will secure the future of his beloved.[21]

Laban less generously replies, "It's better that I give her to you than to some other man. Stay here with me" (29:19). The oracle and Isaac's first blessing had predicted that Jacob would rule, but in chapter 29 Jacob is seven times said to serve.[22] So Jacob does the time, but the years and the labor are no great burden to him because he loves her: indeed, "they seemed like only *a few days* to him" (29:20). The author forces the reader, with the cumulative effect of numerous references to the previous story, to hear this chapter as the aftermath of Jacob's deception. Rebekah, counselling flight during darker days, sent him to Laban to stay "*a few days*" (27:44). Seven references to serving for seven years indicate the completeness of his work. He has served his sentence, paid his penance. His moment of happiness has arrived.

Payback

Jacob tells Laban, "Give me my wife. My time is completed, and I want to make love to her." With these winsome words, Jacob demands his pay. Laban prepares a public celebration, providing witness to the nuptials by bringing "together all the people of the place" (29:22). But, to our ongoing amazement, he secretly substitutes Leah for Rachel, gives her to Jacob, "and Jacob made love to her" (29:23). And in the morning, "there was Leah!" (29:25).

One of the most bewildering accounts in all Scripture, this episode raises without answering a host of questions. Did Laban entertain the possibility that Jacob might simply pack up and go without Leah? How long

20. Walton, *Genesis*, 586. Wenham, *Genesis 16–50*, 235.

21. Bride-price refers to wealth provided by the groom's family to secure the bride, while a dowry is wealth originating from the bride's side. A dowry generally features in cultures that depend on the plough, work performed largely by men. The bride price, on the other hand, features in societies that grant inheritance only to males, so that wealth moves from a groom to the father of the bride, and is not necessarily for the benefit of the bride. This, again speaking broadly, is thought to occur primarily in cultures that engage in manual farming practices, where women do much of the agricultural work, polygamy is common, and the loss of a woman's labor can come at a significant cost to the bride's family. See esp. Goody, *Production*, 6–7, 27–34.

22. Gen 29:15, 18, 20, 25, 27 [x2] and 30: so Waltke, *Genesis*, 403.

was Leah aware of the plan? Where was Rachel on her wedding night, and was she party to the scheme? Did Rachel worry that Jacob, settling for Leah, might leave without her? Did she—and for that matter, does she ever—love Jacob? Whom would she resent more, Laban or Leah? This was a high-stakes gamble.

And how can we accept Jacob's inability to distinguish Leah from the woman he loves? Some assert that it defies belief. Others blame wedding wine for clouding his faculties.[23] But one can deceive even a father who touches, kisses, questions, and doubts. One needs only the veil of darkness, the clothes of a sibling, and a few smooth words. Jacob, unsuspecting, is outmatched by his relatives. So Genesis, having provided the answer in an earlier story, can discreetly omit the details of the wedding night.

The next morning, Jacob rages against his father-in-law with words spoken by the deceived pagans Pharaoh (12:18) and Abimelech (26:10) when the patriarchs present wives as sisters: "What is this you have done to me . . . Why have you deceived me?" Laban, presenting a sister as wife,[24] shrugs off Jacob's challenge with the words, "It is not our custom here to give the younger daughter in marriage before the older one."[25] He in effect says, "I don't know about where you come from, but we don't do that here"—unwittingly speaking two truths. First, Jacob does not belong here. Even after seven years, Harran is not home. Second, and tied to the first, now Jacob learns what we already know. The entire betrothal and marriage account teaches that sin is following him.[26]

Four terms thus bear witness against Jacob as they link the story back to his defrauding of Isaac and Esau: first, Jacob in 29:25 uses a cognate of the verb that expressed deception in 27:35; second, 27:31–34 is about the *berakah* (blessing) while this event is about, says Laban, the *bakar* (firstborn, 29:26);[27] third, Jacob *serves* for seven years, using the language of

---

23. So Waltke, *Genesis*, 405; Wenham, *Genesis 16–50*, 236; Walton, *Genesis*, 587. See esp. Diamond, who notes parallels with the story of Lot and his daughters, including sisters, alcohol, and deception ("The Deception," 211–13). He makes nothing, however, of the fact that while Gen 9:21 speaks of both wine and Noah becoming drunk, and 19:32–35 speak of wine and Lot's loss of awareness, Gen 29 says only that Laban "gave a feast" (29:22). One must import the notion that feasting implies the groom's intoxication: the text does not so much as hint at it.

24. Turner, *Genesis*, 128–29.

25. Gen 29:26.

26. Ross, *Creation and Blessing*, 502–3.

27. Turner, *Genesis*, 128.

the stolen blessing; fourth, Rebekah had counseled flight for "a few days," and for Jacob the seven years were like "a few days." Jacob can run from Esau, but distance cannot separate him from his sin.[28] Sin has an advertised price: the actual cost is always higher.

At the same time, the story, because it does not teach impersonal cause and effect, offers hope for a positive side to Jacob's pain. Sin doesn't pursue Jacob; God does. He simultaneously opposes and blesses him. Through the good and the bad, and without even a passing mention since Bethel, the LORD works out his purposes in Jacob's life.

Laban's words, however, as always, mix truth and falsehood. While they apply as much to Jacob's usurping of Esau's place as to the wedding night, they relate with far greater complexity to the larger story. God himself does exactly what Laban condemns.[29] For he, against custom, exalts the lowly and advances the one without claim.

Laban's Little Flock

Laban has passed the point of no return. He tells Jacob to finish the celebrations, and then he can marry the "younger one" (29:27). All she will cost is another seven years of work. The blessed one, heretofore a contract laborer, is thus reduced to an indentured servant in the house of his own uncle, a father who cares nothing for the happiness of his daughters and nephew. This man of the East sounds like a pimp who sells his own daughters. Modern sensibilities find many ancient customs and practices repugnant; but this story, despite Laban's feigned indignation, does not portray the outworking of typical Eastern marriage practices. Laban cheats, deceives, and shows no concern for the family that he is destroying. But he is not a pimp. He has two daughters, the older named "cow" and the younger "ewe." He treats them not like prostitutes but cattle. And they, we'll soon discover, know it (31:15).

Jacob has met his match. She is beautiful, and he loves her. Jacob has met his match, and he is grotesque. But what can he do? Until Bethel, our every encounter with Jacob saw him cheating the firstborn. When Laban appeals to the rights of the firstborn, he has no recourse. His cunning has been matched, its ugliness exposed. Does he learn the lesson, or is he too close to events? Does life obscure for participants truths readers discover?

28. Laban's vocabulary further heightens the connections between the stories.
29. Turner, citing Gen 25:23 (*Genesis*, 128).

Jacob completes the week of celebration and then receives his second wife (29:28–29). Two other women accompany his wives: Zilpah (29:24) and Bilhah (29:29), attached as maidservant to Leah and Rachel respectively. Verse 30 concludes this section by specifying Jacob's relationship with each member of his suddenly enlarged family: he "made love to Rachel," preferred her to Leah, and "worked for Laban another seven years."[30]

Jacob's Little Flock

How does Scripture evaluate these events, and who should we regard as Jacob's wife? The structure of the story of Abraham's marriage to Hagar conveys the author's judgment and can offer insight into his evaluation of Jacob's marriages. Due to her barrenness, Sarah proposes that Abraham seek children through the slave girl. In response Abraham agreed to what Sarah said.

Sarah's plan, according to 16:3, results in Abraham gaining a second wife. Note the terms, "Sarai his wife took . . . Hagar and gave her to her husband to be his wife." The biblical evaluation of this event emerges as events in the garden reassert themselves. Genesis 16:3 virtually repeats the events of the fall as Sarah enacts, in the same sequence and with the same words, the events of 3:6: the wife "took" and "gave to . . . her husband."

Once again a wife grasps the initiative while her husband passively responds to her action. In 3:6 Adam eats fruit; in 16:4 Abraham sleeps with Hagar. When the plan goes awry, as with Eve in the garden,[31] Sarah shifts the blame. In her anger she shouts, "You are responsible for the wrong I am suffering." She then invokes the LORD with the words David used when he spared Saul at the cave in En Gedi. Like David but with less cause, she cries, "May the LORD judge between you and me" (1 Sam 24:12). Sarah plays the victim well.

These parallels with Genesis 3 suggest that chapter 16 presents another fall narrative.[32] But what is the nature of this fall? Is it bigamy itself or something else? The Abraham/Sarah story, with its motif of faith in impossible promises, makes a direct comment on trying to advance divine

---

30. Genesis relates, during the seven years of work, almost exclusively the fruitfulness of Jacob's family (29:31—30:24). From there it will recount an additional six years of contracted labor for Laban by focusing almost exclusively on the fruitfulness of Jacob's herds (30:25–43). God upholds his end of the bargain.

31. Gen 3:12–13.

32. Wenham, *Genesis 16–50*, 7–8, following Berg, "Der Sündenfall," 10.

purposes without respect for divine promises. Sarah, despite the passing years, will bear the promised one. But for now, lack of faith has created a situation only redeemable through God's gracious intervention. Just as the garden was spoiled for Adam and Eve, and the renewed land for Noah and his family, so the microcosm of universal salvation represented by Abraham's tents has been tarnished. The issue is bigger than polygamy, but it does not exist apart from it.

While these links between Genesis 3 and 16 have been observed, generally unnoticed in the progression of "fall narratives" is that the Hebrew terms in play are repeated in order in Gen 29:23. When the details are filled in, the structure is seen to repeat 16:3–4.

16:3–4: "And *she took* Sarai wife of Abraham Hagar the Egyptian maidservant . . . and gave *her to* Abraham her husband to be a wife *and he came to* Hagar."

29:23: "And it was at night *and he took* Leah his daughter and brought *her to* him *and he came to* her."

The order runs from subject (she/he) to verb (took) to object (Hagar/Leah) to description (the Egyptian maidservant/his daughter) to verb (gave/brought) to indirect object (to Abraham/to him) to verb (and he came) to indirect object (to Hagar/to her). As the serpent deceived Eve, so Laban deceives Jacob. A third generation of the line of kings is—in its very formation—plunged into darkness.

Leviticus 18:18 applies directly to Jacob's situation: "Do not take your wife's sister as a rival wife and have sexual relations with her while your wife is living." But there are complicating factors when it comes to Jacob's household. This later text, therefore, while it may convey a moral evaluation of the situation, does not provide an after-the-fact answer to our question concerning Jacob's true wife. So we return to Genesis.

Jacob's Wife?

Who then is Jacob's wife? If Leah, should he have been content with her? On the other hand, if anybody ever had grounds for annulment, surely Jacob does. The text nowhere deals in such terms. Indeed, as we have just seen, Genesis earlier revealed the biblical perspective on a patriarchal relationship with a slave girl by, in a single verse, describing both Sarah and Hagar as wife (Gen 16:3). If Hagar is a wife, how much more Rachel (and what of Bilhah and Zilpah)? Leah, as the first, believes herself to be Jacob's wife, accusing Rachel of stealing *her* husband (30:15). Jacob, however, behaves as though Joseph, the son of favored Rachel, is the promised and long-awaited child—suggesting that he in this, as in other things, considers her his true wife.

Furthermore, Jacob, ever insensitive to his family, tells his adult children as they depart for Egypt to save his clan, "You know that my wife bore me two sons" (44:27). While this does not prove that Jacob regards Rachel alone as his wife, one wonders how the ten sons would have received the words of 42:38, "My son will not go down there with you; his brother is dead and he is the *only one left.*" Clearly Rachel's place, at least in his heart, is hers alone. And his sons know their place all too well.

Jacob appears ultimately to accept Leah as "a chosen matriarch"—or is this a case of us finding symbolic meaning in mere circumstance? Rachel is buried on the way to Bethlehem (35:19), having died while delivering Benjamin. Leah, however, is buried beside Abraham, Sarah, Isaac, and Rebekah (49:31) in the family plot, the Cave of Machpelah.[33]

Most importantly, God won't overlook Leah. Joseph inherits the double portion of Jacob, as, in Genesis 48, Jacob lays hands on Joseph's two sons.[34] Furthermore, Joseph plays a unique role as savior of his people. But the birthright and blessing, split asunder by Jacob, do not merge in Joseph. He establishes neither the line of the proto-messiahs, Moses and David, nor the Messiah himself. Through Judah, the fourth son of Leah, born before slave girls and mandrakes color the story, the line of promise advances.[35]

Before we finish we will see that God elects the first wife and older sister—obtained through extraordinary circumstances—along with her fourth son. From the despised and rejected will come a king.

---

33. Walton, *Traveller*, 136, and n. 33.

34. That is, Joseph receives the prerogatives of firstborn. See also 1 Chr 5:1.

35. Duguid, *Relentless Grace*, 88; von Rad, *Genesis*, 291.

Chapter 5

All My Children

Genesis 29:31—30:24

COULD THE OUTWORKING OF God's promise to Jacob seem farther away? First his "few days" became seven years of contracted labor. Now he faces seven more years of servitude. The land remains far off. In many ways, however, not far enough. For he inhabits a family like the one he fled, with a father and two siblings at cross purposes. Having abused a father who advances his eldest son, he serves a father who advances his eldest daughter. But now, as Jacob's own family moves to the fore, Laban vacates the stage. Perhaps fulfilment is at hand.

The LORD Sees Leah

But Leah knows no fulfilment. Despite its control over the subsequent story, Genesis almost in passing related Isaac and Rebekah's parental preferences (25:28). Now again with few words we learn that Jacob prefers Rachel. But God sees and grants children to the unloved wife (29:30).[1] With barely a glance in Rachel's direction, the author adds that she was barren (29:31). Thus with light touch the story introduces circumstances

---

1. "The LORD saw" quietly reinforces a lesson that Israel often forgot: God is not limited geographically. Centuries later, Jerusalemites remaining after early waves of captivity falsely declare that the exiles are far from God—believing themselves, in Jerusalem, to be near him. The LORD disagrees: "Although I sent them far away ... I have been a sanctuary for them in the countries where they have gone" (Ezek 11:16). As Jacob learned at Bethel, sanctuary is not a place but a divine presence.

that overshadow coming events and the women who must endure them. Leah has children but desires Jacob's affections. Rachel has his affections but desires children.

Leah dominates the stage in 29:32–35. The unloved bears a son named Reuben, building on the Hebrew root of the verb "to see." She explains: "Because the LORD has seen my misery . . . . Surely my husband will love me now" (29:32). The rejected bride vainly hopes that bearing children will win her husband's affection.

Then, "She conceived again, and when she gave birth to a son she said . . . ." She sounds less optimistic when she names him Simeon, this time building on "to hear." "Because the LORD heard that I'm not loved" (29:33). Translations remove some of the sting: Leah says, "because the LORD heard that I am hated."

A third time we hear, "Again she conceived, and when she gave birth to a son she said . . . ." She dreams that this son will forge a link between mother and father. The name Levi (i.e., attached) reflects her naïve hope. Yet again, as Leah bears her fourth son: "She conceived again, and when she gave birth to a son she said . . . ." This time the name she gives to her son, Judah (praise) and thus the comment on her situation, relates not to divine activity but to her own response: "This time I will praise the LORD" (29:35).

But the refrain abruptly ends: "Then she stopped having children" (29:35). Why? And what is Jacob's role in this? The first pregnancy raises few questions because of the peculiarities of their wedding night, but subsequent births indicate that Jacob continued relations with Leah. If 29:35 or 30:1 had spelled the end of the story, we might assume that Jacob cut off sexual contact,[2] or even that Rachel put a stop to it. But this explanation founders upon 30:9, where Leah, recognizing her own infertility, gives her maidservant to Jacob to bear more children. Clearly the explanation is not that Jacob reserves intimacy for Rachel.

The section running from 29:31 to 30:24 is headed, "Jacob's Children" in the NIV, making it all the more remarkable that Jacob is un-named in the verses recounting the birth of his first four sons (29:31–35). When Leah refers to Jacob, she always says "my husband," reflecting her claim on that which eludes her. The effect is as follows: with Reuben she acknowledges the LORD and then tragically concludes, "Surely my husband will love me

---

2. So Turner, *Genesis*, 130. This, however, fails to account for the role of the maidservants (30:17, 19, 21) and the fact that Leah will bear three more children before the chapter ends.

now." Upon Simeon's birth, she refers only to the LORD. Levi reflects again her concern for her husband, without mention of the LORD, and Judah evokes the claim that "This time I will praise the LORD." She thus alternates between acknowledging the LORD's goodness and her desire for her husband's recognition. She receives only the former.

The story seems at first glance to affirm Laban's contention that the older must have the priority, for she bears first and repeatedly. But the truth is somewhat different: God actively cares for the unloved, the text stating that "the LORD saw" and responded to the fact of Leah's loveless existence. The center of the Jacob cycle, during which he produces a large family and abundant flocks, teaches this over and over: God alone gives life.

Jacob, Rachel, and Bilhah

Rachel is barren. Of all God's promises to the patriarchs, the promise of numerous children, fruitfulness, would seem to be the most easily fulfilled. For most people until about a generation ago, not multiplying was the greater difficulty in marriage. We assume much about both preventing and facilitating reproduction that was irrelevant before the 1960s. But in the poetry of covenantal promise, the refrain is "so and so was barren," demanding recognition that the promised ones are born not of natural means but of God. Each patriarch marries a barren wife, just as each faces the consequences of famine. Barren wives and barren lands are insurmountable obstacles to the promise—unless God himself intervenes.

Simultaneous with Leah's pregnancies is Jacob's physical relationship with his beloved Rachel. In 29:31 the LORD sees, with a clear result. In 30:1, Rachel sees, but without result. She remains childless. Does this mean that the LORD looks away from Rachel, or that she pays a penalty because Jacob loves her? The barren-woman motif meets with varying degrees of faith. Abraham had turned first to Eliezer of Damascus and then, at his wife's suggestion, to Hagar, in pursuit of an heir. Rebekah turned to the LORD and bore twins. Rachel turns to Jacob. "Give me children, or I'll die!" (30:1).[3]

Rachel despairs. In some contexts, the bride stayed in the father's home until becoming pregnant. From its earliest detection, then, barrenness could be a public humiliation. Her plea recalls Esau begging for blessing (27:36, 38) and Jacob's demand to Laban. Both made their requests;

3. Her desperate demand is all the more heart-wrenching when Jacob's preference, which no doubt extended to sexual activity, is recalled.

both received an answer; neither got what they wanted. Now Rachel makes her demand, "give me children," with the same form as Jacob's "give me my wife" (29:21).[4] She too does not receive what she desires. Laban had the power to give or withhold Jacob's wife; Jacob lacks the corresponding power to give or withhold children. He is incensed. He is failing. At home his father and brother were no match for him. But in Harran people and events fall outside his control and overwhelm his ability to manipulate. He can only reply, "Am I in the place of God?"[5]

Jacob in "the Place of God"

These are Jacob's only recorded words during his seven years of forced labor. They at first glance have a pleasing ambiguity. Jacob lives in Harran, far from God's chosen country, and from God's house, Bethel. Jacob is not in God's place. On the other hand, Jacob lives where, events at the well suggest, God has brought him. He is indeed in the place God would have him. But the words contain no such ambiguity. They refer neither to God's house nor to God's chosen residence for Jacob. They refer more directly to deity: Do I play the God role? Am I the one "who has kept you from having children?" (30:2). Do I exercise power over life?

When it really matters, when it comes to producing children, Jacob is impotent. His confession born of frustration reveals not a trust in God as much as an acknowledgement of his own limitations. This is the first expression of weakness from a man who sometimes displays great strength, always comes out on top, and regularly leaves devastation in his wake. We will return to these words below.

Bilhah in the Place of Rachel

Frustrated and jealous (30:1), Rachel desperately offers her maidservant to her husband so that "I too can build a family through her" (30:3). God can build a family through Jacob, but can Rachel build one through Bilhah? For that matter, can she build a family at all?

Earlier, the refrain ran, "she conceived again and gave birth to a son." Here the crucial parts reappear: "and she became pregnant and bore him a

---

4. Wenham, *Genesis 16–50*, 241. See 29:21 and 30:1.
5. Gen 30:2.

son" (30:5). Repetition highlights the fact that everybody Jacob sleeps with becomes pregnant except Rachel.

Nevertheless, Rachel rejoices, for in giving a son, "God has vindicated me" (30:6). She therefore names him Dan.[6] She maintains that God has provided this child, and that he judges and vindicates those who look to him.[7] In this outburst of spiritual insight she seems to surpass her husband. But when the names of her two sons are brought together, that impression collapses. She claims that God has given her, the victim, justice.[8] When Bilhah has another son, Rachel names him Naphtali, exclaiming, "I have had a great struggle with my sister, and I have won."[9] Her words could be rendered, "with the struggling for God, I have struggled (*niptalti*)."[10] To this point, jealousy has motivated her (30:1). She now reduces her son's birth to the conquest of Leah. Indeed, like Leah, she names her children as an intra-family commentary on her relationship with her sister or husband.[11] The sisters gloat or bemoan. In wrestling with "God and man" she sounds much like her husband.[12] Like him, she struggles and overcomes, but it is not clear that this is commendable. Again she appears as a suitable match for Jacob.

Furthermore, Laban's daughters are seen to share his vices. Having been used by their father for economic advantage, Leah and Rachel use their sons for relational advantage.[13]

Zilpah in the Place of Leah

Verse 9 returns to Leah. Like the LORD and Rachel, it is her turn to see. God has seen that she was unloved, so he opened her womb. This gave her

6. From *dannanni*, "God has vindicated me." So Waltke, *Genesis*, 411. Walton (*Genesis*, 588) infers that Rachel "feels a need for vindication because her infertility would bring at least the tacit accusation that she is suffering for (undoubtedly) secret sins."

7. How does God view the birth of Dan? His name does not appear in, e.g., the list of Israelite tribes in Revelation 7, but this may relate more to subsequent events (in which Dan becomes a center of idolatry) than to the circumstances of his birth.

8. Waltke, *Genesis*, 412.

9. Gen 30:8.

10. Waltke, *Genesis*, 412.

11. Wenham, *Genesis 16–50*, 240.

12. Compare with Gen 32:28. Jacob struggles with God and man and prevails (the same word for overcoming).

13. Waltke, *Genesis*, 412.

children, but left her dissatisfied. The birth of her sons—her only hope in the contest with her sister—failed to win her husband's affections. Now she "stopped having children" (30:9). In her moment of barrenness, she presents her maidservant Zilpah to Jacob. At this point, we can pause to ask some questions. Does Leah think that a certain number of sons will make Jacob love her? What causes Rachel's jealousy? Does it arise, as the placement of 30:1–2 suggests, because Leah has been bearing children? Or because, already prior to that, she resented Leah for the loss of her wedding and exclusive claims on her husband? (Whether Leah was culpable would make little difference to Rachel.) Has Jacob been marginalized except for sex?

The lack of answers accomplishes two things. First, it compounds the impression that each acts only in reaction to her sister's status. Leah calls her boys Reuben, Simeon, and Levi because she competes not for God's blessing but for Jacob's affections. Rachel's response of jealousy, the names Dan and Naphtali suggest, expresses her fear of losing her sole advantage over Leah. The giving of maidservants heightens the competition. Thus the one who destroyed his parent's home through sibling rivalry endures a corresponding misery caused by the sibling rivalry of his wives.

Second, it reduces Jacob. His only words, an expression of inability, are a response to his wife (30:2; he doesn't even name his children). And his only action is meeting his wives' sexual demands. He, as much as his wives and children, has become a pawn in other people's conflicts. Matters only become worse from here.

Leah's servant, Zilpah, bears two sons, Gad and Asher. The refrain attending the birth of Leah's first four sons generated a momentum around God's goodness to Leah, suggesting that the LORD is the true, loving husband who is sensitive to her plight. He, rather than Jacob, seemed to increasingly become the focus of her private life. But we see again that hints of spiritual insight are a mirage. She refers not to the LORD but to fortune and happiness as she names her next two children. In this too, matters are about to become worse.

Rachel and Leah among the Mandrakes

We arrive at the center of the Jacob-story, chapters that transfer the blessing from Abraham to Jacob. And here, at the center of the center (30:14–17), events unfold in a festive season. During harvest, Reuben unearths some mandrakes (30:14). His supposedly magical plants, considered both an aphrodisiac and antidote to sterility, catch Rachel's eye.[14] With the courtesy of one bargaining from weakness, she implores, "Please give me some of your son's mandrakes." But Leah is in no mood to share. Claiming Jacob as her own, she accuses, "Wasn't it enough that you took away my husband? Will you take my son's mandrakes too?"[15] Without responding to Leah's claim on Jacob, Rachel proposes, give me the plants and tonight Jacob will share your bed (30:15).[16] Rachel, with respect to Jacob's sexual life, lords over him. And, in her desperation, she resorts to superstition to produce a child.

Leah hastens to meet Jacob.[17] She speaks to her husband only twice in Scripture, both times pointing to degrading transactions. Here she says, "You must sleep with me . . . I have hired you with my son's mandrakes" (30:16). The only other time she addresses Jacob (31:15), she joins with Rachel to say of her father that he has sold them and spent the proceeds.

Rachel and Leah were bought and sold: Jacob purchased them with fourteen years of hard labor. But Jacob, already diminishing in v. 2, is now also bought and sold. Laban had reduced Jacob from nephew to hired hand. Now Leah reduces Jacob from husband to hired hand.[18] Marriage, intended as blessing, has become servitude to his father-in-law and feuding wives.[19] This is reflected nowhere more clearly than in 30:16 when Leah says, "I have hired you with my son's mandrakes," and in the fact that she names the resulting son Issachar (i.e., reward). The wives were pearls of great price; Jacob came cheap. The man who was to be served by family and nations (27:29) has been bought to serve even his unloved wife, the price being something worthless.[20] Everyone shrinks in this story.[21]

14. Hepper, *Baker Encyclopedia of Bible Plants*, 151. See also Song 7:13. On the difficulty of identifying the plant, see Wenham (*Genesis 16–50*, 246–47).

15. Gen 30:15.

16. See Sarna, *Genesis*, 209.

17. Is he alone? Is she? Does she lessen her shame by distancing the conversation from her children? Does she want to eliminate the possibility of public rejection? Or is she a meet-him-halfway wife?

18. See esp. Fokkelman, *Narrative Art*, 138.

19. This is one of four great "exchanges" in the Jacob story: the sale of the birthright for beans, the theft of the blessing, the exchange of wives, and the sale of sex for mandrakes (Waltke, *Genesis,* 413; Fokkelman, *Narrative Art*, 137). The first pair is to Jacob's advantage, the second to his loss (Waltke, *Genesis*, 413). The first and last swap something precious for something of no value; the middle two involve the theft of something priceless through deception.

20. Turner, *Genesis*, 132.

21. Leah's words contain further tragedy. Esau and Jacob had been referred to as "his

The account would seem to end with the anti-climactic words, "So he slept with her that night." But the saga continues. Though Rachel holds the mandrakes, Leah becomes pregnant. She correctly attributes the child to God, but wrongly views it as a reward (the son's name playing with the words "hire" and "reward") for "her idolatrous shortcut of presenting her maidservant to her husband" (30:18).[22] A second time, now without mandrakes, Leah conceives and attributes the child to God. She thinks that this time Jacob will honor (*zbl*) her (i.e., acknowledge her as wife), so she names him Zebulun.[23] If Issachar represents a "reward," Zebulun's birth is a gift. But it is not clear that Leah speaks of the child: she seeks, and believes herself to have now attained, recognition from her husband. Such is the gift she believes God has granted. Thus, her confusion of her husband's love and honor with God's love and honor—and with it the tragic dimension of the story—continues.

This incident, in which God grants children to the one who forfeits the mandrakes, alters the rhythm of the larger account and therefore has been dismissed as "a minor episode that acts as a delaying device to avoid tedium," words written to keep the hearer's attention.[24] But this understates its importance and, literally, its centrality. It also overlooks its uniqueness. This is the only time a child acts. It is the first of only two instances of Leah speaking to Jacob (along with 31:14). And it's the only account of Rachel and Leah speaking to one another. Crucially, it occupies the center of the birth narrative. The boundaries are 29:31, where God saw Leah's rejection and "enabled her to conceive," and 30:22, where "God remembered Rachel . . . and enabled her to conceive." The center and ends of the birth narrative thus teach that Jacob's disastrous household is amazingly fruitful, and the promise to Abraham is fulfilled, only because God, the source of life, chooses to bless this family.[25]

---

son" and "her son" respectively (27:5–6), indicating rivalry in the home. The source of Leah's mandrakes is not "your son" but "my son." Jacob despises his wife and, so she thinks, has no regard for her son either. The text offers no reason to disagree. Moreover, her verb, "sleep with me" (30:16) never in Genesis reflects marital love: it relates to rape, incest, and other forms of inappropriate sexual relations.

22. Duguid, *Relentless Grace*, 87.

23. Waltke, *Genesis*, 414.

24. Sarna, *Genesis*, 209.

25. In what seems like little more than an addendum, Genesis informs that "some time later" Leah gave birth to a girl (30:21). This child stands outside the flow of the story in that (1) Dinah is the only one of Jacob's daughters to be mentioned; (2) she

The narrator stresses Leah's unloved status. But the focus is not really on Leah. The story recounts her husband and the misery that engulfs him. Concentric rings of opposition encircle Jacob, from the customs of the place to the clan headed by Laban to his more immediate family. He fled his nuclear family only to find a radioactive situation in Harran.[26] But at the center of this new life is an unloved woman who bears children by the grace of God.

The Lord Remembers Rachel

The birth narratives, 29:31—30:24, consist of four blocks of text alternating between Leah and Rachel. Each one begins with a major verbal idea. In 29:31, the births begin "when the LORD saw . . . ." Four children follow his seeing.

The second block begins in 30:1 with "when Rachel saw . . . ," followed by the story of her producing children through Bilhah. First comes her vindication in the birth of Dan, the son she claims as her own (30:6, "God has . . . given me a son") and then her triumph over Leah as commemorated in the name Naphtali (30:7).

The third block, like the first two, begins with seeing, only this time it is Leah's turn. In 30:9, "when Leah saw . . . ," she mimics Rachel's plan by means of her slavegirl, Zilpah. The text quietly observes the multiplying tragedy: Leah's predicament arises because her husband has more than one wife. The number of wives, presumably outside her control, became three in v. 4 at Rachel's command. But now, by Leah's own machinations, in v. 9 it becomes four. She gambles big because she plays for high stakes. The resulting births leave her feeling lucky (Gad) and happy (Asher). This block to this point is a godless narrative, and will remain so until v. 17.

Block three continues with a sub-unit that includes the extensive narrative wherein the verbal action is not performed by God or one of the wives, but by Leah's son, Reuben. This again highlights resources Rachel lacks.

---

is not born during the seven-year period of servitude circumscribing the other births; and (3) her name is not explained. Her birth, which prepares for the events of chapter 34 takes the number of Leah's children to seven, six of whom were born in seven years (Sarna, *Genesis*, 210).

26. Turner, *Genesis*, 129.

Reuben could only be a few years old as he stumbles upon the mandrakes and brings them to her mother. Leah in turn barters them away for a night with Jacob. Rachel, who now has the mandrakes, once again disappears from the story. Leah, without mandrakes but with God listening (30:17), gives birth to three more children.

In block four, as in the first, the verbal opening is again performed by the LORD, "Then God remembered Rachel" (30:22). At last her own son arrives, and with him the climax of the birth narratives. Sarah waited more than twenty-five years and Rebekah twenty for a son. In both cases, the longed for child becomes the main character in the subsequent narrative. This one will do the same.[27] God remembers Rachel, who conceives and gives birth (30:22–24). Divine remembering refers not to an act of consciousness but to the LORD acting favorably.[28] Deliverance is imminent. The phrase first occurs in Genesis 8:1 where, after 150 days of flooding (Gen 7:24), God remembers Noah and the animals, and with a delivering wind sweeps away the waters of judgment. In Exodus 2:24 God hears the groans of Israel in Egypt, "remembered his covenant," and sends Moses to deliver his people. Now God "remembers Rachel" and delivers her: Joseph is born.

Her words, like the narrator's, credit God with rescuing her (30:23). As had Leah at the arrival of her first child (in 29:32), Rachel utters the word YHWH, thus framing the birth narratives with the holy name.[29] God's name supplements the births of Issachar and Zebulun and the placement of the birth of Dinah, three births that create significant narrative distance between the mandrakes and the birth of Joseph. The cumulative effect of the name and the space serves the author's argument: it is the God of the covenant, not magic, who provides Jacob's children.[30]

27. Turner, *Genesis*, 132.

28. See also Neh 5:19; 13:22, 31. Nehemiah in the face of adversity prays that God would remember him. Not all divine remembering yields deliverance. Nehemiah also prays that God would remember in judgment those who have corrupted the priesthood (13:29).

29. Sarna, *Genesis*, 210.

30. "Joseph" forms a pun first on the word "take away," and then its opposite, "add," as Rachel appeals to the LORD for another child (Walton, *Traveller*, 143). As such, it looks ahead in two directions: to the birth of Joseph's brother Benjamin; and to Joseph himself being taken away and then "added" (So Waltke, *Genesis*, 414, following Fox, *In the Beginning*, xvi). Rachel's longing meets with grace, yet she remains dissatisfied. Tragically and ironically, the one consumed with bearing children—who says "give me children or I'll die" (30:1)—will die in bearing her second son, the boy who is the answer to this prayer (Hamilton, *Genesis*, 270; Alter, *Genesis*, 158; see Walton, *Traveller*, 144).

"In the Place of God" Again

We know Jacob as a tireless worker. The birth stories supplement this picture as he resists neither his marital obligations nor the wishes of his wives. Through the same misdirection employed in recounting the wedding night, the story conveys exactly what transpires without referring to sexual activity, Leah's words to Jacob being nearest to an exception. Further, the text offers no explicit commentary on the ethics of these arrangements, and within the story itself reveals nothing of the emotional state—apart from Jacob's rebuke of Rachel—of the man whose household simultaneously grows and deteriorates. The story develops sibling rivalry and a dwindling Jacob alongside God's blessing. In this, Jacob's limitations drive attention to God.

Jacob answers Rachel's demand for children with, "Am I in the place of God?" This phrase appears in Genesis, indeed in Scripture, only twice. The present passage, concerning the generation of life within Jacob's family, runs parallel to the family crisis triggered by Jacob's death. In that moment, Joseph's brothers fear that he will judge them, exacting vengeance for betraying him (50:15–18). Joseph replies like his father had a lifetime before: "Am I in the place of God?" (50:19). By setting these references side by side we uncover the essence of deity. Unlike competing notions of the surrounding world, the biblical God stands at an absolute beginning as a source of life and at the end as its judge. Genesis with this phrase draws together life-giving and judgment as the defining prerogatives of the divine. This understanding permeates Scripture.

God as Giver of Life

From the beginning, life comes from the living God: "The LORD God formed a man from the dust of the ground and breathed into his nostrils the breath of life, and the man became a living being" (Gen 2:7). Of the various promises in the patriarchal narratives, none appears more often than descendants.[31] Job recognizes the LORD's control over life: "You gave me life and showed me kindness, and in your providence watched over my spirit" (Job 10:12). Ecclesiastes agrees: "It is appropriate for a person to eat, to drink, and to find

31. Mitchell, *To Bless*, 34. Relatedly, God promises as the people enter the land that if they worship him alone and carry out all his instructions, "none will miscarry or be barren in your land" (Exod 23:26; see Deut 7:13–14; 28:4, 11).

satisfaction in their toilsome labor under the sun during the few days of life God has given him—for this is their lot."[32]

Hannah, in the line of Rebekah and other barren women, vows: "if you will . . . remember me, and not forget your servant but give her a son, then I will give him to the LORD for all the days of his life" (1 Sam 1:11). The Psalmist, listing the blessings of those "who fear the LORD, who walk in obedience to him" (128:1) writes: "Your wife will be like a fruitful vine . . . your children will be like olive shoots" (128:3; see also Ps 127:3).

God as Judge

The one who at the beginning gives life stands at the end as judge. A day is coming when he will impartially[33] judge all humanity to assess deeds (Eccl 12:14), thoughts, words, and secrets of the heart.[34]

God Judges in Righteousness

From early days, Scripture announces that God judges justly: "Far be it from you to do such a thing—to kill the righteous with the wicked, treating the righteous and the wicked alike. Far be it from you! Will not the Judge of all the earth do right?" (Gen 18:25).

In the Psalms, this hope sustains those who crave justice: "He reigns forever; he has established his throne for judgment. He rules the world in righteousness and judges the peoples with equity" (Ps 9:7–8; see 50:6). "He will judge the peoples with equity" (Ps 96:10). "He will judge the world in righteousness and the peoples in his faithfulness" (Ps 96:13).[35]

Thus is God vindicated: "But the LORD Almighty will be exalted by his justice, and the holy God will be proved holy by his righteous acts" (Isa 5:16).[36]

---

32. Eccl 5:18. The same phrase with minor variation appears in Eccl 8:15 and 9:9: "days [or life] God has given him [or you] under the sun." God is not mentioned directly in the Hebrew or Greek of any of the three passages, though by means of a divine passive, the meaning is clear.

33. Rom 2:11; 1 Pet 1:17; Jas 2:1.

34. Jer 17:10; Rom 2:16; see also Ps 44:21.

35. This is repeated nearly verbatim in Ps 98:9.

36. So also Ps 58:10–11: "The righteous will be glad when they are avenged, when they dip their feet in the blood of the wicked. Then men will say, 'Surely the righteous still

OT talk of judgment shapes NT teaching. Jesus speaks of "the Son of Man" whose angels "will weed out of his kingdom everything that causes sin and all who do evil" (Matt 13:41). This Son of Man's separation of the sheep from the goats will result in eternal punishment or eternal life (Matt 25:46) based on how one treats the needy.

Paul assumes that God will judge. It is a trump card rather than something to be argued ("If that were so, how could God judge the world?" Rom 3:6). Furthermore, Paul instructs that God will judge rightly,[37] and that his judgment has already begun.[38] The judgment he speaks of, like that described by Jesus, scrutinizes works: Romans 2:6 echoes Proverbs 24:12 and Psalm 62:12 in asserting that "God 'will repay to each person according to what they have done.'"[39] In Hebrews, the Lord is designated "God, the judge of all" (12:23). Jude declares, "the Lord is coming with thousands upon thousands of his holy ones to judge everyone, and to convict all of them of all the ungodly acts they have committed in their ungodliness, and of all the defiant words ungodly sinners have spoken against him" (14–15). Peter says "the Lord knows how to . . . hold the unrighteous for punishment on the day of judgment" (2 Pet 2:9).

For John, as for Paul, matters of life and judgment can be condensed into the single question: do you know God through his Son?[40] "Now this is eternal life: that they know you, the only true God, and Jesus Christ, whom you have sent" (John 17.3). Indeed, "God has given us eternal life, and this life is in his Son. Whoever has the Son has life; whoever does not have the Son of God does not have life" (1 John 5:11–12). To know God does not reduce to a group affiliation or even to claimed faith in Christ: it encapsulates new birth and generates the fruit of new relationships—first with God, and then with one another.

---

are rewarded; surely there is a God who judges the earth.'"

37. "Based on truth," Rom 2:2; "his righteous judgment," Rom 2:5; see Gen 18:25: "Will not the judge of all the earth do right?"

38. Rom 1:18, 24. It is also significant that, according to the Pauline epistles and in the Petrine and Pauline speeches in Acts, the resurrection is God's vindication of Jesus. That is, the people having judged Jesus, now God announces his verdict in the resurrection.

39. See Schreiner for discussion of Paul's citation (*Romans*, 112). He also cites numerous extra-biblical Jewish sources that relate judgment to deeds (112 n.1).

40. Rosner observes that for Paul it is more important that God knows him than that he knows God ("Known by God"). See Gal 4:9.

Jesus as Judge and Giver of Life

Genesis, by means of the question "Am I in the place of God?" describes deity: God is Lord over life and judgment. These twin aspects combine in the person of Jesus.

NT teaching concerning judgment confronts the unbeliever[41] and the believer alike.[42] But for the latter, confidence abounds.[43] The Christian has hope in the face of judgment because the assessment relates to relationships. Those who know the Father through the Son, having been reconciled and thus spared divine wrath (Rom 5:9–11), enjoy life now and forever. Those outside this relationship know only the death of separation now and forever, for the judge is the Lord who has already given life.

The LORD Who Judges

Israel's ancient hope grew increasingly specific until it took the shape of a Davidic King who judges by the Spirit's wisdom and with justice. This messianic expectation finds expression in Isaiah 11:1–5:

> A shoot will come up from the stump of Jesse;
> from his roots a Branch will bear fruit.
> The Spirit of the LORD will rest on him—
> the Spirit of wisdom and of understanding,
> the Spirit of counsel and of might,
> the Spirit of the knowledge and fear of the LORD—
> and he will delight in the fear of the LORD.
> He will not judge by what he sees with his eyes,
> or decide by what he hears with his ears;
> but with righteousness he will judge the needy,
> with justice he will give decisions for the poor of the earth.
> He will strike the earth with the rod of his mouth;
> with the breath of his lips he will slay the wicked.
> Righteousness will be his belt and faithfulness the sash around his waist.[44]

41. Matt 7:21–23; 25:41–46; John 12:48; Rom 2:12; Rev 20:12–15.
42. Matt 25:34–36; 1 Cor 3:10–15; 2 Cor 5:10–11.
43. See 1 Cor 3:15, where even the one who suffers loss is nonetheless saved.
44. Note the similarities with Jer 23:5–6; 33:15.

John 5:22 and 30 present Jesus as this divine agent, exercising judgment as a role granted by the Father to the Son. However, unlike Isaiah 11:3 ("He will not judge by what he sees with his eyes, or decide by what he hears with his ears"), Jesus says he will in fact judge by what he hears. Both passages, despite their surface tension, point in the same direction. The eyes and ears of Isaiah 11:3 indicate the weakness of human judgment (a prominent theme in the book of Isaiah), which will in messianic judgment be overcome by divine wisdom. In contrast, Jesus' ears hear the Father in matters pertaining to judgment (i.e., he relies upon divine wisdom). Therefore Jesus is a judge whose verdicts accord not with appearance but justice.

The Lord Who Gives Life

In the New Testament, the Father exercises authority over life: He "made us alive with Christ even when we were dead in transgressions" (Eph 2:5). Where Jesus is central, it is still the Father, through the Son, who gives life: "God has given us eternal life, and this life is in his Son. Whoever has the Son has life; whoever does not have the Son of God does not have life" (1 John 5:11–12).

So does the NT attribute life-giving to Jesus? In a word, yes. Paul, who carefully distinguishes between Father and Son, speaks of "the last Adam" as "a life-giving spirit."[45] In John, Jesus is Lord over life, the one who tells the woman at the well, "Whoever drinks the water I give them will never thirst. Indeed the water I give them will become in them a spring of water welling up to eternal life."[46] This water is the Holy Spirit whom Jesus gives (John 7:37–39). In the raising of Lazarus, Jesus shows that life is in his hands and linked to his word (John 11:43, note too 5:24, 28). Ironically, within John's narrative and throughout his theology, it is for giving life and in order to give life that Jesus must die (John 11:47–50; 12:9–11). Chapter 5 especially points to Jesus as the holder, and therefore the source, of spiritual life: "For just as the Father raises the dead and gives them life, even so the Son gives life to whom he is pleased to give it" (John 5.21); "For as the Father has life in himself, so he has granted the Son to have life in himself" (John 5:26).

Judging and life-giving, arising from Genesis as a definition of deity, reach their christological heights here in John 5. The Jews accuse Jesus, who healed on the Sabbath, of claiming equality with God (John 5:16–18). He

45. 1 Cor 15:45.
46. John 4:13–14.

answers with a two-pronged reply. First, he is no competing deity. He is a son who does nothing on his own initiative (John 5:19, 30). His deeds are his Father's deeds and his judgments accord with his Father's words (5:19–21, 30). Thus, Jesus defends the unity of the godhead within a framework later labelled trinitarian monotheism. Second, he replies to the charge by proving that he is in fact God. This he achieves with two further claims: he (within his Father's will) gives life (5:26); and he will judge everyone on the last day (John 5:28–30). He is the alpha and omega, sovereign over the beginning and the end, meaning, as John argues throughout, that his readership's response to Jesus defines their eternal destiny.

As we draw the birth stories to a close, we see that the same words on the one hand reveal the glory and grandeur of Jesus and on the other an ever-shrinking Jacob. He may be the great patriarch, embodying in many ways the strength of the nation, but only the one scarcely hinted at in the story can generate and preserve life—both physical and spiritual. Jesus, put on trial in John 5, takes hold of the understanding of deity offered already in Genesis and applies it to himself. He is God, the one who gives life and is judge.

Chapter 6

Streaks, Specks, and Spots

Genesis 30:25–43

Jacob has experienced the fulfilment of God's promise. For better or worse, he now has a family that surely exceeded his expectations. Born into a small family—one of two sons granted to Abraham's single heir[1]—he is in seven years associated with twelve children, the offspring of four wives. It is far from the perfect family, but it is his—and it is large.

Jacob's Request

With the appearance of Joseph, Jacob remembers home. Fourteen years is long enough for Esau's anger to cool. Further, prior to Joseph's birth, Rachel would have been vulnerable. Custom dictated that paternal relations protected, and were in some ways responsible for, a woman without children who was all too easily considered disposable property by a callous husband. Rachel had lived for seven years with the alloyed joys of marriage to Jacob and the reduced security of childlessness. Her jealousy and ill-will toward Leah were not mere self-pity. And Jacob, had he left with her before Joseph's birth, and despite his best intentions, would have been in an equally fraught situation. But Joseph's arrival means freedom.[2]

---

1. While Abraham had several other children, they were sent away with gifts, while "Abraham left everything he owned to Isaac" (25:5–6).

2. So Walton, *Genesis*, 589. This instability makes Sarah's life and Rebekah's departure to marry Isaac all the more remarkable.

Once his beloved is recognized as his wife, Jacob feels sufficiently confident to think of home. He asks Laban for his wives and children, the wages of fourteen years labor, but his current situation corresponds to Rachel's former dilemma. The terms of his contract included only wives as payment. They did not mention children. Surely one of the greatest horrors of slavery is the master's ownership of the slave's offspring. To whom do Jacob's children belong? Laban apparently thinks, and will continue to think (see 31:43), they are his.[3]

Negotiations

Having exposed magic in the incident with the mandrakes, the story similarly derides Laban's superstition. By divination he has discerned God's blessing of Jacob. Divination?! He need only open his eyes.[4] Laban has clearly benefited from the excess of Jacob's blessing. This is clear too from Jacob's response in v. 29: they both know Laban's livestock has prospered under Jacob's care. Laban's uncovers not, however, that blessing has occurred; he learns the source of the blessing.[5] Just as Lot flourished because

---

3. The request, "send me on my way," contains a sting (30:25). Jacob uses a term that indicates the release of a slave (Sarna, *Genesis,* 211). He lists the following passages that use this Hebrew term to speak of manumission: Exod 21:26–27; Deut 15:12, 13, 18; 21:14; Jer 34:9, 10, 11, 14, 16; 50:33; Isa 58:6 (*Genesis,* 365, n. 13). Jacob is a hired hand, a contract laborer, who is not free to leave apart from his master's permission (McKeown, *Genesis,* 147).

4. Waltke, *Genesis,* 418.

5. Five times the promises indicated that all nations would be blessed through the descendants of Abraham. Laban is, despite his treatment of Jacob, a recipient of this divine blessing. Laban therefore does not want to release him. Jacob affirms much of Laban's statement by pointing to the increase in the livestock under his care: the formerly small herd has multiplied, "and the Lord has blessed you everywhere I have been" (30:30). Mitchell observes that "The phrase [*legarli*] describes God's blessing as following Jacob around (cf. BDB 919b–920a). Yet blessing is not some contagious, mysterious power which a man who is [*baruk*] possesses and which he exudes onto others. . . . Jacob does not possess blessing power; he possesses the blessings God has bestowed on him. Both v 27 and v 30 clearly state that it is Yahweh who has the power to bless. Jacob does, however, possess God's promises; since God has promised to bless him he can expect God to bless his undertakings even though it may benefit others more than himself" (*Meaning of* "To Bless," 70). He further notes Gen 39:5, which speaks of God blessing the household of Potiphar on account of Joseph.

of Uncle Abraham, here Uncle Laban prospers through his nephew.[6] But this too is not Laban's lesson.

He has discovered the source of his abundance: *Jacob's God*. Did Laban ask his gods if they had enriched him, only to be told "No, Jacob's God is blessing you"? Did he thank them, only to be told, "Don't look at us. The LORD did it"? By this absurdity, Laban communicates the inferiority, indeed the uselessness of his own gods.[7] Jacob, agrees, observing that his arrival coincides with Laban's prosperity (30:30).

Such benefits supplement God's own promise at Bethel, where the explicit focus fell on families (28:14). Furthermore, the words of Isaac's blessing, especially the notion that all who bless Jacob will be blessed, and all who curse him will be cursed, are cast in a strange light. Laban has not blessed Jacob. He has opposed him at every turn, yet prospers through Jacob's presence. Today this begins to change.[8]

Laban ignores Jacob's intention to depart, possibly hearing it as the opening round of new negotiations. Jacob has sojourned with Laban for fourteen years, and has acquired a family. He has not, however, been otherwise enriched by his labors. The prosperity has gone to Laban. It is now time to "do something for my own household" (30:30). As long as Jacob serves in the house of Laban, there is no "House of Israel."

Laban responds to Jacob's announced departure by asking "What shall I give you?"[9] For reasons never voiced, Jacob's concern shifts easily from home to wages. Perhaps, having been outsmarted too many times by Laban, Jacob sees his chance to get something back. Maybe, overcome by the realization that Laban's wealth really does spring from his presence, he decides that he therefore should have some say in its distribution. Doing "something for my own household," in any case, means not a journey but a new contract. And this will mean twenty years in Harran.

In Jacob's first round of bargaining with Laban he, from a position of weakness, exceeded reasonable generosity in offering seven years of service to acquire a wife. He is still the employee, but his stock is rising. He thus appears stunningly inept when he says, "Don't give me anything" (30:31). And in the end, Laban gives just that. But Jacob has learned from Laban's previous invitation to suggest wages (29:15). He does not want Laban to

6. See Gen. 13:5; McKeown, *Genesis*, 147.

7. McKeown, *Genesis*, 147.

8. Waltke, *Genesis*, 419.

9. Gen 30:31.

"*give* [him] anything."[10] Instead, he proposes an arrangement by which he can *earn* according to his own stipulations. Near Eastern sheep, the fat-tailed Awassi, were normally white, the goats black or dark brown.[11] Jacob requests as wages sheep not completely white (*laban*), and goats not completely black, that is, all the animals that represent an aberration in terms of color and pattern, and make up a generally fixed percentage of the flock.[12] As numbers increase due to God's blessing of Jacob, Laban will prosper, and Jacob will grow correspondingly richer too, albeit from a smaller base. The conditions set forth have the added benefit for Laban that if the flock falters, Jacob suffers to the same degree, thus ensuring motivated service. Jacob has offered an appealing and safe bargain. Or so it would seem.

The art of the deal is that Jacob's property will be instantly verifiable.[13] If he had been, as Laban implied, somehow unclear about the object of his former labor, this time with extreme specificity he ensures that Laban understands his wages. Uncle White shall have the white. Inasmuch as the sheep would have been predominantly white, the majority goes to Laban. After all, he is both lord and owner. In terms of goats, the black will go to Laban. Again, the easily verifiable majority. Only let me go through the flocks and separate out the minority—the oddities. This way, Jacob gets a respectable but reasonable payment for past services, and will provide for his own from the few animals Laban now gives him.[14]

10. Walton (*Genesis*, 589) possibly bases too much on v. 31, "Don't give me anything." If this is the same gambit employed by Ephron when Abraham purchased the cave of Machphela (see Gen 23:3–16, esp. v. 11), then it should be regarded as conventional. As in that negotiation, so here it does not become part of the agreement.

11. The sheep are Ovis Aries, the goats Ma'az Jebali (or Capra Hircus). Firmage, "Zoology," 1126–27. See also Sarna, *Genesis*, 212; Waltke, *Genesis*, 419; Wenham, *Genesis 16–50*, 256; Walton, *Genesis*, 589.

12. Finkelstein provides evidence that typical agreements paid the shepherd 10 to 20 percent, plus wool and milk. Jacob's percentage would have almost certainly been less than that (Finkelstein, "Old Babylonian Herding Contract"). Also Walton, *Genesis*, 589; Arnold, *Genesis*, 272.

13. Duguid, *Relentless Grace*, 94–95.

14. Jacob has asked Laban to grant him livestock that was unusually marked. What is less than clear, however, is if Jacob expected such animals to belong to him from this day, or only those that will be born under his watch. This ambiguity allows Laban dangerous leeway, and makes it difficult to know if Laban is acting deceitfully. On the ambiguity here, see Walton (*Traveller*, 152). It may be that Jacob was not proposing that the variegated go to him yet, but that in the future, when the sums are totaled, he receive the mixed animals. In that case, Laban's reaction is less one of theft and more one of distrust. He, the deceiver, will not be deceived by Jacob (McKeown, *Genesis*, 148).

As a postscript to their agreement and its remarkable transparency, Jacob adds, apparently without irony, ". . . my honesty will testify for me in the future."[15] The term used here for "honesty" points to his moral uprightness, not something on which you'd expect Jacob to place a lot of weight. As such it perhaps suggests that those who deceive others are equally gifted at deceiving themselves.

Laban's Duplicity

Laban agrees (30:34) but then immediately removes many of the animals that were to go to Jacob. Jacob asked for the "speckled or spotted sheep," and there is no mention of Laban taking them (30:32). But Jacob specifically requested "every dark-colored lamb", and Laban removes "all the dark-colored lambs" (30:35). Jacob stipulated "every spotted or speckled goat," and Laban removes "all the speckled or spotted female goats" as well as "all the male goats that were streaked or spotted."

Thus, in addition to the stock outside the terms of the agreement, Laban took the dark colored lambs, spotted male goats, and all irregularly marked female goats. With anomalous animals removed, and with them the possibility of cross-breeding reduced, Jacob has long odds on producing variegated flocks. In effect, Jacob's flocks—goats and sheep with unusual markings—will have to arise from a foundation virtually free of unusual markings. Laban's hopes, by eliminating particular animals from the breeding process, to alter the percentages. If the flocks thrive but their coloring favors Laban, he gets the greater good. Moreover, Jacob cannot complain, for he himself set the terms.

Jacob seems destined to remain poor forever. Or if not destined, then consigned to it by his father-in-law/uncle. Jacob had said, "Give me my wife" (29:21), and Laban had withheld Rachel in violation of their pact. Now Jacob knowingly says, "Don't give me anything," and yet Laban takes the flocks in violation of this agreement. In both cases, Jacob ultimately gets what he wants, but not on the terms he expects.

The narrator now discloses another variable. Having earlier portrayed the younger daughter doing the heavy lifting until replaced by Jacob, it now quietly emerges that Laban has sons (30:35).

---

15. Gen 30:33.

Jacob's Superstition

Red had been Esau/Edom's undoing—in connection with a pot of stew. A similar play on names colors the story of Laban's undoing. Both his name and the related word rendered poplar trees (as used in Jacob's breeding program), are based on a root meaning white. Jacob who wants black, streaked, speckled, or spotted sheep, not *laban* (i.e., white) ones, sets up poles that are correspondingly streaked, speckled, or spotted (30:37). When females in heat arrive to drink, they find themselves face to face with these poles. There they mate, and lo and behold, kids emerge with markings to match the poles. Similarly the sheep look upon multi-colored or black goats as they mate so that they produce lambs favorable to Jacob. This scheme amounts to a "folklorist"[16] magic, which assumes that an animal's appearance is affected by what its parents see while mating.[17]

As his plan gains momentum, Jacob's concern moves from quantity to quality. He now enacts a strategy for when the stronger females are in heat (30:41).[18] Unlike the first step, this aspect has a firmer basis: vigorous parents generally produce vigorous offspring. Furthermore, Jacob, in a detail withheld till the last possible moment, places the rods in front of the healthiest of the mixed animals, but not the feeble ones. The combination of the two strategies generates stronger animals for his flocks and weaker ones for Laban's. Jacob launches not a get-rich-quick scheme but a contest involving winners and losers. And having been alerted to Laban's sons, we know that losing extends to subsequent generations.

It may come as a surprise that Jacob's home teems with magic. This, however, conforms to his culture and to the religious life of his ancestors. Jacob's great-grandfather Terah was an idolator according to Joshua 24:2. His mother Rebekah would have come from this idolatrous background. His uncle Laban practices divination, asks which god brings blessing, and

---

16. Sarna, *Genesis*, 212.

17. Wenham, *Genesis 16–50*, 256; Waltke, *Genesis*, 420. Sarna offers the possibility that Jacob's dilemma centers upon Laban's removal of his flocks at mating time (*Genesis*, 212). Thus, Jacob's goal must be the mating of combinations favorable to him before they are removed. The reason the plan works is that the toxicity of the three trees "could have had the effect of hastening the onset of the estrous cycle and so heightened their readiness to copulate." The difficulty with this view is that Laban seems to have removed the relevant animals immediately (30:35, "that same day") and kept them away, the subsequent mention of "Laban's flocks" (30:40) referring only to those animals in Jacob's care that belong to Laban.

18. Walton, *Traveller*, 154.

maintains idols. His wife robs temples, or at least steals gods. And Jacob himself will neither for some time claim the LORD as his God nor rid his household of idols (35:2). Indeed, the ancestors of Israel are said to have worshipped other gods while in Mesopotamia *and* in Egypt (Josh 24:14). That is, even the generations after Jacob were not strict Yahwists.

Jacob's wives thought that through magic they could bear children. Jacob apparently shares their worldview as he sets up his plan to breed the sheep and the goats. With respect to the wives, the narrator makes it clear that magic and mandrakes have no bearing on children. With respect to Jacob, the narrator once again indicates that scheming has nothing to do with reproductive success. Strange plants and striped poles accomplish nothing.[19] Plainly, as Jacob will subsequently tell his wives, God is the one who enriched him at the expense of their father (31:9). His methods in this light look as silly as theirs—as the narrator intends.

This is the story of Israel writ large. The nation repeatedly lapses into idolatry. When understood as the attempt to control the divine, as the failure to acknowledge the true and living God, it is seen that the nation failed in this regard from its birth to the birth of its Messiah. Jacob's story speaks of jealous brothers, jealous wives, and jealous sons who have no concept of a jealous God.

God's Overruling Grace

We already know what Laban will learn: neglecting Jacob to chase animals around the countryside has a price. Esau had paid in like circumstances, and now Jacob plunders his uncle's wealth. The attempt to defraud, a three-day journey, provides the means of Laban's undoing.

With a summary sentence, 30:43 informs that Jacob, an active investor, has parlayed his flocks into slaves, camels, and donkeys. Away from his father-in-law's watchful eye, his diversified portfolio grows.

Jacob's fortune comes from genetically modified lamb, but the story fails to explain the abundance. Selective breeding may play some role in the flock's growth, but can hardly explain how, in six years, a flock makes recessive traits dominant. In various ways this is hardly a sufficient conclusion to the Jacob/Laban story.[20] The next chapter, the longest and possibly most overlooked section of the Jacob cycle, provides answers.

19. Longman, *How to Read Genesis*, 141.
20. Turner, *Announcements*, 141.

Chapter 7

On the Road Again

Genesis 31

THE BIRTH STORIES HAVE set mandrakes and human claims (communicated in the names of children) alongside the truth that the LORD alone grants life.[1] But the narrator weaves little evidence of God's work into his account. And the tale of Jacob's agrarian conquests says even less about God, deferring explanation until the four stories that comprise much of chapter 31. In this chapter, members of Jacob's family finally talk to one another, and in so doing, to the reader. Their conversations pinpoint the true source of Jacob's prosperity. This allows each, in their turn, to affirm that just as mandrakes cannot produce children, so striped branches do not produce striped goats. And they don't stop there.

The chapter does at least two more things. First, it conveys the means and schemes by which Jacob and his family extricate themselves from Laban's grasp. Second, in so doing it continues to mercilessly mock idolatry.

An Ominous Report

Strife marks Jacob's existence as much as success. These past years, though, contained in a single paragraph and seeming to locate Jacob in the place he fares best—amongst the flocks and away from his bickering relatives—initially appear as a relatively quiet time. But looks are deceiving.

---

1. Brueggemann, *Genesis*, 255.

First, we heard a bit late that Laban had sons—and, with Jacob, learn that they are at least jealous if not accusing. Jacob, true to form, is plundering their inheritance. Hearing then yields to seeing as Jacob observes Laban's face (31:2).[2] Jacob finds there only "hostility and suspicion."[3] This is surprising, since from our angle Laban has never appeared otherwise.

Jacob Tells His Story to Rachel and Leah

As Laban scowls, the LORD speaks. At last, after twenty years, he sends Jacob home (31:3). He who had promised Jacob's safe return now commands it, repeating enough of 28:15's promise ("I am with you") to indicate that while Laban has changed, the LORD remains the same.[4] Yet again, however, when commanded to return, family obstacles must be overcome. Jacob six years earlier had expressed a desire to leave. Will he this time gain his freedom?[5]

He sends for Rachel and Leah to say that God appeared to him some time earlier, as he began acquiring his wealth. It is not his fault that Laban's herds are now his. But there is more. Jacob had a dream that revealed first that God blesses him and second that this blessing provides a counterweight to Laban's wretched treatment. Laban stands against Jacob, so God stands against Laban. The telling of it compels Rachel and Leah to take sides.[6] With whom will they stand?

Rachel and Leah Tell Their Story

For various reasons, the sisters might have wished to remain in Harran. But they do more than fully endorse Jacob's story. They also offer their own account of life with Laban. The bride-price was intended for a wife's security should circumstances remove her from her husband's care. Jacob gave not cash, but fourteen years of hard labor, which—the women charge—was never of benefit to them. In short, Laban has sold his daughters rather than

---

2. Walton, *Traveller,* 160.

3. Alter, *Genesis,* 166.

4. Mathews, *Genesis 11:27—50:26,* 511.

5. Walton, *Traveller,* 160.

6. Humphreys, *Character of God,* 182.

provided for their welfare.[7] While Laban's sons think Jacob prospers at their expense, Laban's daughters insist that Laban prospers at their expense. This is a serious charge, and provides Jacob with a third motivation to go home: Laban's sons, God's instructions, and his wives' affirmation.

But the sisters have more to say. When Laban worked his worst, robbing Jacob on his wedding night, his explanation included the implication that Jacob was a foreigner. Now the wives accuse Laban of treating *them* as foreigners. At last a unity is forged. Rachel and Leah stand together. And they recognize in their defrauded state a shared experience with not just one another but also with Jacob. Jacob's report never mentions his wives, and theirs never mentions Jacob. Both stories speak of Laban and of God, for both recount divine intervention on behalf of the oppressed.[8] Perhaps their shared status as delivered victims is all that unites them against a common foe.[9] But what could be a greater basis for unity than the shared experience of divine rescue? And such unity ought to generate community. Furthermore, if reconciliation is ultimate, the abuse at Laban's hand has been providentially instrumental in achieving this outcome. Miraculously, Jacob, Rachel, and Leah stand as one.

Laban Tells His Story to Jacob

At last Jacob's family moves in the right direction. But now Laban's agrarian interests afford Rachel access to his home. While he fleeces his sheep, Rachel steals Laban's *terafim* (31:19).[10] If these household gods are linked, as is often suggested, to the inheritance, then Jacob and Rachel steal the same thing from their own brothers.[11] Jacob may be the champion, albeit a bruised one, but Rachel plays his chosen sport well enough.[12]

---

7. Walton, *Genesis*, 590.

8. Humphreys, *Character of God*, 183.

9. Humphreys, *Character of God*, 178.

10. Elsewhere this merchandise can be bigger (1 Sam 19:13). Here, given the way they are hidden, the gods must be quite small.

11. Hamilton cites texts from Nuzi and Emar, but is reluctant to explain Rachel's theft in such terms (*Genesis*, 294–95). Longman similarly suggests that she merely wanted to rob her father of something he valued (*Genesis*, 142). Sitting on Laban's gods may reflect Rachel's evaluation of his culture and religion. Her separation from his clan is complete. See Brett, *Genesis*, 96.

12. Sailhamer, *Narrative*, 197; Zucker and Reiss, *Matriarchs*, 217–18.

A second crime occupies the author as interest returns quickly to Jacob. In an unusually direct instance of moral evaluation, the author writes, with the same verb as used of Rachel's theft, that "Jacob deceived Laban" (31:20).[13] Despite twenty years of battling in Harran, Jacob remains the fugitive, the thief, the deceiver. His past still stands, and his present is unreformed. But now the deceiver's home is permeated with jealousy, frustration, and the sort of theft he excels at. Is Canaan ready for a family like this?[14]

After twenty years, Jacob's story is marked by greater continuity than discontinuity. The deceiver is returning home. To indicate that this flight reverses the earlier escape, the narrator reverses the verbs. Rebekah warned Jacob to "arise and flee." Now, to conclude the story of his sojourn, the narrator announces, with an anatomically challenging construction, "he fled and arose."[15] Deceit and theft sent him to Harran; now theft and deceit send him home again. Will this cycle ever end?

Just then Laban appears, twice robbed, to tell *his* story. He overtakes Jacob in the hill country of Gilead, bearing his own accusations and pressing Jacob's family against the edge of death.[16] He opens the attack with, "What have you done?"—probably forgetting that Jacob shouted these words at him the morning after he married Leah.[17] He then charges Jacob with taking his daughters "like captives in war" (31:26), unaffected by the reality that they are Jacob's wives, earned by fourteen years of hard labor. Additionally, we know, as Laban does not, that his villainy toward them means they fully support this exodus.

Still dwelling on family, and advancing questions of custom and propriety, Laban a second time speaks of Jacob as the deceiver. He supplements his hints at kidnapping with the assertion that he just wants a going-away party. Is he serious? Hasn't Jacob attended enough family feasts. But his daughters must be sorely aggrieved if they willingly leave without so much as a farewell to brothers or father.

Laban next asserts his superiority—but only in passing. This becomes a concession that "the God of your father" warned him to exercise caution. It

13. The cognate also appears in 25:20; 27:35; 28:5; 29:25; and 31:24.

14. Walton, *Genesis*, 594.

15. So Sarna, *Genesis*, 217. The parallel is lost in the NIV.

16. On the challenges of the chronology, see Walton, *Genesis*, 591. Laban pursued for seven days, but preparation might have taken a while for an old man and his retinue.

17. Wenham, *Genesis 16–50*, 275.

could only be Jacob's God since Laban's gods were travelling incognito. That is to say, while Jacob may not have a God, Laban definitely doesn't. The LORD protects Jacob. Laban's gods can't even protect themselves.

Finally, Laban imputes a positive motive to Jacob's departure—a longing for home—even while asking why Jacob stole his gods. Thus he brings two overlapping charges: kidnapping and "godnapping."[18] As he accuses he omits any reference to the last twenty years. But he does, as did Jacob and the wives in their own stories, credit blessing to God. In the previous chapter he testified that prosperity was due to the LORD. Now he also attributes protection to God. While the gulf between them remains vast, in this Laban and Jacob are moving toward one another as well.

Looking for gods in All the Wrong Places

Laban demands a response, providing Jacob the opportunity to disrupt the soliloquy. Jacob answers the charges in order. I took my wives, inverting Laban's accusation, because I thought *you* would treat *them* as captives. I feared that you would steal them from *me*. And about your gods: I had nothing to do with that. If anyone in my caravan has them, "that person shall not live" (31:32). Tragically, this curse will ultimately find its victim.[19]

Jacob Tells His Story to Laban

Laban searches, groping blindly, as Isaac had once done.[20] But he finds nothing. Now Jacob has had enough. His resentment tumbles out. You've chased me. You've ransacked my tents. Let's get this out in the open. What have you found? For twenty years I could have robbed you. For twenty years I was your slave. I had opportunity and motive. But WHAT HAVE YOU FOUND? When things *were* stolen, *I* paid. *I* never robbed *you*. But *you* robbed *me*. Over and over and over. Ten times over.

And God saw.

God saw that Laban is the villain.[21] Jacob had said, "Don't give me anything." Now he contends that Laban hasn't—that *God* gave all he possesses.

18. See Isa 30:22 for a somewhat different pairing of idols with menstruation.
19. Humphreys, *Character of God*, 200.
20. Wenham, *Genesis 16–50*, 276.
21. Wenham, *Genesis 16–50*, 274.

Where Laban withheld payment, God was generous (31:42). And not just materially. God, through the dream, protects him.

Subsequent Scripture provides indirect commentary on these events in describing the proper treatment of slaves. One finds a profound incongruity between Laban's callous behavior and the Law of Moses that came later.

Jacob, by referring to wives and children, puts himself outside of at least a particular type of slavery, since, according to Exodus 21:4, wives given to slaves, and children born to them, remain the property of the master when a slave is released.[22] So is Jacob a slave or not? On the other hand, the Law instructs concerning one who on completing indentured service is released: "And when you release them, do not send them away empty-handed. Supply them liberally from your flock, your threshing floor and your winepress. Give to them *as the LORD your God has blessed you*."[23] Jacob's complaint contains this same language when he says, "You would surely have sent me away empty-handed" (31:42).[24] So Laban treats Jacob as a slave only when it suits him. On one hand, he lords it over Jacob, deprives him of freedom, and speaks of everything as his own (31:43). On the other, he does nothing to ensure the prosperity, or even subsistence, of his own family. Of course he might reply that Jacob, by stealing away secretly, robs him of that chance.

Jacob stumbles toward understanding. In Harran, when he exhibits the traits that comprise his character, he experiences only misery. But when, despite himself, God acts on his behalf, genuine blessing abounds. Indeed, by now we see the danger in Jacob's methods, whether employed by Jacob, Rachel, or Laban.[25] In terms of contracts, Jacob's share is constantly reduced by Laban's treachery, and the daughter's inheritance dissolves. Yet Jacob leaves with Laban's flocks and daughters.[26]

Together at Last

Laban's charges glide past stolen daughters to stolen gods, to the rather desperate claim that all of Jacob's gain corresponds exactly to Laban's loss

---

22. Sarna, *Genesis*, 211.

23. Deut 15:13–14.

24. Sarna, *Genesis*, 211; Wenham, *Genesis 16–50*, 278.

25. Walton, *Genesis*, 594.

26. Walton, *Genesis*, 594. Furthermore, Isaac takes credit for the earlier blessing (27:37), including international honor (27:29). By the time Jacob leaves Laban, it is the LORD (31:49; see also 53) who is the guarantor of blessing.

(31:43). Everything Jacob possesses came at his expense. But he can do nothing against one whom the LORD blesses and protects.

The pair join together with the help of their relatives (mentioned already in 31:23) to build a pillar. For the first and only time they pursue a common goal.

As he had before arriving in Harran, Jacob sets up a monolith, a pillar (v. 45). He then instructs his relatives to erect a second memorial—a heap of stones (v. 46). "His relatives" in what follows denotes Laban's party, not Jacob's own wives and children. Thus, Jacob and Laban each erect a memorial—that is, each "sign the contract." Each names its "witness heap," Laban in Aramaic and Jacob in Hebrew, reflecting their genuine differences in customs and cultural views, which Laban had exploited in his own country.

Despite these differences, a form of equality emerges. When Laban arrived a few hours ago, he was the chief of a single clan, dealing with Jacob from a position of superiority. Now they are equals, each head over distinct households.[27] Jacob's children aren't yet the children of Israel, but neither are they the sons of Laban any longer.

Laban, making concessions as he goes, does all the talking from this point. He invokes Jacob's God (is it because he cannot find his own?) to "keep watch when we are away from each other" (31:49). He who did nothing (at least after Leah's wedding) to provide for his daughters now obligates Jacob to not add to his pair (quartet?) of wives (31:50). Furthermore, adds Laban, the two memorials stand as a nonaggression pact between the two, in effect a boundary marker. Events conclude with a sacrifice, a meal, and a night's rest. With v. 55, Laban says his farewells, blesses his daughters(!) and returns home.

At last Jacob and Laban find *shalom*, having established boundaries and relieved seemingly insuperable tensions. Reconciliation here too has been achieved. Suddenly, it seems, Jacob has gone from war on all sides to peace with his wives, his father-in-law, and perhaps even God. Will he fare as well with Esau?

Naming God

This chapter provides a reckoning—a chance to recount, summarize, and comment on life in Harran. Numerous references to God drift to the surface. The last time he was mentioned, Rachel was speaking at the birth of

27. Wenham, *Genesis 16–50*, 274.

Joseph. Theological language appears nowhere among the sheep and the goats of chapter 30. That changes in chapter 31.

In 31:3, Yhwh sends Jacob home.[28] As Jacob shares his story with his wives, he five times refers to El or Elohim. The wives reply that Elohim has taken from their father—so do what Elohim says. Thus seven times Elohim has been named as the God who blesses, provides, and directs. Laban, as he pursues Jacob, is visited by Elohim in a dream (31:24). Despite his superior strength, Laban avoids threatening Jacob because Elohim has warned him—as stated first by the narrator and then Laban himself in 31:29, bringing to nine the number of times Elohim is named.

References 10, 11, and 12 occur in 31:42: "If the God of my father, the God of Abraham and the Fear of Isaac, had not been with me . . . ." Jacob speaks of Elohim's provision and protection. Laban's treaty invokes Yhwh as watchman (31:49) and Elohim as witness (31:50). In 31:53, Laban three times invokes Elohim as judge, and Jacob then swears by the "Fear of his father Isaac."

Thus, after a section without mention of God, and after four significant narrative blocks in which references to the divine betray only ignorance and superstition, the dam breaks. Twelve times Elohim is named as the God who works in the life of his people. Three times he is asked to judge. Once Yhwh speaks, and once he is asked to watch. And once "the Fear of Isaac" is the God of an oath.

This profusion of the divine name does not primarily show that Jacob and Laban share a religious experience. It states forcefully and finally the means by which Jacob prospered, was protected, and obtained an extraordinary abundance during his years of captivity. It testifies that success arose not from Jacob's strength, ingenuity, magical practices, or various gods. As Jacob leaves Harran alive, rich, and with a large family, the text insists that God, and God alone—the God of Israel, the God who watches and speaks—has accomplished what he promised. Twenty years earlier, Jacob had left Canaan, as ill-defined as a human could be. And for him on that day, God was equally ill-defined. But at last he is coming home.

---

28. The instruction reverses, with repetition of keys terms, elements of the command given in Gen 12:1, where Abram is told to leave his relatives and father's household. See Brett, "Politics," 54.

Chapter 8

Facing the Future

Genesis 32

RUNNING FORMS THE GREAT bookends of Jacob's wilderness years. Just as he had run from Esau toward Laban, so now he runs from Laban toward Esau. Leaving his father-in-law on settled—if not good—terms would bring great relief. But relief is fleeting. A still greater anxiety settles on Jacob, for physical strength and great wealth mean nothing if Esau remains angry. Has time softened his rage? God has fulfilled seemingly impossible promises during twenty years in Harran, but how does Jacob, without our vantage point, interpret his past and, for that matter, his future?

Another Ominous Report

Laban returns home at the end of chapter 31. Jacob, as he does the same, meets (again) "the angels of God."[1] As before, he declares the place to belong to the LORD, and names it to reflect that reality. At Bethel, he had spoken of the "gate of heaven" and named the place "the house of God." Now he speaks of the "camp of God" (32:2) and names the place Mahanaim (i.e., two camps).[2] At Bethel the angels were an unveiling, revealing to fleeing Jacob the presence of the divine as protector and savior. Now

1. Gen 32:1.

2. Fokkelman, *Narrative Art*, 199. See 32:10, where Jacob says that he himself, through God's kindness, has become "two camps." The pair of camps in the Hebrew may refer to the number of angels, the angels on Jacob's side, or even the angels alongside Jacob's abundance.

upon his return they once again speak of God as protector and savior. Has he learned to trust?

Jacob, himself approaching a century, has reason to think that Isaac is dead (though see 35:27–28) and that Esau—given his own long disappearance—has inherited everything. So he sends a message that serves several purposes. First, his twenty-year absence isn't particularly noteworthy. It was merely an extended visit with relatives. Second, his extraordinary wealth shows that he needs nothing from Esau or even from their father's estate. From his surplus he can give, whether needed or not, a gift that would establish Esau for life. Third, he wishes to start afresh with Esau.[3] The return message, however, is ambiguous. David, when angry with Nabal, approaches with four hundred men (1 Sam 25) and would have attacked if not for Abigail's intercession.[4] Esau approaches with an equal number. Obviously Esau has also fared well, but how can it be good for Jacob that such a large band accompanies him? It is time to pray.

Plan A

God has been with Jacob throughout, and has at least by implication promised to restore Jacob to his homeland. Promises, often considered convertible debt, easily become demands. Jacob now offers his first recorded prayer.[5] He begins by addressing the "God of my father Abraham, God of my father Isaac." This resembles God's own words at Bethel: "I am the LORD, the God of your father Abraham and the God of Isaac" (28:13). Jacob is calling upon God to honor the promises made then.

Remember, God, Jacob continues, that you commanded me to return: "Go back to the land of your fathers and to your relatives, and I will be with you" (31:3). Jacob confronts this advancing army only because he is obedient.[6]

Remember too that you have promised that you "will surely make [me] prosper and will make [my] descendants like the sand of the sea,

---

3. Walton, *Genesis*, 603–4.

4. Bar-Efrat, *Narrative Art*, 123–24.

5. Waltke further notes that this is the "only extended prayer in the book of Genesis" (*Genesis*, 443).

6. Wenham, *Genesis 16–50*, 291. Similarly, Adam in Gen 3:12: "The woman you put here with me . . . ."

which cannot be counted" (32:12).[7] If this army slaughters my family, the promise is empty. Have you a plan to rescue me?

The God of Kindness and Faithfulness

In the midst of this prayer, however, with its fearful bargaining, Jacob uncovers a marvelous truth. "I am unworthy of all the kindness and faithfulness you have shown your servant" (32:10). Always true no matter who utters them, these words reveal that Jacob at last explores the depths of his being over against the heights of God's character. A night that ultimately is about seeing God begins with self-discovery.

The first of Jacob's two great words, *hesed* (here "kindness"), indicates an undeserved and enduring favorable disposition, often tied to a covenant.[8] The nature of that relationship can be more precisely delineated. It is sometimes argued that the term looks to a mutually obligating relationship that arises from a covenant,[9] suggesting that God's covenantal love emerges from God's choosing activity. This, however, reverses the flow of God's favor. Deuteronomy 7:7–9 indicates that God's choice of "you . . . the fewest of all peoples" (7:7) arises from his love. Love precedes choice. *Hesed* is that facet of God's character that moves him to work on someone's behalf, to enter into a covenantal relationship. He fulfils promises not from obligation but because of the very attribute that compelled him (if one may so speak) to establish that relationship. It is God's loyalty in the face of challenges, culminating in deliverance.

Kindness combines with faithfulness two other times in Genesis. In 24:26, Abraham's servant "bowed down and worshipped the LORD" in response to God's leading him to Rebekah: "Praise be to the LORD, the God of my master Abraham, who has not abandoned his *kindness and faithfulness* to my master" (24:26–27). Here already, the words speak of God's constancy in blessing the chosen one and relate to a present event, which presages future fruitfulness. The third instance of the collocation in Genesis

---

7. See also 28:14.

8. *Hesed* has been rendered "lovingkindness" (ASV), "steadfast love" (ESV), "unchanging love," (NASB), "faithful love" (NJB), "mercy" (Geneva Bible, NKJV). In Mic 6:8 the same word is more often translated "mercy" (KJV, NKJV, NIV), but "kindness, (ASV, NASB) and "loyalty" (NJB) also appear.

9. Glueck, *Hesed*, esp. 81.

finds Jacob entreating Joseph, with death imminent, to "show me *kindness and faithfulness*. Do not bury me in Egypt" (47:29).

Leaving Genesis for a moment, we find Jacob's words informing another "seeing God" event. Moses, who asks to see the Lord's glory (Exod 33:18), hears God reply that he will parade his goodness before Moses and utter his name. "You cannot," however, "see my face, for no one may see me and live" (33:20). The next day, while passing in front of Moses, God proclaims his name, and in the words that follow says, "the Lord, the Lord, the compassionate and gracious God, slow to anger, abounding in *love and faithfulness*."[10] "Love and faithfulness" are the same as Jacob's "kindness and faithfulness,"[11] for God clothes his justice in mercy, kindness, and love when he establishes his covenant with Israel.

Rahab, having protected the two spies in Jericho, requests protection when the city falls. They reply, "If you don't tell what we are doing, we will treat you *kindly and faithfully*, when the Lord gives us the land."[12] At an equally decisive moment in Israel's covenantal history—as the men of Hebron anoint David king over Judah—David sends word to the men of Jabesh Gilead who have buried Saul: "May the Lord now show you *kindness and faithfulness*, and I too will show you the same favor because you have done this."[13]

David uses the phrase again when, driven from Jerusalem by Absalom, he discharges Ittai the Gittite from service with the words, "May *kindness and faithfulness* be with you."[14] The divine character in this instance stands in for the divine name. In effect, David says, "the Lord be with you." Ittai replies, "I will be with you," recognizing that the Lord is with David despite current events. The LXX clearly understood David's words to refer to God as much as to his attributes: it renders them with the equivalent of, "the Lord treat you with mercy and truth."

In Psalm 25, David praises God's faithfulness and willingness to forgive. Between references to his own sins and God's forgiveness (Ps 25:7 and 11) he inserts the words, "All the ways of the Lord are *loving and faithful* toward those who keep the demands of his covenant" (25:10). This statement of God's covenantal character precedes the hope of deliverance

---

10. Exod 34:6.

11. These words are most directly glossed as, "and great in love and truth."

12. Josh 2:14.

13. 2 Sam 2:6.

14. 2 Sam 15:20, my translation.

for king and people (25:16–22). Another Davidic psalm entreats the LORD to "increase the days of the king's life; his years for many generations. May he be enthroned in God's presence forever; appoint your *love and faithfulness* to protect him" (Ps 61:6–7).

Later, in successive psalms, first the Korahites and then David appeal for deliverance. In the midst of national crisis the psalmist recalls God's former deliverance and implores him to forgive. "*Love and faithfulness* meet together; righteousness and peace kiss each other" (Ps 85:10). David appeals to the same qualities enunciated by Moses in Exodus 34:6–7: "But you, LORD, are a compassionate and gracious God, slow to anger, abounding in *love and faithfulness*" (Ps 86:15).

In a request for God to renew his covenant with David, the psalmist pronounces, "Righteousness and justice are the foundation of your throne; *love and faithfulness* go before you" (89:14). Once again the character of God is tied to his covenant and becomes legitimate grounds for petition.

In Proverbs, exhortations arise from these divine qualities and become the foundation for harmonious relationships. The king instructs his son, "Let *love and faithfulness* never leave you; bind them around your neck, write them on the tablet of your heart. Then you will win favor and a good name in the sight of God and man" (3:3–4). "*Love and faithfulness* keep a king safe; through love his throne is made secure" (20:28).

Though the construction under consideration never appears in the Prophets, the sentiment does. For example, building again on Exodus 34:6, Joel writes, "Rend your heart and not your garments. Return to the LORD your God, for he is gracious and compassionate, slow to anger and abounding in love, and he relents from sending calamity."[15]

Genesis 32 and events at Bethel resembles Exodus 34 in that both combine the impossibility of seeing God with the recitation of divine attributes. Both also incorporate the covenantal elements of *hesed*. But they differ in that Moses receives more than Jacob, for the shrouded God of Genesis 32 graciously, indeed dangerously, reveals his glory to Moses.

John weaves these threads into a coherent tapestry when, with a glance at Moses (John 1:17), he speaks of Christians receiving blessing (1:16). These blessings are intertwined with seeing the full disclosure of divine glory in Jesus, "who came from the Father, full of grace and truth" (1:14). *Hesed*, rich with nuances of love and grace, indicating God's unwavering commitment to covenantal relationships, finds its parallel in

---

15. Joel 2:13.

χάρις (*charis*), the Christian notion of grace.[16] John, with this material, moves from seeing God (1:14a, 18) to the witness of Moses (1:17a) to "grace and truth" (1:17b, also in 1:14b). At the center of it all stands the one who from "his fullness" bestows "grace in place of grace" (1:16). Thus John recalls God's revelation of himself in terms of grace (i.e., covenantal love) and truth (Exod 34:6). He continues, "No one has ever seen God, but the one and only Son, who is himself God and is in closest relationship with the Father, has made him known" (1:18). God shows Jacob unmerited favor. God gives Moses a glimpse of his glory. And God reveals himself to children of faith. With mercy exceeding any shown to Jacob, and revelation outshining any granted to Moses, he discloses his love and kindness, offering this blessing in the crucified one.

The Man without Faith and Truth

Jacob, confessing his own unworthiness (literally and ironically perhaps, "smaller-ness," or is it "younger-ness"?) in the face of God's provision of family and flocks, at last produces a statement worthy of God's faithfulness. Setting his status alongside divine grace, he observes that God has blessed him with "kindness and faithfulness." Words hardly do it justice. Jacob's prosperity defies the imagination.[17] He who twenty years before had fled with only a staff now returns as "two groups." Furthermore, his words reflect the lavishness of God's blessing: the construction that we have been considering appears in dramatically heightened form. Here alone in the Pentateuch is *hesed* in the plural (kindnesses), and here alone is it prefaced with "all these."[18] Jacob rightly says that all these kindnesses and all this faithfulness are undeserved (32:10). The plurals speak to God's blessing, but can't approach the sum of it.

These groups are his possessions, but even more, the objects of his love. And they are vulnerable. How can Jacob protect them against the advancing army? "Save me, I pray," he petitions God, "from the hand of my brother Esau, for I am afraid he will come and attack me, and also the mothers with their children" (32:11). This prayer is as it should be. Jacob responds to God's character and his own weakness, pours out his fears

16. Dodd, *Interpretation*, 175–76.

17. Ross, *Creation and Blessing*, 543.

18. The plural of 32:10 (32:11 MT), *hesadim*, expresses intensity. So Mathews, *Genesis 11:27—50:26*, 551.

before the LORD, and asks God to save him "from the hand of my brother, from the hand of Esau."[19] Esau's hairy hands. Jacob's hands had grasped the heel (25:26). Jacob's hands were covered with hide (27:16). Savory food was placed "into the hand of her son Jacob" (27:17, ESV). Isaac says Jacob's "hands are the hands of Esau" (27:22). But now Jacob fears the hands of Esau. His prayer reminds us why he needs rescue.[20]

His blindness, furthermore, has not been fully cured. His manipulative character returns as he reminds God—"But you have said . . ."—that he had promised prosperity and numerous descendants (32:12). Jacob has grown in that he comes to God for aid; his failing is that he still thinks he needs to wrestle it away. He remains short-sighted. To be sure, his horizon has broadened. He is less self-centered regarding his family now than when he left. But seeing outside his own interests, necessary for seeing God, remains beyond him.

Plan B

Having prayed, Jacob launches his scheme. He sets his possessions in parade ranks—multiple groups totaling 550 animals with attendants. These proceed with gaps between them (32:16). The leader of the first herd will answer Esau's inquiries by confessing that Jacob is Esau's servant, that Esau is lord, and that the animals are tribute for "my lord Esau" (32:17–18). Subsequent herd-leaders will give the same answer, repeating the words, "Your servant Jacob is coming behind us."[21]

In 32:20 (32:21MT), Jacob's thoughts reveal his purpose. A more direct rendering of his words reads, "I will cover his face with these gifts which walk to my face; later, when I see his face, perhaps he will lift my face." A moment ago it was hands. Now, four times in this verse Jacob refers to faces, alternating between "his face" and "my face." Laban's face, Esau's face, and God's face all feature large in preparing Jacob for the encounter.[22]

19. My translation.
20. Turner, *Genesis*, 144.
21. Gen 32:20.
22. Just as hands had been a recurring motif through the earlier story, so now "face" moves to the fore. This is not a new feature: Gen 4:5 and 6 refer to the face of Cain; in 4:14 the curse on Cain means that God will hide his face; Sodom's sin has risen to the face of the LORD (19:13); Abraham in 19:27 stood before the face of the LORD; Jacob left Isaac's face in 27:30; Laban's face is less friendly to Jacob than before (31:2, 5); Jacob anticipates meeting Esau "face to face," so he hopes his gift "pacifies his face" (32:20–21); when they meet, Jacob can say that "to see your face is like seeing the face of God" (33:10).

The use of messengers delays the face-to-face meeting, but Jacob is preparing for tomorrow with sacrifices. His gifts and words are theologically loaded. "Gift" is the common word for an offering.[23] To pacify is *kipper*—the language of atonement.[24] And the verb translated "accept," which can mean simply "lift," is often used for forgiveness in sacrificial contexts. Taken individually, this use of "offering" or "atone" might be surprising. The combination of terms demands that we hear the language of sacrifice.

Furthermore, having just spoken of God as Lord and himself as servant, Jacob now speaks of Esau with the same relational words, repeatedly calling himself Esau's servant. This implies a rather disturbing equating of God with Esau such that the appropriate response to the former is to deal properly with the latter. Waltke writes, "It is no less appropriate to pacify an offended brother than to appease an offended God."[25] A similar drawing together of reconciliation toward God and toward one's brother informs Jesus words: "if you are offering your gift at the altar and there remember that your brother or sister has something against you, leave your gift there in front of the altar. First go and be reconciled to them; then come and offer your gift."[26]

But our story pushes harder than that. Further, it invests little in Jacob's rehabilitation. In Harran, Laban was a mirror reflecting Jacob back to himself. Now at the edge of the land, Esau will serve to reflect God to Jacob. But can Esau, the offended brother, stand in for the offended God? And would it be enough for Jacob to be conciliatory? While Jesus insists that it is necessary to make amends with an offended brother before offering a sacrifice, he does not teach that what is necessary is sufficient. Instead, he presents brotherly reconciliation as a preliminary to engagement with the LORD. With Jacob, that engagement still waits.

If sacrificial language does not here represent a solution to the problem of Jacob's sin, how then should we interpret events? The way forward is once again to probe deeper into the structure of the story. In Genesis 29, the narrator attacked a particular view of atonement, or at least of reconciliation. Jacob had worked for seven years. Seven times he was said to have

23. So the MT of 32:14, 21.

24. Face as object of *kipper* appears only here. The phrase transliterates an Akkadian expression (*kuppar pane*) meaning "wipe the face"—i.e., wipe away the implicit anger. So Wenham, *Genesis 16–50*, 444.

25. Waltke, *Genesis*, 444.

26. Matt 5:23–24.

served during those seven years. The flight was to have lasted "a few days." The seven years "seemed like a few days." The emphasis on serving and completion indicates the fullness of Jacob's penance. But it accomplishes nothing with respect to the bigger issue. The shape of the story undermines the notion that working could somehow atone for sin, that payment can appease God. In fact, we go on to read that even if Jacob triples the years of labor, even if he experiences God's blessing along the way, the reality of sin still stands before him.

But that was four chapters ago. Now Genesis cuts off another false path to atonement and reconciliation. Jacob resorted to all manner of bizarre and dishonest behavior. He intruded into the domain reserved for the LORD himself. He variously rejected or accepted the role of God. He has been a chameleon who, whatever the circumstances, advanced his own agenda. And now again Jacob adopts that familiar role of the "planner and schemer."[27] Jacob has, in the first instance, offended God: "against you, you only, have I sinned" (Ps 51:4). To equate Esau too closely with God as the offended party is inappropriate. A problem with that approach, a problem Jacob creates for himself, is that he gives to Esau what belongs to God. Jacob sounds too much like Israel in that just moments earlier he had addressed God, not Esau, as Lord—but now transfers allegiance for political reasons. God himself had promised that the older would serve the younger. Jacob's superiority, like God's Lordship, here given away in an hour of fear, is not his to give.

Furthermore, the animals that Jacob now gives away are those that God took from Laban to give to Jacob. Jacob had asked Laban, just before the animals began to multiply, "when may I do something for my own household" (30:30). Having been enriched by God as provision for his own household, is it right that Jacob gives the blessing away?

Finally, how do we distinguish a gift from a bribe? Jacob evidently thinks Esau either needs the offerings or will be impressed with the giver. He errs in both cases.

The language of atonement shows that gifts are no more effective than work. If sin cannot be paid off with efforts, neither can it be paid for with gifts—even sacrifices. Such things have value when they orient the giver to a future fulfilled by Christ. They have none when the giver supposes that God somehow benefits from bulls and goats.

27. Sailhamer, "Genesis," 209.

We are witness to an extraordinary development. Jacob, from knowledge or ignorance, speaks in a way that interacts with the author's theology of reconciliation. But any progress on his part has limits; and its value is limited by the fact that Jacob remains, despite talk about the face of Esau, more concerned with saving his own face, or at least his own skin. Jacob's actions to this point, and the subsequent arrangement of his family, reveal his motivation.[28] The final presentation of wives and children moves from maidservants and their children to Leah and her children to, at last, Rachel and Joseph. That is, Jacob arranges the family from most expendable to most precious (33:1–2). As night falls, he sends everything and everybody across the river, and now, standing alone, occupies a vantage point from which to witness events. If Esau and his army accept Jacob's gifts and family, then all is well. But if they attack, Jacob can revert to form. He ran from the land; he ran back to the land. He can run again. He hasn't changed that much. As Esau closes in, Jacob keeps his options open.

"You Must Be Born Again"

By nightfall, Jacob stands as he had twenty years earlier: alone, empty-handed, at the border. All he possesses is opposite him. Expecting solitude, he finds an adversary, one described here only as "a man."[29] This is the third great event of Jacob's life to unfold under the cover of darkness. Twice before he was caught up in wrestling under blinding influences, first with Isaac and Esau and then with Laban. He was one for two in such matches, though in the subsequent engagements with Laban, Jacob built up a statistical superiority. He wrestles like he runs. That is to say, very well.

But now his spiritual wrestling is reflected in a physical wrestling. This has generated all manner of questions and speculations. The reality is, however, that only one verse speaks of a match that took all night, and it does not seek to satisfy our curiosity. In this, it is like other "seeing God" events. When Isaiah sees God, he talks about the size of the

---

28. Walton lists "three strategic advantages": (1) should Esau intend attack, receiving and assessing five groups of animals and continually regathering for combat would leave the army less alert than at the first; (2) incorporating so many animals into Esau's band would be cumbersome and noisy, robbing him of speed and surprise; (3) absorbing members of Jacob's household into Esau's ranks would render any military strategies ineffective (*Genesis*, 605).

29. Gen 32:24; he is also designated "a man" in 32:25, 26, and 28.

hem of his robe.[30] When Moses and the seventy elders see God, we learn that "under his feet was something like a pavement made of lapis lazuli, as bright blue as the sky" (Exod 24:10). It is like meeting the president and reporting on the carpet in the oval office. They give nothing away. When Ezekiel reports his strange encounter, he says he saw something much like something resembling something else. Each account turns out to conceal more than it uncovers.

In Genesis, God sometimes seems simultaneously near and far. Other times he is tangibly present. God is here, of all the chapters of Jacob's life, most clearly present. Surprisingly but fittingly, ambiguities are not reduced.[31] He is at once hidden and revealed.[32] In fact, at least as much as in any other event, we are left asking what happened, how, and why. The more God reveals himself, the more we flounder.

How much anthropomorphism can we accept? At Bethel, God stands, speaks, "has a form," and is seen.[33] Is it too much if God now wrestles with a wrestler, apparently as with a near equal, and is to a degree manipulated by a human? And is this the nature of us all when we deal with God? Is there some measure of self-interest in even our most pious and earnest exchanges?

In Genesis 32, God, as close as he ever gets, remains hidden to us. Perhaps the most we can know is that he struggles with us and that he suffers. And perhaps the nearest we come to a glimpse of God as he really is—deep within himself—is when we see his suffering. These verses offer no snapshot of God; but they point to the very essence of the one who dies on the cross.

Adding to the disorientation, the Hebrew sentences contain few nouns. Until it is virtually over, we cannot be sure who does or says what. We learn mostly in retrospect. Jacob wrestles with a man, but then no mere man; he can bless and re-name. Finally, from Jacob's words we discover that he has been wrestling with God. When presenting God's conversation with Abraham concerning Sodom, Genesis reveals at the outset that the LORD has appeared, but then speaks of three men. Concerning Jacob, he similarly delays

---

30. John seems to consider the glimpse of God in Isa 6 to be a revelation of Jesus. Compare John 12:41 with the language found in Isa 6 and 52–53, esp. 52:13.

31. Walton, *Traveller*, 90.

32. Walton, though "present" and "absent" go too far (*Traveller*, 92). Arguably God is always present—and always to some degree hidden.

33. Walton, *Traveller*, 90.

information. For seven chapters we thought Jacob had been wrestling with men. Now the narrator slowly lifts the veil to reveal that Jacob has all along been wrestling with God himself. At last dawn is breaking.

The match begins at night (32:22). They wrestle until daybreak (32:26). Only after the dialogue will the sun rise (32:31). Jacob has for twenty years toiled in deep unlit shafts. He has lived much but seen little. And now change is at hand. It is physical as well as mental. Most of all, it is spiritual.

Not surprisingly (or is it?), the man cannot overpower Jacob. But neither is Jacob able to overpower his opponent. At first light things reach their climax. This opponent does not wish to be seen—any more than Jacob did in his encounter with his father, or Leah did in her encounter with Jacob. The man, in seizing control of the situation, wrenches Jacob's hip (or is "hip" a euphemism?). He then commands Jacob to let him go.

We must again ask—with whom does Jacob wrestle? The narrator speaks of "a man" but Jacob of *elohim* (32:30). It might be an angel, mentioned already in 32:1.[34] This agrees with Hosea 12:4 which, reflecting on this event, speaks of "the angel."[35] This does not, however, do justice to the names Israel (32:28) and Peniel (32:30), which identify the opponent with God. Jacob has seen angels before, but this event reaches a higher plane: he responds in amazement that he has seen "God face to face, and yet my life was spared" (32:30). Only the Angel of the LORD provides a suitable answer, for he alone simultaneously represents a sufficient threat and a source of blessing.[36]

The adversary commands Jacob to let go, to stop grasping. Jacob, true to form, refuses. In his grasping he demands a blessing. The opponent asks him his name (32:27), and in so doing repeats earlier events. Had Jacob answered honestly when his father asked the same question, he

---

34. For discussion see Moberly, *Genesis 12–50*, 31.

35. Walton, *Genesis*, 606.

36. Other interpretations come from Alter, who psychologizes: "Jacob's opponent is the embodiment of portentous antagonism in [his] dark night of the soul . . . and he may equally well be an externalization of all that Jacob has to wrestle with within himself" (*Genesis*, 181); and Kunin, who suggests that Jacob wrestles with Isaac (*Logic of Incest*, 129). A carefully nuanced answer holds that since Jacob's assailant opposes Jacob's return, and only Esau has reason to oppose—but it is clearly not Esau—then "he must stand for Esau in some manner. He is, as it were, Esau's alter ego." Jacob thus wrestles with Esau's angel, "the celestial patron of Esau-Edom who is the inveterate enemy of the people of Israel" (Sarna, *Genesis*, 404). Sarna's reading is provocative, but ultimately unconvincing. Though conceivable that in his current crisis Jacob might appeal for blessing to Esau's representative, it is inconceivable that he receives the special name Israel, as part of a blessing, from "the inveterate enemy of the people of Israel."

would not be contemplating death. This time the truth tumbles out: he is Jacob, the grasper, deceiver, fraud, liar.[37] But the truth is met with grace: the man replies, "it shall no more be called Jacob, but Israel."[38] The former name has all his life functioned as a label, as a marker of character. But now that old character is under assault.[39]

Having identified himself, Jacob then enquires after his adversary's name. He hears only, "Why do you ask my name?"[40] Explanations for the evasion vary: one should not presume to ask God's name; God has no name; God will not provide something so powerful that Jacob could weaponize it against Esau.

Each of these has value. But the most straightforward explanation is best. The reply to Jacob's question—"Why do you ask my name?"—forces recognition: Jacob, don't you know who blesses you? Don't you know who has watched over you for all these years? It now settles upon Jacob that throughout his life he has been wrestling with the God who longs to bless him. He hadn't needed to grasp and fight, only surrender. His adversaries— Esau, Isaac, and Laban—were family, pushed to the brink by his grasping and wrestling. Now he clings to God, knowing there is no other hope. The blessing robbed from Esau meant nothing (as will be seen in the next chapter); the blessing obtained from God means everything.

So how has he prevailed against God and man? How can one suffer so much, yet emerge as victor? His wrestling with Isaac and Esau were for blessing. In this wrestling with God he again fights for blessing. He prevails in that in each instance he wins what he fights for.[41] To overcome, though, is not to escape injury. Wrestling away the blessing in chapter 27 had a

---

37. So Wenham, *Genesis 16–50*, 296. Walton maintains that "this probably go[es] beyond what the text allows, especially as the explanation of Jacob's new name seems almost to make a virtue of Jacob's struggle with Esau and Laban" (*Traveller*, 94–95, n. 65). But can we accept that the text is ambiguous, almost positive, concerning Jacob's wrestling with at least Isaac and Esau? If wrestling (i.e., "grasping," "deceiving") is good, then why is Jacob changed by God in precisely this element of his name (and presumably character)?

38. Gen 32:28, my translation. How different is the new name? The first relates to his wrestling with Esau, the second to his wrestling with God. The activity is the same but the opponent changes.

39. Waltke, *Genesis*, 446.

40. Gen 32:29.

41. Sailhamer, *Narrative*, 198.

price; so here again, attaining a blessing comes at a cost.[42] This time, however, the blessing will be as good as promised.

Why does God wrestle with Jacob? Yes, God wants to rescind his ability to run. But God could have achieved this through less dramatic means. Speaking narratologically, a more substantial answer emerges as several details of Jacob's life reappear in this event. Jacob wrestled with Esau at birth. Now he wrestles again. Jacob held on to Esau at birth. Now he holds on again. Jacob's name, given at birth, reflected his wrestling with Esau. Now he is named again, to reflect his wrestling again. Twenty years preceded Jacob's birth. Twenty years have passed again. The numerous parallels carry the meaning: we're reading a birth narrative. If the seeds of salvation were sown in Genesis 3, then the seeds of new birth are sown in Genesis 32. Jacob has been "born again." He has undergone a new, spiritual birth, as he encounters God, faces death, and emerges no longer as Jacob but as Israel.[43]

Jacob had kept his options open, but now God is closing them. Jacob must enter the land and meet his brother. The God who eliminates options has touched Jacob's life and removed his ability to run, and with it elements of his scheming nature. In giving himself up, Jacob discovers who God is. This will equip him to face Esau.

The Dawn of a New Day

Jacob, having been made weak, experiences his greatest victory. This notion that God triumphs through weakness stands at the center of biblical teaching. The boy David—overlooked because he lacked stature—replaces the king who stands a head taller than his countrymen. After his anointing, while Israel's giant-king shrinks in fear, that boy faces a still greater giant who brandishes Iron-Age paraphernalia, and defeats him with Stone-Age weapons in the name of the living God. David's greater son triumphs at the cross, not despite weakness, but in and through it. Paul, immersed in God's sufficient grace through weakness, says "for Christ's sake, I delight in weaknesses . . . . For when I am weak, then I am strong" (2 Cor 12:10).

---

42. Walton, *Traveller*, 94.

43. Has he changed? See Driver, *Genesis*, 297 (cited in Walton, *Traveller*, 94 n. 65). Fokkelmann relates the event to Christian baptism (*Narrative Art*, 215–16). Wenham speaks of new courage, humility, and penitence (*Genesis 16–50*, 304). There are, to be sure, changes in Jacob, some of which are immediately apparent (including his new name and his new strategy). But this event speaks of something more.

Paul, like Jacob, stopped resisting God, was overcome by him, and, with a new name to match his new relationship, grasped God's power to deliver. Scripture assaults self-sufficiency. It drives people to God, sometimes graciously crippling them in the process.

If these have become clichés to us, they are not for that reason less true or necessary. They lie at the heart of the gospel, and find their ultimate expression in Jesus and his cross.

Israel Wrestling with God

How does the reader wrestle with God? One scholar suggests that "God is someone who calls for our active engagement. Someone who honors us in the struggle as long as we don't let go."[44] Another writes, "faith may involve situations where the believer seems to be thrown onto their own resources or even onto fighting against what might seem to be the divine plan."[45] True? In fact, Jacob fights *for* the divine plan, not against it. But with his "own resources." And God doesn't approve.

Others equate Jacob's wrestling with prayer.[46] While it can be a struggle, it is not clear that God opposes us, threatening our lives, when we pray.

What then if wrestling is not about us—about some existential issue—and the text doesn't seek to correlate so directly with our life? What if it is about the forming of the nation. The name "Israel" appears here first, twice. And in these appearances it is already linked with the Israelites, [lit. "sons of Israel"]. This is Israel: at risk, isolated, struggling with God, strong, tenacious, God being simultaneously friend and foe because of both sin and his remarkable grace.[47] For Israel as for Jacob, being chosen means being wounded.[48] It also means possessing the promises.

Here the nation begins when God, taking the form of a man, shrouds his dangerous glory. He drags Israel back to the moment of birth, both revealing and hiding himself, giving a crippling blow, and offering a blessing—all the while finding little faith. In this he reveals that sometimes those not entirely "pure in heart . . . will see God."[49] And in this we find

44. Longman, *Genesis*, 144.
45. Walton, *Traveller*, 96.
46. Clowney, "Biblical Theology of Prayer," 140.
47. Walton, *Traveller*, 95–96.
48. Walton, *Traveller*, 96.
49. Matt 5:8.

God making promises that establish hope for a better future. This—is it not?—is the OT story of Israel. Jacob is Israel. And this story of simultaneous blessing and downward spiral will repeat until the arrival in Matthew 1 of a king who writes a new chapter.

If this is Israel, then points of discontinuity with the NT abound, which might make it difficult to incorporate Israel's story into our own. But we shouldn't miss the direct lines into what God has done through Jesus to form a new people. Maybe the difficulty stems from a reluctance to admit the truth: that something of Jacob lives in each of us.

Chapter 9

Facing the Past

Genesis 33

THE LAST TIME WE heard from Esau he was threatening murder. The last time we heard about him he was seeking a wife who satisfied Isaac. Maybe he tends toward magnanimity; perhaps a cooling-off period serves him well. The characterization is too thin to draw firm conclusions. Clearly Jacob, who knows him better than we do, remains fearful. They have not been presented together since the stew incident.[1] But now, after twenty years, meet they must.

The Meeting

Esau does what Jacob cannot: he runs to greet him. God has bent Jacob into a subservient posture.

---

1. Scenes were arranged around pairs. Scene 1 features Isaac and Esau; 2, Rebekah and Jacob; 3, Isaac and Jacob; 4, Isaac and Esau; 5, Rebekah and Jacob; 6, Isaac and Jacob. In scene 1, Isaac launched a scheme to bless Esau which was rerouted when Rebekah, the transitional figure, inserted herself into affairs. She, hearing the plan, spoke to Jacob (scene 2), moving him from outside the events to the inside. Jacob, in scene 3, kept his appointment with Isaac, but only until the moment when Esau arrived. Scene 4 placed Isaac and Esau together again. A narrator's comment relating Esau's disposition toward Jacob, and a quotation showing his intentions, formed a bridge to scene 5, where Rebekah, again hearing the plan, spoke to Jacob in a way that again subverted the intention of the elder male. This served to place Jacob once again before Isaac. In all this, Jacob and Esau never met. So Bar-Efrat, *Narrative Art*, 99.

Siblings typically address one another as "my brother" or "my sister," as in Genesis 33:9 and 2 Samuel 13:11. Repeatedly, however, in Genesis 32–33 Jacob speaks of lords and servants. Kings also address one another as "my brother."[2] So Jacob consciously rejects a doubly egalitarian vocative—fraternal and political—to express submission. Recall Aaron's response to Moses after the incident with the golden calf: "Do not be angry, my lord" (Exod 32:22). Guilt and the desire to appease elicit "my lord."[3]

The Value of the Stolen Blessing

Jacob's theft pushes him from the land promised in the blessing. Isaac's references to family mock Jacob as he exchanges one dysfunctional unit for another. Isaac blesses his son in terms of being served by family and by nations, but then in every reference to serving in the ensuing events, Jacob—where the term relates to him—always serves and is never served—ten times (30:26, 29; 31:6, 41; 32:5, 10, 18, 20; 33:5, 14).[4] The elements of Isaac's words are upside down within the Jacob story—as though it has brought curse rather than blessing.[5]

But the new blessing, the one from God himself, is not about what Jacob will receive. It defines who he will be. The change of names is more than an altered designation: it is saying that he no longer is the deceiver; he is Israel. And while this has problems of its own, it promises an ongoing relationship with God.

Now, in v. 11, Jacob presents his gift to Esau. But he changes the term for gift from *minhah*, used five times from 32:13 to 33:10,[6] to *berakah*. Further, he exhorts Esau to "*take* my *berakah*." Echoes of Jacob's theft abound. Both Esau and Isaac had identified as *berakah* that which he stole (27:35, 36).[7] Indeed, at Esau's appearance Isaac had reported, "your brother came deceitfully, and *took* your *berakah*." Thus when Jacob here says, "take my blessing," both "take" and "blessing" repeat the harrowing words of 27:35. Additionally, according to Isaac's blessing, Esau would bow down to Jacob (27:29). Bowing has not reappeared until 33:3, where

2. Bar-Efrat, *Narrative Art*, 67–68.

3. Bar-Efrat, *Narrative Art*, 67.

4. Turner, *Genesis*, 129.

5. Turner, *Genesis*, 129.

6. See MT of Gen 32:14, 19, 21, 22 and 33:10.

7. Sarna, *Genesis*, 230.

Jacob bows to Esau. The sum of Jacob's words and action is that he does not merely offer Esau a gift. He now returns the stolen blessing, giving back that which has brought nothing but trouble, destruction, and curse from the moment he took it.[8]

And while Jacob was away slaving, Esau has been home prospering.[9] He has grown into a successful and powerful clan of his own. In 27:28 Isaac spoke of abundance (*rob*) in the blessing. Here Esau says he has enough (*rab*).[10] In this too it appears the promises are fulfilled as much in Esau's life as in Jacob's.

The Impossible Ending

That went well! After all those years and fears colored—now it seems un-necessarily—by flight and fight, Jacob returns to find *shalom*. The drama that permeated the story since our first glimpse of the adult Jacob, a tension induced by narrow escapes, threatening brothers, shrouded activities, looming neighbors, arguing wives, stolen gods, accusing relations, divine visitations . . . the list goes on, dissolves with a fraternal embrace. It all seems too easy. And once again, our author does not answer so many of our questions. Why does Esau change? Does he yet again display his impetuous nature? Does his previous insensitivity to the future now meet with a corresponding disregard of the past? Do events unfold thus because God answered Jacob's prayer? Is it because God had been working behind the scenes—in this case, in the life and heart of Esau—all along? How does the moment of prayer relate to God's work over twenty years?

This is the great unexpected ending. Indeed, it establishes a paradigm of sorts for impossible endings. It speaks of grace, of favor that we know to be, despite any sympathy for the protagonist, completely undeserved, the sort of forgiveness associated with God himself. Thus it comes as little surprise when Jesus borrows this too-good-to-be-true sequence

8. Westermann describes the meeting as "remarkably ceremonialized," unfolding as if it were "a public ceremony with fixed protocol"; in fact, he suggests that the account is brought into conformity with a "familiar court ritual," pointing to 33:3 and its resemblance to the wording of the Amarna letters: "Before the feet of my lord I bow, seven times and seven" (*Promises*, 81–82). The narrative portrays a vassal submitting to his lord, desiring reconciliation after some offense. The climax of Jacob and Esau's "reconciliation involves Jacob's submission, a submission that he almost forces on his brother."

9. Turner, *Genesis*, 145.

10. Turner, *Genesis*, 144.

of running, embracing, kissing, and forgetting past offenses (33:4) to tell of the prodigal who returns to a father who (inappropriately, some will argue) runs, embraces, kisses, and forgives (Luke 15:20).[11] The impossible ending becomes the paradigm of impossible grace.

11. In chapter 32, Jacob as Israel was presented as both an individual and as representative of a nation. This will increase over the next three chapters, and will be true of Esau as well. On the future of Edom, see Gen 36. Should we therefore say that this story would have been heard in the context of strife with Israel's neighbors, the Edomites? Is it intended to comment on cross-border relations? If so, it would provide a controversial answer. If Jesus' describing a Samaritan as neighbor offends, so would Edom's presentation as the nobler brother.

Chapter 10

Raising Up and Tearing Down, Part One

Genesis 34

ANOTHER STORY PROMISING BLOODSHED has ended peacefully. Two decades ago Jacob fled, wrestling with Esau prior to meeting a well-disposed God. On his return, he wrestles with God prior to meeting a well-disposed Esau. Tribulation has been his constant companion, but along the way his family has become numerous and he has made the acquaintance of God. Now he is home.

Indeed, though the LORD promised Canaan to the patriarchs, ever since Abraham arrived there (12:6–9) and just kept going (12:10), much of the narrative concerns activities unfolding elsewhere. Abraham travelled from Harran, arriving first in Shechem where, in response to the LORD's appearance and the promise of the place to his offspring, he builds an altar (12:6–7). From Shechem he travels to Bethel and builds another altar (12:8) before continuing south until, due to famine, he arrives in Egypt. The timing and spacing of these events differ for Jacob once he returns to Canaan, but his movements mimic his grandfather's as he travels from the lands of the east via Shechem to Bethel, and ultimately to Egypt, again due to famine.

To this point, Jacob's story within the land concerns only three days versus twenty years without. While events in Canaan occur over decades, the narration is episodic and says little about time. On the other hand, external events bear multiple time-stamps, underscoring their duration. So also with Joseph's story, which largely unfolds abroad. In Genesis, land-promises require patience; already in 12:7 God indicates that it will go to subsequent generations: "To your offspring I will give this land." But for now Jacob is back, and chapter 34 offers a glimpse of life in Canaan.

At chapter 33's conclusion, Jacob exchanged one hundred sheep for property in Shechem (33:18–19). Now settled in Canaan, he is primed to enjoy the fruits of his labors. Thus, the end of chapter 33 offers a mini-prologue to 34, with hints of peace and prosperity. But Shechem's streets will soon run with blood. Somebody always opposes Jacob. Chapter 34's adversaries include those already in the land and even his own sons. Israel's trouble is sometimes international, but often local. And it crosses generational lines.

Home at Last

In Canaan, as head of a large nomadic family, Jacob settles among people as alien to him as he was to Paddan Aram. In the long term, as with his father and grandfather, someone must choose the recipient of blessing. There is, however, a more pressing need: much of Jacob's story has dealt with wives and sons, but now it is time to attend to sons and wives. At least, that is what we might expect. Instead, and this may come as a surprise given the birth-order of his children and the priorities of the story to this point, this chapter will shine a light on a daughter and a potential husband. More pressing still, Jacob's growing family needs secure and stable relations with the neighbors. Can these be established without jeopardizing their distinct identity as God's people? We will discover that before Jacob can even settle in, these things threaten to collapse because of Shechem, Dinah, and Jacob's sons.

The story before us is disturbing. "The rape of Dinah" concerns private and public violence, deception and betrayal, and murder. It may also present neglect, rivalry, and deliverance. The chapter, like others before it, leaves many questions unanswered, and never mentions God. But it movingly displays some of Israel's abiding challenges. Laban had exploited the space between Jacob's expectations and the customs of Paddan Aram (29:26). Now we encounter similar tensions in Canaan, for the house of Jacob has settled in a populated region. And unlike his son Joseph, who accumulates friends wherever he goes (ultimately even his brothers), Jacob finds adversity at every turn, including in his own tents.

Meeting the Neighbors

All those years ago, while fleeing Esau, Jacob swore that if the LORD would bring him home in *shalom*, then the LORD would be his God (28:21). He has met Esau and parted peaceably. Had he continued in the line running from Gilead, where Laban overtook him (31:25), to Peniel, he would have landed near Bethel. But instead, upon leaving Esau he deviates to Succoth and builds a house for himself and shelters for his animals (33:17). That is, he stays a while. Then the clan journeys to Shechem, explicitly declared to be in Canaan (33:18).[1] With actions reminiscent of Abraham's journey, Jacob arrives at Shechem (33:18; cf. 12:6), builds an altar (33:20; cf. 12:7), and pitches his tent (33:18; cf. 12:8).[2] So Jacob has returned to the land and, miraculously, has arrived in peace (*shalem*, 33:18).[3] He lives near Bethel— though he won't go there for another chapter.

Dinah now steps forward at about fifteen years of age.[4] She, presented initially as Leah's daughter, goes out to visit the "daughters of the land."[5]

1. Shechem is identified with modern Nablus. The ancient town is about a mile east, designated Tel Balatah. So Wenham, *Genesis 16–50*, 460. See also Mathews, *Genesis 11:27—50:26*, 574–75, with bibliography, for further discussion of Shechem/Tel Balatah.

2. Though note that Abraham "pitched his tent" elsewhere in 12:8. See Mathews, *Genesis 11:27—50:26*, 574–75.

3. On the ambiguity of the Hebrew, see Waltke (*Genesis*, 460, including n. 232): it could mean that Jacob arrived safely, or that he entered Shechem peacefully. The words could also mean "at Salem the city of [prince] Shechem." See the similar use of the word at 29:6. For a (somewhat reluctant) defense of the reading that Jacob came in peace (rather than to a town named Salem), see Parry, *Old Testament Story*, 134–35, n. 32.

4. On the chronology, see Waltke (*Genesis*, 459). The destruction of Shechem occurred about ten years after leaving Laban, allowing for the sons to be aged sixteen to twenty-two, with Dinah being the last birth recounted in chapter 30 before Joseph's. That is, she was born after Leah and the handmaids produced their sons and before Rachel gave birth to her sons. Relevant texts include Gen 30:20–24, which indicates that Dinah was born after Zebulun and before Joseph, and 37:2, which gives Joseph's age as seventeen when the story focusses more directly on him. McKay ("Making a Difference," 226) considers the implications of Dinah being fifteen rather than say twenty-five, and further, asks about Shechem's age and marital status ("Making a Difference," 233).

5. The same construction is used of the "daughters of the land" in 27:46 as Rebekah vents her frustrations and arranges for Jacob to marry elsewhere. See 24:3, 37, and also 28:1: "do not take a wife from the daughters of Canaan" (my translation). The identification of Dinah as daughter of Leah and Jacob is by my count one of twelve references in Genesis to particular daughters, the majority of passages referring more generally to "sons and daughters" rather than individuals, or metaphorical daughters (as in e.g., Gen 49:22, where the same form as we find in 34:1 [i.e., plural of "daughters"] is appropriately rendered "branches"). Each of the particular daughters but one is significant due to her

Where references to hands and faces bound together previous chapters, here the most notable repetition is a pair of verbs. We will see that "take" appears throughout the chapter. The other verb is "go out."[6] This phrase appears five times in the chapter, in vv. 1, 6, 24 (twice), and 26; it is the first word of v. 1 and the last of v. 26.[7] Many, including some from a feminist perspective, read "went out" as a trigger that foreshadows the disgrace about to befall Jacob and his clan.[8] In some cases, "going out" has been over-developed to the point of blaming Dinah even for the massacre of Shechem.[9] But this is unlikely. She neither pours gasoline nor strikes a match. Rebekah went out, spoke with strangers, and even invited one to her home—resulting in a successful marriage.[10] Rachel tended flocks away from home and gathered them in a public space, again leading to marriage.[11] The sister and daughter of Laban were

role in the founding of tribes and nations: Israel, the Moabites, the Ammonites, Ishmaelites, the Edomites, and the tribes descended from Joseph. The exception is the seventh of the twelve, Dinah, who plays no role in subsequent generations. Particular daughters are Milcah (of Harran, 11:29); Lot's daughters (Gen 19); Rebekah, "daughter of Bethuel" (24:24, see also 25:20); Esau's wives Judith (of Beeri) and Basemath (of Elon); Mahalath (of Ishmael, 28:9); Laban's daughters Rachel (29:6 et al.) and Leah (29:16); Dinah (30:21 and 34:1); Esau's daughters in the genealogy of Gen 36 (e.g., 36:14); "daughters of Jacob" (37:35, note the plural; see also 46:7); Judah's wife, daughter of Shua; Asenath of Potiphera—Joseph's wife (41:45, 50); and the daughters in Jacob's genealogy in Gen 46.

6. Parry, *Old Testament Story*, 127–28.

7. Vrolijk, *Jacob's Wealth*, 262.

8. Frymer-Kensky, "Virginity", 86. Waltke (*Genesis*, 461) writes, "This is an improper and imprudent act." Those who find hints of sexual scandal in "going out" include Sarna, *Genesis*, 233; Neusner, *Genesis Rabbah*, 3:146; Wenham, *Genesis 16–50*, 310. For a demolition of this view see Parry, *Old Testament Story*, 229–32.

9. For a brief history of interpretation, focusing on those who blame Dinah, see Parry, "Feminist Hermeneutics," 36. Wenham, in his treatment of the moral dimension of the chapter, offers insight into early Jewish interpretations, and then discusses the views of Calvin and Sternberg (*Story as Torah*, 110–11).

10. Stiebert, *Fathers and Daughters*, 41; McKay, "Making a Difference," 227.

11. On the other hand, Leah never "went out" on her wedding night: she stayed in, under a veil. However, while Leah is never loved, we read that Shechem loved Dinah. So Sheres, *Dinah's Rebellion*, 90.

able, and in this they differ from Moses' wife, to go out in peace.[12] Through no fault of her own, Dinah will fare worse than all three.[13]

Daughter Dinah goes to see the daughters of the land.[14] Instead she is seen—by Shechem, the prince who bears the name of the city. He sees her, "takes her," "lays her,"[15] and "disgraces her."[16] As the chapter unfolds we learn of Dinah's youthfulness,[17] Shechem's nobility (34:19), Dinah's detention (34:17 and 26), Shechem's love for and desire to marry her, and his willingness to pay a high price. This is a marriage story, though it unfolds without courtship prior to a ceremony or even bargaining followed by a festival. Instead, it moves from sexual violation to kidnapping to negotiation. This is a story of marriage by abduction, a practice with a widespread history that remains all too common in many places (including Europe, Asia, and Africa).[18] That is, this story describes not rape as we usually define it,

12. The same language of "going out" appears in Ruth (2:22). Scholz, *Rape Plots*, 131; Schneider, *Mothers of Promise*, 142. Leeb argues that the situation is more problematic, suggesting that the term *na'arah* used of Dinah "connotes a girl or young woman who is away from home, perhaps in danger or at risk in some way." See Leeb, *Father's House*, 125. For a withering critique, see, Gruber, "Review of *Away from the Father's House*."

13. Leeb (*Father's House*, 136) observes that wells and water sources are the only place known to us where ancient women gathered. Compare Acts 16:13.

14. Gen 34:1. Dinah is here presented as "the daughter of Leah" (my translation). For some, this designation, coupled with the naming only of Simeon and Levi (29:31–34), Dinah's full brothers also born to Leah, suggests that parental struggles continue to the next generation. So, for example, Vrolijk, *Jacob's Wealth*, 262.

While this is a natural reading of the account, with implications for how things unfold, it appears to be peripheral to the story.

15. The construction differs from other similar statements, which are better rendered "lay with her." This is thought to indicate the coercive nature of Shechem's act. Mathews, *Genesis 11:27–50:26*, 592; Wenham, *Genesis 16–50*, 311. Noble ("Rape of Dinah," 178–80) attends to the possible ambiguity of the language.

16. Gen 34:2.

17. Gen 34:3, 8. Much can be made of "young girl" as descriptor of Dinah (see esp. Leeb, *Father's House*, 125), but the same term is used of Rebekah (Gen 24:14,16). So Scholz, *Rape Plots*, 131.

18. Fleishman provides a brief bibliography of bridal abduction in the ancient world ("Why Did Simeon?" 102, n.4).

The Council of Trent, in its attempt to define and regulate marriage and aware of this widespread practice, advised that kidnapped brides are to be married only if they consent "in a safe and free place" (Session 23, chapter 6). See also the account of the Sarakatsani shepherds of the Greek mountains as presented in Campbell, *Honour*. He explains the marriage customs in a subsection entitled "Betrothal and Abduction" (pp. 124–32). For a contemporary account of such marriages and the trauma many women live with, see Hari, "Kidnapped. Raped. Married." It is estimated that in post-Soviet Kyrgyzstan 40

but rather a brutal marriage practice known in their world and ours—including in ancient Israel (Judg 21:19).[19]

Abductive Marriage

Some cultures instinctively recognize what happens to Dinah. To them, rape is a misclassification because Shechem detains her and negotiates a marriage.[20] One study concludes with four contemporary stories of abduction in Ethiopian culture. Of the four, one girl escapes at the outset; one is recovered by her clan after a week; and two end up, after negotiations, enjoying what are described as happy marriages. Three of the stories highlight the shame brought on the clan (even when they accept the outcome). Negotiations balance finite resources. On one side is the life of a girl; on the other a family's honor.[21]

Shechem takes Dinah. Rape does not always mark abduction because merely detaining a woman for consecutive nights suggests sexual impropriety.[22] The damage to her (and her family's) reputation, and thus to her prospects, leaves few options apart from marrying her captor. But this describes neither the common practice nor Dinah's experience. Shechem violates her, and in this he, the text keeps reminding us, degrades her and does something that should not be done in Israel.

---

percent of marriages are initiated with kidnapping. So Hayashi, "Grab and Run." Popular as well as scholarly sources are easy to find, discussing abductive marriage across a wide range of cultures, but somehow this has neither stopped the practice nor made it a leading issue among those concerned with justice for women. Clearly more needs to be done.

19. Fleishman, "Why Did Simeon?" 102–3.

20. For a look at abductive marriage in the context of Gen 34 see Hankore, *Abduction*, 228. He offers a thorough discussion of abductive marriage against the backdrop of the Hadiyya of Ethiopia. His work is most helpful, though I question his assessment of Gen 28:10—35:15 as a "votive narrative."

21. Hankore, *Abduction*, 232–35.

22. Whether Dinah was raped is an ongoing debate. While many conclude that she was, this has been challenged by Ararat, who suggests that the narrative presents a seduction. See Ararat, "Reading"; Zakovitch, "Survey," 19–38; Bechtel, "What If," 19–31. For the argument that coercive rape is not on view, see Frymer-Kensky, *Wake*, 274, n. 34. Others, unpersuaded, maintain that she was indeed raped: see esp. Sternberg, *Poetics*, 445–81. Sternberg's important work has been critiqued by Fewell and Gunn who nevertheless conclude that Sternberg is correct to read the account as a rape ("Tipping the Balance").

Shechem's Love

Dinah suffers. We therefore recoil when Shechem claims to love her. Can love behave thus? But Shechem is not the first to speak of love. The narrator tells us that his "heart was drawn to Dinah daughter of Jacob; he loved the young woman" (34:3). Then Hamor states that his son has set his heart on Dinah (34:8). Finally, the narrator repeats Shechem's delight in her (34:19).[23]

This love can be contrasted with Amnon's feelings toward Tamar after raping her. Amnon hates her, is repulsed, and sends her away despite pleas not to do this still greater wrong (2 Sam 13:16).[24] Shechem behaves differently. This again conforms to abductive marriage. The groom, having violently taken the girl, often claims that love compels his actions.[25]

Honor Issues

Modern westerners define rape in terms of consent. How then should we assess other cultures, past and present? Where does consent factor into an arranged marriage, even one negotiated before birth? Whose consent? In Dinah's world, such rights belonged to the father, not the daughter.[26] To defy a father by imposing one's will thus instigates a battle for honor. To rape a girl assaults the father's, and therefore the clan's, prestige. And so we read in v. 2 that Shechem humiliates Dinah, with the same verb used to describe Amnon's treatment of Tamar in 2 Samuel 13:14. Despite its frequent rendering as "rape," the word refers primarily to shame rather than sex (and therefore is not exclusive to contexts of shameful sexual activity).[27] In both Genesis 34:2 and 2 Samuel 13:14, the LXX speaks of humbling her, and then with a separate verb indicates the sexual nature of

---

23. Fretheim, "Genesis," 580.

24. Williams, "Insult to Injury, " 103–4."

25. See again the disturbing article by Hari ("Kidnapped. Raped. Married").

26. Leeb, *Father's House*, 136, n. 33.

27. It is rendered as "raped her" or a near equivalent (NIV UK of 1984, NIV US of 2011, HCSB). The NET Bible reads, "sexually assaulted her." Similarly, it is translated "lay with her by force" in the RSV, NRSV, NAB, and NAS. The KJV says, "defiled her" (though NKJV has "violated her"). The ESV offers the more literal rendering "humiliated her." It was used of Hagar's misery at the hand of Sarah (16:6), and will encapsulate Israel's oppressive slavery in Egypt (prospectively in Gen 15:13; retrospectively in Exod 3:7). In her suffering Dinah is said to anticipate "Israel's own violation at the hands of other outsiders (cf. Isa 53:4)." So Fretheim, "Genesis," 580.

the assault.[28] That is, modern translations and our understanding of the event can cause us to overlook a primary concern of the text: the *dishonor* heaped upon Dinah and her household.[29]

Shechem defiles Dinah (34:5, 13, 27), which is described as an "outrageous thing" (34:7). As the chapter ends, Simeon and Levi assert that Shechem has treated Dinah "like a prostitute" (34:31).[30] Or do these words indict Jacob, who bargains after sex, trying to settle on a price? Such a charge would assault Jacob's prestige within his own home. The measure of a man was his protection of women; their security within his household reflected his ability to safeguard the clan, especially since the honor of the family was tied to the virginity of its daughters, with social and economic consequences when it was lost.[31] To fail here "unmans the man"[32] and might invite a challenge to his authority over both land and kin.[33] Thus, unwanted sex was more than an act of sexual violence. It could threaten the head of the clan, as in the case of Reuben in chapter 35, or even the king, as in the case of Absalom.[34]

This assertion of honor-issues never lessens the theological implications of rape within Israel: the Scriptures consistently regard inappropriate sexual activity as a sin against the LORD himself. The refrain in both

28. Gen 34:2 (LXX) can be rendered, "taking her, he slept with her and humiliated her"; 2 Sam 13:14 reverses the order of the verbs: "he humiliated her and slept with her" (my translation).

29. For an examination of the relevant term and its role in similar contexts to this one (including a brief history of major interpretive trends), see Van Wolde, "Does *'innâ* Denote Rape?" 528–44.

30. Fretheim, "Genesis," 580.

31. Benjamin and Mathews, *Social World*, 178; citing Schlegel, "Status," 724. The adversarial nature of clans even within a relatively small people-group (and in the context of securing a wife) is developed in Campbell, *Honour*, 39–42, 51–52, 125.

32. Frymer-Kensky, "Virginity," 84.

33. Benjamin and Mathews, *Social World*, 178. See also 2 Sam 3, where Abner, the kingmaker, shifts from the house of Saul to the house of David when Ish-Bosheth accuses him of sleeping with Saul's concubine (3:7–11).

34. Benjamin and Mathews, *Social World*, 178. They further add (179–80) that biblical rape-stories present "an assessment of the political status of the house-holds to which these men and women belong. The households of Shechem (Gen 34), Amnon (2 Sam 13:1–22), and Absalom (2 Sam 16:15–22) use sexual violence as a bid to control the households of Jacob, Absalom, and David." This seems unlikely in the cases of Shechem and Amnon, who are not, according to the story as presented, trying to gain control of the household of others as much as trying to gain access to Dinah and Tamar because they are attracted to them.

Testaments is "You must purge the evil from among you."[35] Virginity thus indicates "non-pollution."[36] Marriage after rape provides for the victim and rescues the status of an unwed non-virgin within the clan. As appalling as it seems to us, as unbearably inappropriate, Tamar when raped by Amnon asks to remain with him, describing abandonment as worse than the sexual assault (2 Sam 13:16).[37] It defiles him, her, the clan, and the nation.

Fathers or Brothers?

Deuteronomy 22:20–21, legislating cases in which a bride is not a virgin, speaks of the father's rather than the husband's honor.[38] Similarly, laws governing a slandered virgin treat the father as the offended party as much as the woman.[39] So it would seem that the father, the one responsible for his daughter, is dishonored by her violation. But in this story Dinah's brothers step forward.[40] Are they their sister's keeper? Does it fall to them to arrange their sister's marriage?

Unless we retroject subsequent texts, both narratives and laws, onto this chapter, we have only Genesis itself to answer these questions. And here the evidence is ambiguous. Compare Laban's role in the marriage of his daughters and his sister. Clearly, with respect to Leah and Rachel, Laban dictates their marriages.[41] Laban's activity even muddies the wedding type-scene found in Genesis and Exodus: he appears once as brother and once as father, arranging the marriage of his sister Rebekah in Genesis 24:10–32 and his daughter Rachel in 29:9–14 (though to be fair, Genesis 29 nowhere indicates that Rachel *has* a brother to negotiate on her behalf). Further, Exodus 2:15–21, where the same scene plays out, does not suggest that Jethro has sons. When brothers appear, however, things change. In Genesis 24, with Rebekah's father present, Laban negotiates for Rebekah. Abraham, in the role of brother, negotiates with Pharaoh

---

35. Williams, "Insult to Injury," 100. See, for those instances that relate to sexual sins, Deut 21:21; 22:21, 22, 24; 24:7; Judg 20:13. Compare also 1 Cor 5:13.

36. Williams, "Insult to Injury," 102–3.

37. Williams, "Insult to Injury," 103–4.

38. Pressler, *View of Women*, 42; compare Williams, "Insult to Injury," 90.

39. Deut 22:28–29 and Exod 22:16–17. So Pressler, *View of Women*, 29. See also Zucker and Reiss, *Matriarchs*, 215.

40. Stiebert, *Fathers and Daughters*, 50.

41. Jacobs, *Gender*, 161.

concerning his "sister" Sarah.[42] So while our small sample cannot prove much, in each instance when we know of a brother's presence he always heads the negotiations, while in the single account where both brother and father are present the former still leads.

Of course such observations only relate to negotiations on behalf of the bride's family. Who takes responsibility for the men? Of Jacob's family we know only that Isaac's father spared no expense for his son, and Isaac did nothing for Esau and Jacob, leaving them to their own devices. Jacob thus begins without so much as a bride-price to compare with the riches Abraham sent, and Esau fills the house with wives disliked by their in-laws.

So we can scarcely define the various roles in arranging marriages, including the marriage of daughters. Isaac set no precedent for Jacob, and Laban offered none worth emulating. Any talk of normative practices would overlook this variety within the patriarchal narratives. But clearly, however they understand it, brothers show an interest in such things. Just as clearly, Dinah's brothers take their role seriously.[43]

Marriage as Competition

In a world competing for honor, the contest often extended to obtaining wives.[44] And in a polygamous world, men often substantially outnumbered eligible women. Thus family units can be considered adversarial groupings who here oppose and there form alliances with one another (often by marriage). Consider the story of Saul and his daughters Merab (1 Sam 18:17) and Michal (18:21), both of whom are betrothed to David—a shepherd engaged to royalty. These arrangements, concerning which David declares himself unworthy (18:18), are Saul's means to eliminate a threat—on the surface by aligning the people's hero more closely with the king, but underneath, by placing David at risk. The political maneuverings of the palace and their potential dangers differ, to be sure, from common betrothals; but Jacob's dilemma involves a chief's son, a clan's honor, and an offer of alliance. Its political dimension is unmistakable.[45]

---

42. Jacobs, *Gender*, 158 (see also 84).

43. Leeb, *Father's House*, 138.

44. Dickemann, "Women," 945.

45. Moreover, motivations are only known to us because of the narrator's comments (as in 18:17), while in most cases actions are unreflective representations of cultural values and customs—rarely if ever articulated by those who practice such behavior.

In this competitive environment, Jacob's family with twelve sons fights uphill. What can he offer a prospective bride-family? How can his sons display better prospects (to a potential father-in-law) than other men in the vicinity? For that matter, who can his sons legitimately marry?

Give and Take

Each episode of Jacob's story places bargaining near the center. In this chapter, twenty of thirty-one verses present negotiations. They begin when Shechem appeals to his father Hamor, the chieftain, to arrange his marriage to Dinah (34:4), with the demand, "Get me this girl as my wife." But bartering will not be from a position of neutrality. His verb, when he says "take her for me," echoes v. 2.[46] What he has already taken—Dinah—he now demands his father take for him. Verse 4 admittedly accords with the customary idiom, so and so "took a wife." One struggles, however, given the word's link with his assault on Dinah in v. 2, not to take offense.

Against this backdrop, Hamor goes to Jacob with his proposal (34:6). As events unfolded, Jacob's sons were away tending the flocks. Now they appear. We are left to wonder if they arrive in response to Dinah's plight or if they come home in the course of events, only to learn of it upon arrival. That is, the Hebrew of 34:7 could read, "Jacob's sons came in from the field when they heard what happened. The men were grieved and very angry." Or it could mean, "Jacob's sons came in from the field. When they heard it, the men were grieved and very angry."[47] The chronology, and thus the possibilities it throws up, remains elusive. We don't know when they learn of their sister's humiliation so don't know when they devise their scheme. But we do know their reaction. Unlike Jacob's, it is writ large. They seethe. They are distressed (34:7). They will respond to this outrage.

But this comment about the brothers' anger stands between Hamor's "going out" to bargain with Jacob (v. 6) and his words. That is, Hamor goes out to meet Jacob while the brothers come in to meet Hamor (34:7). The story in this way comes to a halt just long enough to express the reaction of both the narrator and the brothers. Only after this double denunciation does

---

46. My translation. This reading is clear in the LXX, where 34:2's verb for "take" is repeated in 34:4 (as in the Hebrew). Few English translations maintain the repetition.

47. These translational options are from Sternberg, *Poetics*, 452. Most English versions adopt some form of the first reading. The LXX and a few translations (NRSB, NAB) tend toward the second.

Hamor speak. He testifies to Shechem's love and asks for Dinah's hand. He proposes intermarriage, shared land, and economic exchange. Hamor thus holds out wives to a man with twelve sons and land to a pasture-less shepherd with great flocks. He further offers to break down the barriers separating a wandering people from the life and benefits of his town. The honor of settled life will cleanse the social stain of being landless herdsmen and even of rape. More to the point, once they exchange wives and land, Israel and Shechem will be one, bound by blood and common property.

Now Shechem speaks. He addresses Jacob and the brothers (34:11), Dinah being his only concern. Thus we learn that though Hamor and Jacob occupy center-stage (34:6 and 8), their sons also stand by. Shechem, less visionary than Hamor and less skilled in negotiation, resembles Jacob in his bargaining for Rachel. He opens with a general entreaty: "Let me find favor in your eyes." This seems unlikely, yet accords with abductive marriage. He recognizes the honor lost by Jacob's clan and the delicate position from which he therefore bargains. But he proposes a path to restoration: "I will give you whatever you ask." Shame will be erased by the payment of an exorbitant bride-price, a sum announcing Jacob's public victory. "Make [it] as great as you like" as an ongoing testimony balancing out the honor of our two clans and allowing us to live together in a settled and harmonious relationship. "Only give me the young woman as my wife."[48] A wife at any price. Because of his love for her. The law will fix the bride-price of a raped woman at fifty shekels (Deut 22:29), an amount presumably sufficient to prevent abduction in most cases, and also, again presumably, to appease an angry clan. But some clans won't be appeased. Realizing his bride won't come cheap, Shechem writes a blank check.

Razor's Edge

Dinah's brothers are enraged. In expansive language the narrator states the reason: because Shechem had lain "with Jacob's daughter—a thing that should not be done" (34:7). It is uncertain that the rage attaches to the crime of rape, and it is even less likely that both brothers and narrator are upset about the mixing of Israel's clan with foreigners. After all, who *should* the twelve brothers marry? Judah will marry a Canaanite (Bath-Shua) and Joseph an Egyptian, while Simeon begets one of his six sons by

---

48. Gen 34:12.

a Canaanite.[49] Marrying internally appears impossible unless one deigns to marry a servant or servant's daughter. Jacob's covenant with Laban closed the door to seeking wives in Paddan Aram.

What then so incenses the brothers? Probably two things. The "thing that should not be done" includes sex apart from marriage with a virgin daughter of Israel.[50] The narrator's valuing of sexual purity, presumably shared to some degree by participants in the story,[51] can be seen in our introduction to Rebekah. We learn first that she "was very beautiful" and then, with a redundant construction, read twice of her virginity (Gen 24:16).[52] Shechem's action cuts against the grain of this moral code.

Further, we are three times told Dinah has been defiled. The first time explains the brothers' fury, the second their deceitful reply.[53] With the third, the narrator observes in the aftermath of death and looting that this happened "where their sister had been defiled."[54] So the brothers' rage, deceit, and destruction of Shechem flow from Dinah's being defiled.[55]

But what does "defile" mean? By probing the nexus of shame and rape, we can see what it here entails. In Genesis 34:2, Shechem sees, takes and rapes Dinah. The third verb points, as proposed above, to shame. The

---

49. Gen 46:10 and Exod 6:15 mention the fact of a Canaanite mother of Saul, son of Simeon, without comment on the other sons' mothers. Waltke (*Genesis*, 575) interprets this negatively.

50. This is close to the view of Schneider, *Mothers of Promise*, 144.

51. Needless to say, one cannot simply assume narrator and characters hold the same values. In many cases in the Pentateuch and beyond, this is clearly not the case. But a high view of virginity and sexual purity was probably shared by the narrator, the sons of Jacob, and even the Shechemites—though each group would undoubtedly express this in different ways.

52. For a negative counterpart in Genesis, see 38:24, where Tamar faces death for being sexually active outside of marriage (So Mathews, *Genesis 11:27—50:26*, 609). One often cannot draw straight lines with respect to moral evaluations because of the inconsistency embedded in the stories. For example, only a flat reading would identify Judah's primary sin as extramarital sex, even though Tamar is condemned for it.

53. The first instance of "defiled" is in 34:5, which explains the brothers' wrath in 34:7. The second instance is in 34:13. In both instances, the text connects defilement with disgrace.

54. Gen 34:27.

55. 1 Sam 13:22 concludes the account of Amnon's rape of Tamar by telling us that Absolom "hated Amnon because he had disgraced his sister Tamar." We should note both the brother's anger directed at the assailant, and the narrator's clear evaluation of the event.

same term appears in the account of Tamar's rape by Amnon,[56] the rape of the Levite's concubine in Judges,[57] and the Babylonian militaristic rape of the women of Zion.[58] In none of these does the term mean rape *per se*, but in each instance, it presents rape in terms of humiliation. In at least one instance, the assault on the woman's honor causes her death.[59] The brothers' response is born of their offense at what Dinah has endured. She is a young, vulnerable girl who has suffered sexual assault, and if, as the story indicates, she has been folded into the home of her assailant, then the brothers can only fear the worst. Who is treating her wounds? What is her mental and emotional state? Is she being properly fed and clothed, or does she wear torn garments? There is no gap between her honor and her physical and sexual well-being.

Words and actions as well as the narrator's sometimes explicit commentary reveal that various family members respond differently to the abduction. Some interpreters suggest that Jacob's reaction reveals apathy— Dinah is the unloved daughter of an unloved wife—while Levi and Simeon act because as sons of Leah they care for their sister and identify with her rejection.[60] But this overlooks the complexity of the situation.

How should Jacob respond? Where nomads and town-folk co-exist, societies often construct a finely calibrated set of rules, which generate a "balance of power."[61] The presenting issue here, Shechem's assault of Dinah, is especially scandalous because Jacob, by purchasing land from Hamor, enters a relationship that implies a degree of security. In assaulting a girl under his own father's protection, Shechem abuses this trust, indeed violates a covenant.[62]

Jacob is pinched between his daughter's abduction and economic partnership with the Shechemites. Now he must navigate both familial and

---

56. 2 Sam 13:13–14.

57. Judg 19:24–25.

58. Lam 5:11.

59. See Parry, *Old Testament Story*, 140–43.

60. Jacob's reaction is explained as a lack of commitment to Dinah by Graetz, *Unlocking*, 31. Waltke views Jacob more favorably, denigrating his passivity but not relating it to Dinah's identity (*Genesis*, 461). While 34:1, with its reference to Dinah as Leah's daughter, receives much attention, less is made of 34:7, where the narrator identifies Dinah as Jacob's daughter.

61. Stiebert, *Fathers and Daughters*, 57, following Zlotnick, *Dinah's Daughters*, 40.

62. Stiebert, *Fathers and Daughters*, 56–57.

political realities.[63] The negotiation surrounding his daughter's marriage differs in many ways from his bargains with Laban, except that each contains traps, and traps tend to be hidden.

Hamor, as we have seen, implores them to give Dinah to Shechem. The resulting alliance would allow Jacob's sons to marry Shechemite daughters and Shechemite sons to marry Jacob's daughters—surely an enticing offer for those battling long odds. Further, the country itself would be available to build homes, travel freely, and acquire land (34:10). In this, Hamor offers what God himself has promised.[64] Is Shechem where Israel will live and move and have his being?

The brothers shift the discussion from economic concerns to purity. They answer deceitfully, and yet again we are told why: because Shechem defiled Dinah (34:13). Hamor has proposed the merger of Israel and Shechem. The brothers reply that giving their sister to an uncircumcised man would be a disgrace (v. 14). But there is a way. If the Shechemites submit to circumcision, then the proposed exchanges, the social union, can go ahead. Jacob's clan will settle in Shechem and "become one people with you (34:16)." They too interpret Hamor's offer as an invitation to merge.

On the other hand, if the Shechemites won't agree to the terms, Jacob's sons will "take our sister and go" (34:17). This together with v. 26 reveals that Shechem has detained Dinah while they negotiated—kidnapped, humiliated, sexually assaulted, and bargained over. If Jacob's seven years seemed like a few days, these few days would have felt like years. Tragically, events still unfold like this. But how will it end? Then as today, blood frequently colors the path to resolution.[65]

Shechem Bargains with the Shechemites

Both sides accept the terms, with Shechem getting his bride and Jacob's clan negotiating a free-trade agreement that will restore their honor. But now Shechem must convince the Shechemites. This should be easy since Hamor rules as tribal chief and Shechem is "the most honored of all his father's family" (34:19), reminding again that honor and shame permeate the account.

63. Stiebert, *Fathers and Daughters*, 57.

64. Gen 28:13–14; see also 17:8; 22:17; 35:12.

65. This differs from so-called honor killings where brothers kill their own sisters because they have been raped and thus brought shame on the family—even in instances where a male member of the family is the rapist.

The people's status derives from their leader's prestige. As before, among their neighbors Hamor and Shechem bargain from a position of strength.

For a third time merging moves to the fore. They will "live with us as one people" so that "their livestock, their property and all their other animals," not to mention their daughters, will belong to us (34:22–23). They will be swallowed up and everything will be ours. Shechem offered to Israel whatever they asked. The brothers responded with a ceremonial request prior to a merger-offer. But as Hamor and Shechem present the deal to the Shechemites, merging floats to the center, and paying something becomes gaining everything. Unity now shapes the negotiations, and inequity defines the unity. Merger becomes acquisition. Shechem will absorb Israel and all he has.

The Family Responds

. . . with Negotiations

In v. 2, Shechem "took" Dinah, beginning the whole tragic sequence. In v. 4, Shechem demands of his father, "take [her] as my wife."[66] A third time the verb "take" becomes prominent. As the brothers negotiate, they threaten to "take" Dinah—their "daughter" (34:17).[67] One might have thought that Shechem, in detaining Dinah, holds all the cards. The brothers disagree.

. . . with Violence

Using circumcision to deceive and disable the Shechemites, the brothers strike. Yet again, "take" surfaces as the brothers rescue Dinah from Shechem's home (34:26). They could of course take her without wholesale slaughter. But they do not; vengeance flows into every crevice of the city. They attack the men, who are temporarily disabled by their circumcision, and kill them all.

Some maintain that introducing Dinah as daughter of Leah in Genesis 34:1 highlights the defective relationships within Jacob's home. Here

66. My translation.

67. Schneider, *Mothers of Promise*, 144. Note that while several translations speak of "our sister," including the NIV, others better capture the brothers' words with the curious and poignant phrase, "our daughter": so NASB, KJV, NKJV, CSB, HCSB, ISV, JPS Tanakh, RSV, NRSV, et al.

only Dinah's full brothers, Simeon and Levi, are implicated in the murder.[68] But to this point the brothers have acted without distinction. Only now do Simeon and Levi stand apart (i.e., 34:25); and even now, while they execute the Shechemites and rescue Dinah, the other brothers sack the city, seizing all the wealth, women, and children.[69]

Treat Our Sister like a Whore?

Jacob rebukes Simeon and Levi for tarnishing his reputation. The pair pointedly reject his admonition. To them, quibbling over the price after sex is to reduce their sister to a prostitute.[70] So in this battle for wealth and honor, Jacob's sons take the first to satisfy the second. In the end, however, the stench of greed lingers longer than the scent of honor. Moreover, Shechem was not offering to pay for sex; he was offering the bride-price for his wife.

Rescuing Dinah

Do the brothers act on behalf of their sister? We are reminded that they murder, plunder, and carry off all the women and children because Dinah was defiled (34:27).[71] But is this for *her*? How does pillaging and kidnapping benefit their sister? She has indeed been defiled, but their actions rescue their own honor, not hers, and so arguably reflect self-interest, with Dinah getting at best peripheral benefits, which may in fact be damages. Such questions can only be answered by delving into her personal reaction, which the text withholds, or her subsequent situation.

After this chapter, Dinah plays no role in Israel's story. She journeys to Egypt in Genesis 46, meaning she lives decades longer. She is however associated with neither spouse nor children.[72] Her rescue from the effects of this tragedy, as far as the text discloses it, is never complete.

Hamor and Shechem have proposed to merge with Jacob and his clan. The brothers' counteroffer involves universal circumcision. The Shechemites submit, and in the end the comprehensive merger they desire eventuates,

68. The relationships are presented in 29:31–34. Vrolijk, *Jacob's Wealth*, 262.

69. For a discussion of who engages in the sacking, Simeon and Levi or the other sons, see Mathews, *Genesis 11:27—50:26*, 607–8.

70. Schneider, *Mothers of Promise*, 141; Scholz, *Rape Plots*.

71. Schneider, *Mothers of Promise*, 141.

72. Schneider, *Mothers of Promise*, 140.

except that Israel retains its distinct identity and the men of Shechem are entirely excluded. The merger thus occurs without Shechemite domination. Ultimately Israel overcomes, acquires the women and girls of Shechem, and is enriched. Is kidnapping how they solve the problem of bachelor sons?

Just as Abraham's wealth increased despite, indeed because of, his ill treatment of Sarah (see 12:14–16), so Jacob's sons prosper in and through their own sins. Their success cannot validate their crimes, but it again indicates that God's larger plans and promises survive the transgressions of his chosen ones.

Why This Story?

Though chapter 34 is often described as "the rape of Dinah," the nature of the crime against her is elusive. Furthermore, Dinah recedes within the chapter, rendering the description ill-fitting. She acts only in a single clause, the rest of the chapter presenting swirling events beyond her control. She says nothing and contributes nothing. She is an object—both grammatically and as a character—always and only acted upon. She lacks voice and options.

Dinah, a flat character, serves as a prop. She is also the daughter of Jacob and Leah, and sister to the heir of promise. The story could be structured to make us weep for her, but instead moves in other directions. It quickly becomes the story of her family and the city of her suitor, Shechem. In this, it continues the story of Jacob.

So how does this story fit within the purposes and narrative of Genesis and the Pentateuch? One possibility is that it doesn't. Two of the most reliable guides to the Pentateuch race past Genesis 34 without mentioning Dinah.[73] Some commentators label it a digression.[74]

Some interpreters pay it forward, arguing that this chapter recounts events not from the patriarchal era (which are often regarded as fictive or unknowable), but from the conquest, giving theological shape to the conflict and triumph of Levi and Simeon over the city of Shechem.[75] This is problematic, however, in that neither Levi nor Simeon acquire significant land-holdings in Israel.[76] Moreover, the Bible's conquest-narrative nowhere

73. Clines, *Theme*; Sailhamer, *Meaning*.

74. See for example, Waltke, *Genesis*, 458.

75. See Boling and Wright, *Joshua*, 251–54; Meek, *Hebrew Origins*, 124–28.

76. Judges 9, which recounts Abimelek son of Gideon's destruction of Shechem, provides a more significant set of similarities, including the location and the brutal slaughter

recounts the taking of Shechem. So this reading explains a conflict that apparently never happened.[77]

It is equally unlikely that the chapter assails intermarriage with Canaanites.[78] The Pentateuch says much about the dangers of "foreign wives," and Genesis has already alerted us to the complications both of marrying Canaanite women (in the case of Esau) and of finding a wife outside the land.[79] But when read against the larger story, this loses explanatory force. As we observed above, subsequent marriages will of necessity reach outside the clan. Judah and his sons (Gen 38), Joseph (41:45), and Moses, all marry outsiders: Joseph (like Abraham) marries an Egyptian, and Moses marries a Midianite.[80]

One interpretation finds in our story a post-exilic recasting of an earlier account: that is, its final shape emerges during a period of Israel's history when collective interests supersede those of the individual. Dinah presents a threat in that she is an assertive "woman with a distinct identity" who pays no heed to "the traditional signals other women use when they undertake similar 'departures.'"[81] She suffers because she is bold enough to mingle with strangers.[82] Thus, an earlier romantic tale of impetuous youths willing "to

---

of nearly a thousand non-combatants (Judg 9:46–49). But this does not relate to the conquest or to Levi and Simeon as demoted tribes.

77. So Merrill, *Kingdom of Priests*, 113–14. See also the analysis of Pitt-Rivers, *Fate of Shechem*, 157.

78. Pitt-Rivers reads the account as reflecting a political and social progression such that Jewish women, who in earlier accounts were given to outsiders (e.g., Abraham and Isaac's offer of their "sister" to foreign rulers in what Pitt-Rivers characterizes as "sexual hospitality"), are now restricted to insiders (*Fate of Shechem*, 157–59).

79. The Book of Judith reads the slaughter of the Shechemites positively because sex with an outsider brought "pollution of [the clan's] blood" (Judith 9:4). While the effects of sex were restricted to temporary ritual impurity, and were thus (normally) viewed less seriously, the concern here, according to Judith, is that if Dinah were pregnant by Shechem she would contaminate Jewish blood with gentile impurities. So Thiessen, "Protecting," 167–68.

80. In this, neither Joseph nor Moses marry "daughters of the land" (Fretheim, "Genesis," 580), but at least Judah and his sons marry a Canaanite, and through her establish the line of kings. The limit of my reading is that the data relates consistently to sons, but the same problems apply unless one is willing to assume Jacob's daughters remain unmarried, that only in the next generation, when the clan is sufficiently expanded (through the marriage of Jacob's sons to foreign wives), do female descendants marry. See Himmelfarb, *Kingdom*, 70. The text says nothing of such things.

81. Sheres, *Dinah's Rebellion*, 46.

82. Sheres, *Dinah's Rebellion*, 47.

merge culturally, politically and religiously," was transformed, politicized into a story concerning "communal blood purity" and a caution to women about the dangers lurking outside the home. In this, it illustrates the later biblical penchant for achieving security through violence.[83] And it is the later layer that adds, so this reading suggests, rape to a story of romance. But this emotionally complex version of Dinah hardly arises from the text. To speak of her assertiveness, identity, or attitudes constitutes an act of pure imagination. Genesis says not a single word about her personality or cognitive processes. Further, the interpretation is speculative in the extreme when it redates and reallocates, and proposes new elements.

Yet another reading, focusing on the morality of destroying Shechem, moves closer to major Pentateuchal themes. If an overarching question is how Jacob and his descendants will bless the nations, then this chapter recounts the failure of the "community of faith"[84] as they replace blessing with annihilation. There are two ways to meet the present crisis: as described in subsequent legislation or with violence.[85] Deuteronomy 22:28–29 offers precise instructions concerning rape and its aftermath, providing for the remainder of the victim's life through marriage.[86] Hamor and Shechem agree to all the stipulations of this legislation and offer generous terms.[87] Scripture thus reflects negatively on the brothers and their cruelty. But this explanation suffers from two weaknesses. First and obviously, the laws didn't yet exist; and once enacted, how often could they prevent a violent response to rape? They did so neither in the time of the judges (Judg 20) nor the reign of King David (2 Sam 13:23–29). Second, the chapter nowhere unambiguously elevates one set of characters over the others. Even the brothers, implicated in a terrible crime, appear to be partially exonerated: they are given the last word in the chapter.[88] Thus, ethical issues permeate Genesis 34 but seldom appear to be the author's primary interest.

83. Sheres, *Dinah's Rebellion*, 47. Sheres writes: "Dinah and Shechem must be seen as a man and a woman who accidently met and, in a rather romantic vein (not too different from Romeo and Juliet), committed themselves to each other" (*Dinah's Rebellion*, 89–90).

84. Fretheim, "Genesis," 580.

85. Fretheim, "Genesis," 580.

86. Exod 22:16–17, which speaks of the seduction of a virgin, offers similar legislation, but includes the notion that the father must consent to the marriage.

87. Walton, *Traveller*, 200–202. Also pertinent is the rape of Tamar in 2 Sam 13; see esp v. 16 for the victim's evaluation of the options.

88. They are not, however, given the last word in Genesis as a whole. See below on Gen 49:7.

Attempts to read it as a morality tale suffer from the narrator's reluctance to offer direct ethical evaluation.

None of the above explanations satisfy. But attending to the central concerns of Genesis and of the Jacob narrative reminds us that in these texts God grows a single barren couple into a great multitude. Further, this God discriminates, repeatedly narrowing the scope of his blessing. Of Abraham's eight sons, the second receives the promise.[89] Of Isaac's twin boys, God chooses the younger. Thus, a central question, perhaps at this point the primary question, is this: which of Jacob's twelve sons will inherit the blessing? The first three are Reuben, Simeon, and Levi. But these are not the great tribes of Israel, the promise-bearers. That honor will be shared by Judah and Joseph. Eventually we learn, when Jacob blesses his sons (Gen 49:1–27), that the three oldest are set aside due to sin. While Reuben's failure takes up a single verse (Gen 35:22; cf. 49:4), chapter 34 recounts at length Simeon and Levi's crimes. All three elicit a curse from their father (49:4–7). Reuben, celebrated as firstborn (49:3) will be celebrated no more (49:4). Simeon and Levi, charged not with voiding a contract or extricating Dinah, but with excessive force against an entire town, will be scattered among the tribes (49:7). This finds fulfilment when Reuben fades into transjordanian obscurity, producing no notable leaders,[90] while Simeon disappears into Judah (Josh 19:1, 9). Even the Levites, more significant to be sure, and re-habilitated perhaps ironically when they once again wield the sword, this time killing their own brothers, friends, and neighbors (Exod 32:27–29), nevertheless inherit mere fragments of land.[91]

Jacob and the Last Words

At chapter's end, knowing that those who live by the sword die by the sword, Jacob charges his sons with bringing "trouble on me" (34:30).[92] The repetition of the first person pronouns in Jacob's rebuke is often said to reflect

89. Gen 25:2 names six more sons of Abraham, born to him by Keturah.

90. Wenham, *Genesis 16–50*, 472–73.

91. See Waltke, *Genesis*, 606–7. More precisely, Levi is "apportioned forty-eight towns and pasturelands among the twelve tribes including Ephraim and Manasseh (Num. 35:1–5; Josh. 14:4; 21:41)." Where the promise centers on land, Levi comes up short. Parry (*Old Testament* Story, 185–96) discusses Genesis 34's numerous parallels with Numbers 25 and 31, and attends to the rehabilitation of the Levites.

92. Pitt-Rivers, *Fate of Shechem*, 135.

self-interest,[93] but the full statement suggests that "I" encapsulates his clan: if the people of the land "join forces against me and attack me, I *and my household* will be destroyed" (34:30). For the head of a clan, "I" becomes representative. This relates to the theme we have been tracing through the Jacob story, the production of the promised family. Obstacles to this promise course through Genesis. First, it was barrenness and then old age. As it had with Sarah, infertility defines the experience of Rebekah and Rachel. Foreign rulers combine with lying husbands three times to jeopardize the promise (12:10–20; 20:1–18; 26:1–11). Even before the nation begins, Israel faces famine (12:10), attempts at murder (27:42), and ultimately the slaughter of newborn males (Exod 1:22).[94] In this unfolding drama, when confronted with Esau, self-preservation had been Jacob's motivation. Now he expresses concern for the clan. In this at least, his priorities align with God's.[95]

Genesis 34, without mentioning God, advances the story by exploring Jacob's relationships with his children and with the Canaanites. Significantly, it begins to explain the elevation of Judah and Joseph over their older brothers. Chapter 35 will further develop Jacob's relationships with his family and with God. In so doing, it clears the way for a son of Israel who will save the nation.

93. See Wenham, who notes Jacob's similar expression of fear in 32:12 (*Genesis 16–50*, 316). Waltke characterizes Jacob's response as "less than honourable" (*Genesis*, 467).

94. Kaiser, *Toward*, 89.

95. Walton observes that the threat of assimilation has been addressed, but the violence has replaced it with the threat of annihilation. God's saving hand is once again required (*Genesis*, 634).

Chapter 11

Raising Up and Tearing Down, Part Two

Genesis 35

GENESIS RELENTLESSLY HAMMERS AWAY at the family of promise, showing that nothing good can possibly emerge from this bunch. As it grows, it becomes worse. But at the same time, Genesis reveals—in every incident—God both tugging at the threads of the patriarch's lives and showering blessing upon them. Chapter 35 in various ways emerges from and complements 34. The latter explains the movement of the clan, the fear of the people of the land, and ultimately, the demotion of Levi and Simeon within Jacob's family. Chapter 35 will add another detail to the ranking of Jacob's sons. Furthermore, where chapter 34 was silent with respect to God's involvement in events, chapter 35 sees him move to the fore once again.

Bits and Pieces

Robert Alter calls Genesis 35 "a collection of miscellaneous notices about Jacob and his household."[1] Brueggemann writes that Genesis 35 and 36 "contain miscellaneous materials not centrally important to the tradition."[2] Von Rad describes the material in 35:16–29 as "the rubble of

---

1. Alter, *Genesis*, 195.

2. Brueggemann, *Genesis*, 280. In his estimation, they are only loosely related but "give closure to the narrative of Jacob."

smaller or very small single traditions, often quite fragmentary in character (cf. v. 21f.!)."[3]

Is it possible to cut against the grain and argue for the coherence of chapter 35, even proposing that it approaches the very heart of Genesis? Consider the following.

Kingship in Genesis

Genesis 3:15 promised a fight. That chapter filled with deception, eating, curses, and promises, looked ahead to offspring, busted heads, and—from the root that gives us Jacob—a "bruised heel" who will bear the brunt in a victorious struggle. Since then, the reader of the OT waits to learn how and through whom this victory takes place. The identity of the serpent-slayer unfolds slowly. In Genesis 12:1–3 we learned that he will come from Abraham.[4] Now, in Jacob, we find a "heel" who struggles and emerges bruised but victorious. How does he relate, and how then does this chapter relate, to the questions of how and through whom?

The structure of Genesis provides clues. Observe that reports of two of the three branches of Abraham's family—Ishmael's and Esau's lines— are dominated by tribal chiefs. The "account of Ishmael" lists the twelve rulers that emerge in his clan (Gen 25:12–18, esp. 16).[5] The "account of Esau"—found in 36:9–43—similarly records the kings and chiefs descended from Esau (36:31–43). Esau's list is even introduced with a glance at Israel, "These were the kings who reigned in Edom *before any Israelite king* reigned" (36:31). From here, the remainder of Genesis, the "account of Jacob," containing the stories of Joseph and Judah, continues Genesis's focus on questions of rule and authority.

In this way, every other account (i.e., each *toledot*) of Abraham's family drives inexorably toward discussions of kings and rulers. But what of

---

3. Von Rad, *Genesis*, 340. More positively Mathews writes that "The idea of completion gives the diverse units of this chapter cohesion, which is organized around the itinerary of Jacob's movements from Shechem to Hebron" (*Genesis 11:27—50:26*, 610).

4. Wright, *Mission of God*, 212.

5. I follow the NIV in rendering the Hebrew *toledot* with the English word "account." It is important to recognize that a given *toledot* does not introduce the story of the person named, but the story of his children. So the *toledot* Abraham (the "account of Abraham") is largely the story of Isaac, and the "account of Isaac" centers on the story of Jacob. The *toledot* Jacob presents events in the life of Jacob's sons, mainly focusing on the stories of Judah and Joseph.

the story of Jacob, the *toledot* Isaac? For obvious reasons, our story does not end with a list of kings, but it does conform to the pattern. God gives Isaac two sons, raising the question of the primary heir. Jacob clearly wins out. This too gives way to sons, for Jacob has twelve. If choosing between two was troublesome, how much more twelve sons from competing wives.[6] Chapter 35 functions as companion to 34, and continues to develop this concern with status in the clan.[7] Who will produce the line of kings and ultimately the seed tasked with crushing the serpent's head?

Back to Bethel

The journey to Bethel is undertaken with elements of Genesis 34 hanging in the air. "Should he have treated our sister like a prostitute." Jacob is fearful: "You have brought trouble on me . . . .We are few in number, and if they join forces against me and attack me, I and my household will be destroyed" (34:30). Once again the promise is in danger. The clan is now a threat to the people of the land: their violent behavior, Jacob fears, is an incitement.

Of immediate concern is the fact that Jacob is afraid. Whither can he flee? Some say that Jacob seeks refuge in the LORD only when afraid, Bethel being his safe-place in times of danger.[8] But in fact Jacob neither turned to God when he fled from Esau (he found God beside him), nor looks for him in the present crisis. We read, "Then God said to Jacob . . . ."[9] The initiative, in Jacob's hour of fear, is God's. And he tells Jacob, who inexplicably has settled about a day away from Bethel, to finally return there.[10]

Moving thus hinges on God's faithfulness, a point emphasized by the repetition in 35:3 of the words of 28:20 and Jacob's desperate prayer. There is no mention of tithes here, but perhaps his gifts to Esau are intended to satisfy this element of the vow. In addition to chapter 28, there are numerous

---

6. Brueggemann rightly notes that "the sons of Jacob pose issues more difficult to resolve than does the brother of Jacob" (*Genesis*, 287).

7. Brett, *Genesis*, 103.

8. McKeown, *Genesis*, 276.

9. Gen 35:1.

10. Since Jacob has been away for so long, and since his renaming of Bethel was a private affair, it is no surprise that the place is still called Luz. The narrator reminds us, though, that the place will be called Bethel because it was there that God had appeared to Jacob.

parallels with Genesis 17 and God's still-unfulfilled promises.[11] After God speaks, it is Jacob's turn: he tells his family of the God who answered him in his darkest hour and shared the hard road with him (35:3). Such divine goodness is enough for this God to be his God.

And so he orders the removal of the "foreign gods" in his entourage (35:2). Indeed, the burial of the gods—the first of four in this chapter—is to be accompanied by the removal of impurity right down to the changing of their clothes. This probably means little to us, but in a culture where garments are handmade and either expensive or labor intensive, wardrobes of semi-nomadic herdsmen were small. Further, in Jacob's exploits, as well as the stories of Judah (38:14) and Joseph (37:3, 23, 31–32), clothes play a key role. Is it going too far to say they touched upon a person's identity?

Upon arriving at Bethel, Jacob builds an altar (35:6–7). Somewhat intrusively, we hear of a second burial. Deborah is an unknown. How long has she been part of Jacob's household? The first burial, pointing to a different sort of progress, was of something virtually worthless. The second one hardly seems more significant to the story, but she is more valuable than false gods. Further, her mention here contributes to a sense of one generation eclipsing another.

Even as time advances, however, the pledge to Abraham is given new life. God reaches back past Abraham to Eden in commanding Jacob to "be fruitful and increase in number" (35:11, echoing 1:28). With those words, initially spoken before the fall, God issued both command and blessing. So here again. A father of eleven sons, Jacob's fruit-bearing days are largely behind him. Israel's are not. The reintroduction of fruitfulness, multiplication, and "kings . . . among your descendants," draws together major theological touchstones of Genesis.[12] It also reminds us that despite the curse, living under God's blessing entails elements of Eden—elements of the past, present, and future. As we'll see, subsequent talk of nations and kings (35:11) similarly points both backward and forward. In this, God connects the earliest of all blessings to his announcement of a coming king and kingdom.[13]

---

11. Turner, *Genesis*, 152–53.

12. See esp. Bartholomew and Gehee, *Drama of Scripture*, 55.

13. Sailhamer, "Genesis," 218.

Called Israel

Esau was renamed Edom. From "Hairy" to "Red." Big deal. Superficial labels for a superficial man. "Red," by forever recalling his levity regarding weighty matters, captures his essence. So also with Jacob. His old name conveyed his grasping. And unlike Abram, Sarai, and Ben-oni, names that immediately fall away, Jacob disappears from neither his story nor the prophetic indictment of descendants marked by this characteristic. He is, however, given a new name, one that defines his life experience.[14] Furthermore, it predicts. He has wrestled with God and man. And the giving of the name Israel implies that this is not just his past, but also the future of those who bear that name.

God had in Genesis 12:2 told Abraham that he would make him a great nation, and in 17:4—as he renames him—that he would father many nations. Now, in 35:10, as God renames Jacob, he promises that he, like his grandfather, will be a nation and a community of nations.

Kings and Land

The mention of kings has been rare. Once again we are brought back to Abraham and Genesis 17: twice in that chapter renaming gave way to the promise of nations, and nations to the promise of kings (17:5–6, 15–16). Now again we move from naming to nations to kings. And kings are naturally associated with land. Chapters 17 and 35 each speak of the land God will give. In 17:8 it is presented as "the whole land of Canaan." Here, further evoking the promises of chapter 17, God says "The land I gave to Abraham and Isaac I also give to you" (35:12). Finally, the Abrahamic promise was from the outset enmeshed with the notion of seed: 12:7 reads, "To your [seed] I will give this land." It remains for us to pursue how this seed relates to the coming king.

Jacob receives divine promises (35:11–12), erects a pillar (35:14), anoints it with oil (35:14), and names the place Bethel (35:15). By focusing the reader's attention on these events, especially Jacob's renaming the city as though for the first time, the text leaves us asking, "Wait a minute. Haven't we read this before?" The narrator thereby draws us back to the place, and therefore the promises, that were central to Genesis 28. This is

---

14. Mathews, *Genesis 11:27—50:26*, 540.

another way of making the unavoidable plain, of theologizing the journey: God has been faithful to his promises.

It also accentuates the new element. Jacob previously received a new name and promises of land, nations, and God's presence. He has not however heard the promise of kings. That is deferred until 35:11, and will be indirectly taken up in what follows.

Benjamin, Bethlehem, and Rachel's Burial

Jacob had extracted a living "through painful toil" and "by the sweat of [his] brow." Now "With painful labor [Rachel] give[s] birth" (cf. Gen 3:16–19). God blesses even as the curse persists. Childbirth adds and takes away, as Rachel herself had predicted at Joseph's birth. Now she bears and is buried near Bethlehem (35:19), on the border of Benjamin.[15]

Her grave later becomes identified with Ramah. As the captives of fallen Jerusalem march into exile, they pass through this village, about six miles (i.e., ten kilometers) north of the capital.[16] And, poetically, by means of the shared location, Rachel's cry swells to a national lament for these lost children:

> A voice is heard in Ramah,
> mourning and great weeping,
> Rachel weeping for her children
> and refusing to be comforted,
> because they are no more.[17]

These words advance two themes. First, Jeremiah in grieving for his nation participates in Rachel's agony. Matthew recalls his words at the slaughter of the innocents.[18]

But second, as life arises from death, so salvation emerges from evil. Genesis doesn't speak of a lost child; it speaks of a lost mother. So much irony: "Give me children, or I'll die" (30:1)! Rachel knew the grief of waiting for a son. In fact, as she waited she refused to be comforted. And yet she hears comforting words as she takes her last breaths: "Don't despair,

15. So 1 Sam 10:2.

16. See also Jer 40:1, which identifies Ramah as the place where the prophet was released. Evidently it functioned as a gathering point for the deportees.

17. Jer 31:15.

18. Matt 2:18.

for you have another son."[19] Some who long for their Messiah know the agony of waiting. And those in the line of Rachel maintain a hope that survives death itself (Heb 11:39). Accordingly, this lament stands out in Jeremiah 31, a chapter that as a whole celebrates the messianic age. Hear Jeremiah's next words:

> This is what the LORD says:
>
> "Restrain your voice from weeping and your eyes from tears, for your work will be rewarded," declares the LORD.
>
> "They will return from the land of the enemy. So there is hope for your descendants," declares the LORD. "Your children will return to their own land."[20]

The movement from Genesis to Jeremiah to Matthew thus achieves two results. The loss of children invokes the pain permeating Israel's story. But it also announces that the time for tears will end. With the birth of Jesus, the wait is finally over.

The death of Rachel marks another sort of ending as well. Rebekah and Rachel are related in a number of ways. The two great women of Jacob's life come from Laban's household. Jacob's mother was sister to his father-in-law; Jacob's wife was his mother's niece. Each bore two sons in deadly circumstances. Rebekah caused Jacob's exile in that she launched the scheme; Rachel caused it in that his love for her rendered him vulnerable to Laban. Jacob's last glimpse of his mother was when he left; his last glimpse of Rachel is here, at his return. Thus, these women delineate the beginning and end of his exile. He is home at last.[21]

The Twelve Sons of Israel

Genesis next, with an event and a list, fills out the picture of Jacob's sons (Gen 35:21–26). He begins with a journey and a place name. The messianic credentials of Genesis 35:21 are at least as old as *Targum Pseudo-Jonathan*, which renders the text thus: "And Jacob proceeded and spread his tent beyond the tower of the flocks, the place from whence it is to be

---

19. The words of 35:17, "Do not be afraid," are pronounced by God in a range of settings, nearly always with some measure of covenantal significance. So Pao and Schnabel, "Luke," 257.

20. Jer 31:16–17.

21. See Mathews, *Genesis 11:27—50:26*, 611.

that the King Meshiha will be revealed at the end of the days."[22] Clearly this eschatological and explicitly messianic dimension doesn't arise solely from the words of 35:21. In the next chapter we will consider the theological explanation of such a mundane journey.[23]

If the christological concerns of 35:21 must be temporarily set aside, the following verse offers a more immediate engagement with the themes of Genesis. We have struggled to identify Jacob's "true wife." Like the women, we wonder about the status of various family members. And if we puzzle over his wives, it will be correspondingly difficult to identify his true heir. Would the sons have inherited their mothers' insecurities? Reuben? What chance would he have—this son of an unloved mother?

Like Absalom, who in an act of political aggression has sex with his father's concubines during an ill-fated coup, Reuben sleeps with his stepmother, Bilhah.[24] Such sin was prohibited already in ancient times. Among the curses from Mount Ebal we find: "Cursed is the man who sleeps with his father's wife, for he dishonors his father's bed" (Deut 27:20). Paul commands the Corinthians to expel a man for this sin, which "does not occur even among the pagans" (1 Cor 5:1), causing us to marvel yet again that God will bring blessing to all *the families* of the earth through a family such as this.

In this sin Reuben resembles Jacob, who had dishonored his own father's bed to obtain blessing. Does Reuben act out because of a growing awareness that Jacob will overlook him, the firstborn? Is he thus, as his own parents had done, contending for position? The result of his grasping, like the brutality of Simeon and Levi in Genesis 34, does not elevate him. It disqualifies him from the blessing.

But there is more. After God changes Jacob's name in chapter 35, the narrator refers to him by name eight times in fifteen verses. All eight refer to him as Jacob except the two in vv. 21–22. By referring to him as Israel here, and only here, the name stands out. It serves to transfer Reuben's crime from the individual to the national stage.[25] Indeed, the consequences of an event that redraws the lines of divine promise are more than national: they are messianic. The one who lifts the curse will not descend from Reuben.

22. As cited in Pao and Schnabel, "Luke," 267.

23. See below on Mic 4:1, 6—also "days of old" in 4:5 and 7:14. Micah looks to the past and the future.

24. 2 Sam 16:20–22. See also 2 Sam 3:7; 1 Kgs 2:22.

25. Mathews, *Genesis 11:27—50:26*, 627.

From Abraham to Isaac to Jacob, the advance until now has always entailed a narrowing down. But Jacob has twelve sons. The man told to be fruitful and multiply has done exactly that. Where, however, Abraham's non-elect sons were sent away, and Esau similarly forms a separate nation, Jacob's sons represent not new nations but distinct tribes within the single entity that is Israel. In that sense, all are chosen. But this doesn't void the question of the special heir of the promise. This question occupies our author's interest in chapters 34 and 35. He has been excising branches from the main line: Simeon and Levi first. Then the oldest, Reuben. So who is left? The next in the line of Jacob, the fourth son of Leah, is Judah.

Isaac's Death and Burial

We arrive at chapter 35's fourth and final burial. Each indicates closing chapters of Israel's history. Idols speak of the past and belong in the ground. Deborah represents Harran.[26] Rachel is part Harran, part Canaan. Isaac, all Canaan, links Jacob to Abraham. Father and grandfather are gone, yet promises remain.[27] Their imprint, for good and ill, will endure.[28]

Isaac's burial magnifies other changes, for Isaac has two deathbed scenes. At the first, Jacob and Esau separated. At the second, they reunite.[29] Esau had promised to kill Jacob at Isaac's burial, but that threat, now forgotten, plays no role in this chapter. They are reconciled, providing a completeness to the *toledot* Isaac. The tensions and fears generated by Jacob's ambition, producing in turn Esau's threats and Jacob's self-inflicted wounds, have been resolved.[30] Jacob is home and with his brother. Obstacles to peace remain, but they arise no longer from the sons of Isaac. From here, at least for the remainder of Genesis, the threats to peace will be from the sons of Jacob. But those crimes fall outside the scope of this book.

26. Mathews, *Genesis 11:27—50:26*, 611.

27. Mathews, *Genesis 11:27—50:26*, 611.

28. This is less obviously true of Deborah, but elements of Harran color the next generation.

29. Turner, *Genesis*, 155.

30. Fears of post-mortem reprisals reappear not with Isaac's death, but at the death of Jacob. See Gen 50:15–21.

Chapter 12

Jacob's Story in Scripture

Jacob's Story in the Pentateuch

AN INITIAL GOAL IN probing Jacob's story has been to answer questions raised by both the primeval history and the promises to Abraham. Who will crush the serpent's head? Who will inherit the blessing? How can God use people like this to accomplish his purposes, and how does faith work if the main characters often don't appear to trust. The structure of Genesis itself points the way: the repeated use of the *toledot* formula, pointing to generations and coupled with numerous genealogies, highlights fruitfulness and multiplication. But Genesis moves beyond mere numbers to trace a single line—from Adam to Noah to Abraham to Isaac to Jacob.

Tracing that line allows the reader to follow the messianic rivulet that trickles out of Eden, flows through the stories of Abraham and Jacob, and broadens as it sweeps through the Pentateuch to the whole of the OT. Jacob's story doesn't end with Genesis 35. The remainder of Genesis, with its focus on Joseph and Judah, presents two saviors. Joseph, who dominates chapters 37–50, saves in the near term—but his benefits end when Genesis ends. Judah, whose chief narratological role is also his chief messianic role, sleeps with his daughter-in-law, mistaking her for a roadside prostitute.[1] Through

---

1. Brueggemann writes of Gen 38 that "this peculiar chapter stands alone, without connection to its context." Further, "It is not evident that it provides any significant theological resource. It is difficult to know in what context it might be of value for theological exposition." He goes on to note, though he doubts it, that the chapter could stand "primarily as a vehicle for the genealogy . . . which leads . . . ultimately, to Jesus" (*Genesis*, 307–8). Alternatively, the chapter is more tightly bound to Genesis, and the trajectory

such means, Judah saves in the long term. Tamar bears Perez who begets Boaz who begets David; and the Son of David is Jesus. We turn now to see what the rest of the Pentateuch says about this messianic savior.

The Pentateuch consists of four great narrative blocks, each concluding with an interpretive poem.[2] The first is Genesis's accounts of the patriarchs, culminating in Genesis 49 with Jacob blessing his sons. The second presents the deliverance from Egypt, concluding with the nation singing a song of praise in Exodus 15. The third recounts the desert wanderings of Numbers, which reaches a crescendo with Balaam's oracles (in Num 23, 24). The fourth is Deuteronomy's account of the initial conquest—leading to the "Song of Moses" in Deuteronomy 32 and Moses' departing statements concerning Israel's future in 33.[3]

Sailhamer attends especially to three of the poems, which he claims stand "at three macrostructural junctures in the Pentateuch."[4] They are Jacob's blessings in Genesis 49, Balaam's oracles in Numbers, and Moses' last words in Deuteronomy 33. Their wide distribution mustn't distract from an interconnectedness achieved by repeated words, themes, and elements of narrative.[5] Via these links the poems carry the Pentateuch along, cementing it into a unified theological whole. In this, they draw Jacob's story forward until it yields—as the heartbeat of the books of Moses—a future-facing royal eschatology.[6]

The Rise of Judah

Let's quickly review how we got here. God's opening promise to Abraham in Genesis 12:3 reads, "I will bless those who bless you, and whoever curses you I will curse; and all peoples on earth will be blessed through you."[7] Further, God had said, "To your [seed] I will give this land" (12:7). Abraham's promise is then explicitly tied to Jacob. Isaac, in his second blessing

---

toward Jesus forms part of its coherence.

2. Sailhamer, *Meaning*, 463, 468, n.8.

3. Sailhamer, *Narrative*, 35–36.

4. Sailhamer, *Narrative*, 36.

5. Sailhamer, *Meaning*, 475, n. 18.

6. Sailhamer, *Meaning*, 467. See esp. footnote 8 on that page, where he likens the poems to "the songs in a Hollywood musical. They are road signs telling the readers where they are and where they are going."

7. Sailhamer, *Meaning*, 474. Sailhamer does not refer to Gen 28.

of Jacob had said, "May he give you and your [seed] the blessing given to Abraham, so that you may take possession of the land where you now reside as a foreigner, the land God gave to Abraham" (28:4). A few verses later God himself added, "All peoples on earth will be blessed through you and your [seed]" (28:14). So Genesis 27–28 intersects with chapter 12, linked by mention of Abraham, blessing, "seed," and land.

These promises then flow into Genesis 49:8 via the words of blessing in 27:29.[8] Clearly, Jacob's successes notwithstanding, he never was presented as "lord over your brothers"—of which, incidentally, he had only one. Whenever someone bowed, it was Jacob. So we witness the transfer of an unfulfilled promise. Genesis 49:8 reiterates precisely this element of Genesis 27.[9]

And once again the promise expands. The veil covering royalty in the stories of Abraham and Jacob is yanked away.[10] The blessing on Judah entails not just fraternal praise but the destruction of enemies (49:8), an eternal rule (49:10), and international recognition (49:10). The promises are global. And this king is a lion. The lion of the tribe of Judah. He crouches and lies down. He is "like a lioness—who dares to rouse him?" (49:9).

Mangling the metaphors, this lion wields a scepter and holds the ruler's staff—and will not let go "until he to whom it belongs shall came." Concerning this difficult phrase—sometimes rendered "until Shiloh comes"—we should observe two things.[11] First, as in Genesis 28, "until" points to certainty, not termination. Second, Ezekiel 21:27 resonates with this phrase as it speaks of the stripping away of sovereignty and the reversal of power structures when a new king arrives: "A ruin! A ruin! I will make it

---

8. In Gen 49, Judah receives the blessing. Jacob gives the birthright, on the other hand, to Joseph, whose "double portion" emerges in pronouncements over his two sons in Gen 48 (as also in 1 Chr 5:1). In this, Joseph, the favorite son, is leader (and savior) among the brothers (depicted in their bowing down to him), while Judah is leader among the tribes (depicted in their bowing down to him—the terms are transferred to Judah in 49:8). See Walton, *Genesis*, 722. Alexander (*Paradise*, 9–11) observes that Ephraim obtains the blessing while Judah receives "the promise of kingship."

9. Though with four wives, the terms must be altered from "your mother's sons . . ." to "your father's sons will bow down to you."

10. Von Rad (*Genesis*, 424–25) rightly maintains that because Judah's place among the tribes arises from the fact of David's kingship, 49:10 must look beyond David. That is, it would mean little to say that "the scepter [that Judah has because of David] will not depart until David comes."

11. "Shiloh" simply transliterates the Hebrew.

a ruin! The crown will not be restored until he to whom it rightfully belongs shall come; to him I will give it."[12]

Genesis 49 indicates the overturning of the curse in the messianic age. Thorns and thistles—and the sweat of the laborer's brow—will yield to such lavish vines that losing one to a donkey is no hardship.[13] The text does not say why the Messiah associates with a donkey or the colt of a donkey during a time when peace overtakes war, but this connection is developed in Zechariah 9:9 and in Jesus' triumphal entry.[14]

Clothing features in this portrait. Targums on 49:11 interpret the Messiah's robes—red with wine and "the blood of grapes"—as the blood-stained garments of victorious battle. *Targum Pseudo-Jonathan* reads:

> How beautiful is the King Messiah who is to arise from among those of the house of Judah. He girds his loins and comes down arranging battle lines against his enemies and slaying kings together with their rulers; and there is no king or ruler who can withstand him. He makes the mountains red with the blood of the slain; his garments are rolled in blood; he is like a presser of grapes.[15]

This battle dress shapes Isaiah's eschatology. Israel's constant opponent is Edom, meaning "red."[16] Edom's ancient capital is Bozrah, meaning "vintage."[17] On the "day of vengeance" (Isa 63:4), God will flex his messianic "arm of salvation" (63:5). That is, he will alone tread the grapes of divine wrath. Isaiah 63 opens with questions and answers concerning the LORD's triumph. From their watchtower the guards of the city initially ask about identity, but their questions center on appearance. First, "Who is

12. So Dumbrell, *Search*, 37. Ezekiel speaks in the larger context of Judah's defeat by Babylon. Ezekiel 22 specifies the cause as shedding blood and idolatry. Ezekiel 24 speaks of "the city of bloodshed." Ezekiel 25 then offers an oracle against Edom (see also Ezek 35:1 "sword of Edom"). But alongside all this, hope is renewed for a day of restoration when "he comes to whom it rightfully belongs"—quoting the cryptic phrase from Gen 49:10. Dumbrell further notes that the LXX reads 21:27 (21:32 LXX) messianically: the individual and personal reading is evident (*Search*, 37).

13. Kidner, *Genesis*, 219.

14. Matt 21:2–5.

15. Citing Maher, *Pseudo-Jonathan*, 159. *Targum Neophiti* and *Fragmentary Targum* are virtually identical. For the text and its analysis see Fitzmeyer, *One Who Is to Come*, 155–56.

16. Isaiah 34 prepares for this reference in that Edom there represented the enemy of God's people. The reduction of Israel's enemies to this one nation results from the frequent confrontations between the two. So Webb, *Isaiah*, 143.

17. Motyer, *Isaiah*, 510.

this coming from Edom, from Bozrah, with his garments stained crimson? Who is this, robed in splendor, striding forward in the greatness of his strength?"[18] Events in the red land, the place of the vintage, have stained the warrior's garments.

The answer: "It is I, proclaiming victory, mighty to save" (Isa 63:1c).

Now they ask more directly about his clothes. "Why are your garments red [*'adom*], like those of one treading the winepress?"[19]

The reply strips away the metaphors, "I have trodden the winepress alone . . . . I trampled them in my anger and trod them down in my wrath; their blood spattered my garments, and I stained all my clothing."[20]

Genesis 49:10–11 and its portrait of a man in blood-red, grape-spattered clothes thus underpins Isaiah 63's presentation of a blood-stained conqueror. This is not, however, its final application, for the imagery undergoes further development in Revelation 19:13–16. Once again we should note differences as well as similarities.

Regarding differences, the savior-warrior who in Isaiah was "striding forward" now rides a white horse. There he fought alone, but now "The armies of heaven were following him, riding on white horses and dressed in fine linen, white and clean."

Regarding similarities, as in Isaiah, the clothes are blood red: "He is dressed in a robe dipped in blood." The warrior's identity is (thinly) veiled in both accounts. The watchmen's question of identity elicited only, "It is I." Here we read, "He has a name written on him that no one knows but he himself" (Rev 19:12).[21] In Isaiah, the warrior's garments were "like those of one treading the winepress?"[22] Revelation, to explain Jesus' clothes being dipped in blood, states, "He treads the winepress of the fury of the wrath of God."

Significantly, while here again Jesus' clothes are covered with blood, his army, which played no role in Isaiah, remains "white and clean". This is because "I have trodden the winepress alone."[23] Despite their presence, the battle belongs to the LORD.

18. Isa 63:1a,b.

19. Isa 63:2.

20. Isa 63:1–3

21. For the identity of the unnamed rider, and the significance of the name, see Osborne, *Revelation*, 681–83.

22. Isa 63:2.

23. The agenda is established already in Exod 14:14, where God fights alone against the chariots of Egypt.

Before moving via the links observed above to Numbers 23, let us note in passing two things about Judah. First, Genesis 49:8–12 is often said to be the first messianic passage in Scripture. Second, Judah is the first person in Scripture to volunteer for slavery to please his father and save his brother.[24] He will not be the last.

Numbers 23–24

Lions rarely feature in the Pentateuch. In fact, only our three blessing poems mention them.[25] Lionesses, rarer still, appear only in the first two poems.[26] The "scepter" is rarest, found only in Genesis 49:10 and Numbers 24:17. This unusual vocabulary, clustering in these distinctly promise-oriented poems, forges links between them.

But Numbers, taking more than just words from Genesis, echoes broad statements. Numbers 23:24 describes Israel in the wilderness with the language of Genesis 49:9: "The people rise like a lioness; they rouse themselves like a lion." Numbers 24:9 then builds on 23:24, "like a lion they crouch and lie down, like a lioness—who dares to rouse them." Obscured by the translation, however, is a pronominal change. Plurals in Numbers 23 become singulars in 24. Balaam describes Israel in chapter 23 as it surges from Egypt to the promised land.[27] He then, in the next oracle, looks ahead to when "*His* king will be greater than Agag / *His* kingdom will be exalted (24:7)."[28] Again, "Like a lion *he* will crouch and lie down / Like a lioness— who dares to rouse *him*?"[29]

---

24. Gen 44:33. Compare 43:9: "I will bear the blame."

25. Gen 49:9, Balaam's oracles (Num 23:24; 24:2) and Moses' blessing (Deut 33:20—speaking of Gad).

26. Gen 49:9 and the Balaam oracles of Num 23:24; 24:9.

27. Sailhamer, *Narrative*, 408.

28. The LXX focuses, without poetic language, on the man who will "be lord over many nations," and Gog rather than Agag. So also the Samaritan Pentateuch: Cole, *Numbers*, 420; Drazin, *Targum Onkelos*, 247, esp. n. 28. "Gog" is presented as the final enemy before the temple's restoration in Ezek 38–39.

29. Num 24:9 a, b. Note too that 24:8 repeats 23:22, again changing from plurals to singulars. "God brought *him* out of Egypt." Is this to be related to Hosea's notion that "Out of Egypt I have called my son" (Hos 11:1)?

This oracle then concludes with words that extend all the way back to Abraham, "May those who bless you be blessed and those who curse you be cursed!"[30]

The particularizing implied by the singular becomes even more specific, and more exalted, in Balaam's fourth oracle. Here he deals in openly eschatological categories, speaking of "days to come" (24:14). He first amplifies his distance from his subject, "I see him, but not now; I behold him, but not near." Then the vision tumbles out:

> A star will come out of Jacob; a scepter will rise out of Israel. He will crush the foreheads of Moab, The skulls of all the people of Sheth. Edom will be conquered; Seir, his enemy, will be conquered, but Israel will grow strong. A Ruler will come out of Jacob and destroy the survivors of the city.[31]

In this portrayal, consistent with Isaiah 63, Jacob finally overcomes his brother. The head-crusher predicted in Genesis 3:15 emerges from Jacob and receives the full measure of authority and blessing promised to the patriarch. To complete the Jacob/Edom narrative, it was necessary for Numbers 24 to speak not of Judah but Jacob. But we can legitimately narrow the line because this star-king was just a few verses earlier linked to the lion of Judah—as one who brings blessing and curse depending on one's response to him (24:9).[32]

Balaam's final oracle addresses the nature of history, for under God (24:23) kingdoms will rise and fall. Amalek will be destroyed. Ashur will capture the Kenites (Num 24:20–24). Eventually, "ships will come from the shores of Cyprus" (Num 24:24) and "subdue Ashur and Eber," but they too will be destroyed.[33]

Daniel absorbed this lesson of passing kingdoms. He even borrowed Balaam's language to predict the ruler behind "the abomination that causes desolation" (Dan 11:31). Immediately preceding his assault on the temple, so says Daniel, "Ships of the western coastlands will oppose him" (Dan 11:30). In Daniel 11, these words repeat the Hebrew of "ships from the shores of

---

30. Num 24:9 c, d.

31. Num 24:17c–19.

32. Sailhamer, *Narrative*, 408–9.

33 Sailhamer (*Narrative*, 409) says that Eber is "probably Babylon." Roland Allen ("Numbers", 913), relates Eber to eastern forces, while Kittim represents the west. The LXX identifies Eber with "Hebrews."

Cyprus." Daniel thus reprises crucial elements of Numbers 24, and like Balaam's final oracle looks far beyond David for its fulfilment.[34]

Deuteronomy 33:7

Jacob's statements were explicitly called a blessing: Genesis 49:28 concludes his pronouncements with "this is what their father said to them when he blessed them, giving each the blessing appropriate to him."[35] Deuteronomy 33:1 also speaks of a blessing: "This is the blessing that Moses pronounced on the Israelites." Brueggemann relates this anticipatory element of the prophet's farewell back to Genesis 35:22–26, and then looks forward, stating that "of the biblical materials, the genre of [Genesis 49's] poem has most in common with Deut. 33."[36] At least formally, Deuteronomy 33 resembles Genesis 49.[37]

But similarities run deeper. The blessing of Deuteronomy 33:7 reads, "Hear, LORD, the cry of Judah; bring him to his people. With his own hands he defends his cause. Oh, be his help against his foes!" For what does Judah cry, and who are "his people"? The most common interpretation looks to the Babylonian exile, with Judah asking to be restored to Israel ("his people").[38] But if 33:7 connects with Genesis 49, as is widely accepted of Deuteronomy 33 generally, then a bigger possibility emerges: Moses sees future-Judah one day growing impatient and praying, "bring him to his people." These words supplement Jacob's grand expectations. In Genesis 49:10, as we have seen, Jacob spoke of Judah's coming king: "until he . . . shall come." The talk was of vines and wine and milk and donkeys; of grapes, eyes, teeth, scepters, and staffs. Jacob dreams in color. On the

---

34. Wenham suggests that each of the four oracles develops an element of the Abrahamic promise, moving from descendants to blessing and protection to land to blessing on all nations (*Guide*, 115–16).

35. Von Rad observes that the content differs from typical blessings (*Genesis*, 421). See also, Coats (*Forms*, 310) who despite their self-designation, argues that both Gen 49 and Deut 33 contain "tribal sayings," which are "intimately related to, but not the same as, tribal blessing."

36. Brueggemann, *Genesis*, 365.

37. I question, however, his assertion that Genesis 49 "is not likely to serve a theological expositor very richly." Brueggemann, *Genesis*, 366.

38. It is not clear that Judah's captivity entails being "separated from his people." This poses problems for the notion that God must "bring him to his people." So Sailhamer, *Meaning*, 470.

other hand, Moses dreams in black and white, presenting a somber vision, for Judah will cry out from a crucible of suffering. Moses maintains hope, but speaks of a time before the end when God's gathered people are beset by foes and plead for one of their own to rescue them.[39] To be God's people is to be blessed. To be blessed is not yet to be at rest.

A final element of Moses's words points toward a distant future. Much like Genesis's climactic blessings before Jacob's death, so these final words, and thus the climax of the Pentateuch, build upon eschatological foundations. Like Jacob who died outside the land trusting that God would bring his people home, Moses looks ahead. Genesis 49 began, "Gather around so I can tell you what will happen to you in days to come" (49:1). Moses with the same phrase ("In days to come . . .") begins his parting comments (Deut 31:29). Balaam had also spoken of the distant future when he told Balak, in launching his final oracle, what Israel will do "in days to come" (Num 24:14, see also 24:17). This eschatological marker, frequent in the prophets, appears just four times in the Pentateuch, the only other one being Deuteronomy 4:30.[40] In this, Moses' final prophecy binds together the messianic material of Genesis 49 and Numbers 23–24.

With these oracles we arrive at the end of the Pentateuch. Our goal has been to demonstrate the significance of Jacob's story, primarily through its messianic content, for the Pentateuch as a whole. But the end of the Pentateuch is not the end of God's promises to and through Jacob. It remains for us to explore how the OT picks up, interprets, and makes use of, the story of Jacob.

Jacob's (and Esau's) Story in Scripture

Compared to Abraham's role in subsequent Scripture, Jacob is—for obvious reasons—less prominent. The best known texts are Hosea 12, Obadiah (with its parallels in Jeremiah 49), and Malachi. In these passages, the use of Genesis material is clear and generally accepted. In what follows we will look at them, but will also introduce other verses that contain fragments of Jacob's story.

---

39. On the place of kings in the context of Deut 33, see Sailhamer, *Narrative*, 477.

40. "In [days to come] you will return to the LORD your God and obey him."

Hosea 12

Hosea rebukes Israel's unfaithfulness and calls for her return. Disloyalty to the LORD (idolatry) and to one another—expressed as social abuses, such as misappropriating wealth (12:7)—draw his ire. Hosea's message mingles tragic elements of his own marriage to a prostitute with numerous incidents from Israel's history. Such living metaphors point to Israel's faith*less*-ness alongside a God who, while bearing the grief, unrelentingly calls for his own bride's return (6:1; 12:6; 14:1–2).

In chapter 12, Hosea preaches from the text of Genesis.[41] In two sections, vv. 3–4, and then vv. 12–13, he engages with the Jacob story. The first covers events unfolding inside the land, the second events occurring outside. Hosea's treatment is not exegesis *per se*, but application of those events to the nation. The story gives him the material to construct, and set side by side, images of both the ancient patriarch and the nation that now bears his name. This comparison is facilitated by an "artful ambiguity" that sometimes makes it difficult to distinguish man from nation.[42] Jacob and those who bear his name share a common character. Hosea hopes they share a relationship with God.

The structure of the text is elusive. Perhaps the best way to visualize the whole is as follows:

Israel is a deceiver (11:12—12:1):

A. God announces a lawsuit against Jacob (12:2).

B. *The Lord's faithfulness (12:3–6).*

C. Commercial deceit (12:7–8).

B. *The Lord's faithfulness (12:9–10).*

C. Religious deceit: Gilead and Gilgal (12:11).

B. *The Lord's faithfulness (12:12–13).*

A. The verdict: guilty (12:14—13:1).[43]

In 12:2, God launches a mock trial indicting Judah and Ephraim. He promises to repay Jacob, here representing the totality of Israel, for his sin.

---

41. Landy, *Hosea*, 145.

42. So McKenzie, "Jacob Tradition," 317. He finds this ambiguity in the larger unit, though not in the verb of his immediate concern.

43. This table reproduces the work of Stuart, *Hosea-Jonah*, 185–86; see also 188.

JACOB'S STORY AS CHRISTIAN SCRIPTURE

The trial then provides a four-line character witness based on Jacob's story, each taking up a key term from Genesis to encapsulate an event.

Hosea begins with Jacob's struggle with his brother in the womb, playing on the pun that forms his name. Jacob "grasped his brother's heel," an idiom casting Jacob as the supplanter (Hos 12:3). Worse, he supplants his own brother. Jacob's nature was at work prior to and during birth, and now continues in the nation named after him.

The poem/trial then advances to adult Jacob, who continues to struggle, now explicitly with God. The verb that shapes the name "Israel" in Genesis 32:28 comes to the fore, reminding us that wrestling is consistent with his past and future character—and with those who share his name.[44]

In the next line, Jacob wrestles with God's messenger and, repeating a second verb from Genesis 32:28, overcomes. To this point, supplanting, struggling, and overcoming derive from Genesis to characterize Jacob, taking us to the point where he was reunited with Esau.

Line four says that Jacob "wept and begged for his favor." This echoes Genesis 33, with its report of weeping (33:4) and attempts to placate Esau. A *leitmotif* of that chapter is the favor that Jacob has already received from God, mentioned in 33:4 and 11, and the favor he hopes to receive from Esau, mentioned in 33:8, 10, and 15. The significance of this event in Jacob's life is thus conveyed with the word "favor."

So in four movements, Jacob wrestles with Esau, God, an angel, and Esau again, until he returns and begs for favor. But now Hosea takes us to Bethel. To this point, Jacob has performed every verb. He grasped, struggled, struggled again and overcame, wept, and begged. Now it is God's turn to act. In "He found him at Bethel," God performs the verb (12:4). The one who is lost is found—by God. The one who is cast out and alienated is found and talked to—by God. The fugitive receives promises—from God. He is told that God will do the impossible. "I will bring you back to this land" (so Gen 28:15). And who makes this promise? None other than "The LORD, the *elohim* of Armies."[45] This is a good God for a refugee in enemy territory. Such was Jacob's plight, and such will be the plight of his descendants, according to Hosea. Both face the disastrous consequences of sin. And yet both are elect of God. From where Hosea stands, Jacob experienced this exile long ago; Israel's exile is imminent; and Judah—unless repentant—will experience it in the near future.

44. Hos 12:3b.
45. So the MT of Hos 12:6. My translation.

Hosea, notably, offers no more moral evaluation of Jacob than does Genesis.[46] If the narrator disapproves of Jacob's behavior in understated terms, the same is true, at least to this point, of Hosea 12. The climax of old Jacob comes at Peniel and in the next day's encounter with Esau. This death-and-life struggle is overshadowed, however, by moments of discovery occurring, anachronistically, at Bethel. Jacob's is no flash-of-blinding-light conversion story; it is a drawn out wrestling match, sometimes frenetic, sometimes excruciating, often hard to watch. But it's also a story that affords glimpses from the mountaintop. Even Peniel gives way, not chronologically, but in the poetry of Jacob's life, to Bethel. Bethel is the mountaintop.

And if Hosea commands Israel's return, then Jacob is the ideal image. For Bethel is a mountain with twin peaks. Jacob did return with the help of God. The impossible ending took place. And God can do the impossible for Israel as well.

Returning is problematic. Would a husband welcome back his whoring wife? Hosea 5:4 says, "Their deeds do not permit them to return to God. A spirit of prostitution is in their heart." But 12:6 breeds hope in the impossible. The preposition rendered "to" is better understood as instrumental: "But you must return *with the help of* God."[47] Hosea knows that returning opposes Israel's nature. But God can conquer. And he can, in his grace, restore the wandering heart . . . as he had for Jacob. There can be an end to exile.

Here is the key to Hosea's use of Jacob's story thus far: Jacob *did* return. The journey back occurred and must occur again. And so, v. 6, "you must return to your God." The moment that matters most is when God met Jacob, speaking a word of hope to the hopeless. Hosea in this way implores Israel to carry Jacob's story to its end. Struggles with God and man are not the last chapter of Israel's life. Becoming a fugitive is not the last chapter. The way the script is written, Jacob returns to Bethel because God both promised it and brought it about.

In this we see Hosea's sensitivity to Genesis' astonishing achievement. How does one portray a character who, as it were, arrives, and yet whose blessing is all of grace? The flow of the story signifies that Jacob's place before God is "always a gift, never a reward for virtue."[48] And if his inclusion does not depend on goodness, neither does exclusion result from his flawed

46. Andersen and Freedman, *Hosea*, 599–600.

47. Daniels, *Hosea*, 37. Carroll, "Hosea," 292.

48. Andersen and Freedman, *Hosea*, 600.

character.[49] Jacob comes good (I think), but that is not what animates the story. Genesis and Hosea look to God's choice—announced before Jacob was born, granted to the only person portrayed as wicked even before birth, and carried forward in God's tender rending of body and soul.

Following Bethel's pivotal word of hope, God presses charges against Israel. Now we find unambiguous moral evaluation. "The merchant uses dishonest scales and loves to defraud" (12:7). The scales, like Jacob, are deceivers (see also 11:12), and the heart, which should belong to God, instead delights in robbing one's brother.[50] Moreover, and resulting from his ill-gotten wealth, Ephraim is arrogant enough to think that his wealth is sufficient to cover his sin—that God will somehow be impressed.

At v. 12, Hosea returns to the Jacob story, now recounting events from outside the land. Jacob flees, serves, and tends sheep. But while these are the bitter fruit of Jacob's deception, they also account for his prosperity as he labors in exile. Once again it is important to recall that the pivotal moment occurs when God, at Bethel, told Jacob "I will be with you." This promise rescues and sustains Jacob during his dark night. And so as the sons of Jacob face exile, they too can turn to a Lord who is present and able to prosper and multiply them even as they bear the consequences of their sin.

As in the first block of Jacob material, Jacob performed all the verbs up till that moment when God speaks. And the poem's fluid transitions reappear as the identity of Jacob again resolves into something more. In v. 12 "Jacob fled" and "Israel served." But in the next verse Moses brings "Israel" up from Egypt. "Jacob" becomes "Israel" and Israel becomes the nation—but the story is singular. And in this singular story, the same God who rescued and enriched the slave Jacob does the same for the slave Israel in Egypt. That is to say, God blessed an impoverished refugee reduced to slave labor. And just as God interrupted Jacob to shine his grace on him at Bethel, so he interrupts slave-Israel in Egypt. In sending his prophet, he expresses compassion and delivers Israel from slavery (Hos 12:13). This develops beyond the promise of 12:6. There God announced that he would do the impossible in changing the heart. Here we discover the means of transformation: a prophet sent by God to deliver his people. But because they refuse to heed the prophets (including Moses), Hosea's Israel, swaddled in luxury, unwittingly faces slavery

---

49. Andersen and Freedman, *Hosea*, 600.

50. The prophets, like Jesus, frequently relate love of God to love of neighbor: Amos 5:15; Mic 6:8; Zech 7:9–10.

once again. And still the new prophet persists, holding up a mirror to Israel. Jacob's image reflects back.

So Jacob serves Hosea's purpose. The God who called flawed Jacob now calls flawed Israel because, despite themselves, they are elect. Jacob's defective character is the character of the nation. Now Jacob's story must become the story of the nation.

Before leaving, it may be helpful to step outside Hosea 12 and make two more observations. First, in a book featuring one reversal after another, chapter 1 teaches how high God raises his people. The name Lo-Ammi, "not my people" (1:9) gives way not to the standard "children of Jacob" or "children of Israel" but to "children of the living God" (1:10). This new name, through omission, draws the reader to think of Israel—even while proposing to recast the family likeness in far loftier terms. This mingles with the promise that "the Israelites will be like the sand on the seashore, which cannot be measured or counted" (1:10). Commentaries generally take this as a reaffirmation of the promise made to Abraham after his offering of Isaac (Gen 22:17). But in fact, the quotation more closely resembles the plea of Jacob in Genesis 32. He rehearses his fears and then adds: "But you have said, 'I will surely make you prosper and will make your descendants like the sand of the sea, which cannot be counted.'"[51]

One might say that Jacob is asking, "what becomes of the promise if the family of promise is destroyed?" The same logic informs Moses' intercession in the context of the golden calf. In Exodus 32:13, Moses appeals to God's promises to Abraham, Isaac, and Israel. How can God fulfil his promises if he destroys the bearer of the promise? Moses doesn't manipulate God. He calls for mercy from an all-powerful, loving Lord. And Hosea, recalling not faithful Abraham but fearful Jacob, looks to a God who is rejected again. He will punish harshly, but will let go of neither his promises nor his people.

Second, and more briefly, I have suggested that Jacob as a type points to Israel, not Jesus. But divine math sometimes becomes complicated. In Hosea 12, Jacob in Harran = Israel in Egypt. But this chapter stands in the shadow of chapter 11's claim that, "When Israel was a child I loved him, and out of Egypt I have called my son." This is famously taken up in Matthew 2:15 and applied to Jesus. So at least for a moment in Matthew, Jacob = Israel can be extended to Israel = Jesus.

51. Gen 32:12.

So what conclusions can we draw from Hosea's dependence on Jacob's story? First, Jacob then and now is by nature deceitful. Nevertheless, God loves Jacob and will reverse his fortunes.

Second, God's character is expressed throughout the book of Hosea. He is husband (Hos 2:2–5, 14–16, 19–20), father (1:10), and shepherd (4:16). As Jacob learned, to love is to be vulnerable. God is jilted and wounded, yet loving.[52] He was no less the vulnerable God when he chose Jacob; and he is no less vulnerable as he, in Jesus, weeps over his dead friend in John 11:35, or over doomed Jerusalem in Luke 9:41–44. Jacob experiences an immediacy in his relationship with God. The prophets in many ways emphasize the distance and barriers between sinful humanity and a holy God. Hosea shortens that distance until God himself suffers for the sins of his people. Ultimately this suffering will take him to the cross. For only by such means can he finally remove the barriers.

Third, the character of Jacob is under-developed. God's character, not the deeds of the elect, is determinative. The elect son must therefore guard against arrogance and presumption, but is permitted to—indeed must—stand on the promises of God.

Fourth, Hosea develops the transition from Israel to the sons of Israel—present already at the end of Genesis 32—to probe the ongoing nature of the people of God. If we find lines of identity that run through Israel into the church, it will be necessary for us to consider how Christians appropriate Jacob's character and story.

Jacob the Deceiver: Jeremiah 9

Jeremiah warns the people, "Beware of your friends; do not trust anyone in your clan, for every one of them is a deceiver, and every friend a slanderer" (Jer 9:4). Behind the term "clan" is the Hebrew for brother, so that the thought runs, "every brother is a deceiver." Such words might recall, in themselves, Jacob's defrauding his own brother. But there is more. The text could be rendered, ". . . do not trust your brothers. For every brother is a deceiving Jacob."[53]

The appraisal continues: "You live in the midst of deception; in their deceit they refuse to acknowledge me, declares the LORD." The prophet here mimics the Hebrew form used in both Genesis 27:35: "your brother came

52. Hos 7:13, "I long to redeem them." Also 11:1, 4, 8, 9.

53. See NIV text note.

deceitfully and took your blessing"; and 34:13: "Jacob's sons replied *deceitfully* as they spoke to Shechem and his father Hamor."

Like Hosea, Jeremiah foregrounds Israel's deceitful character as a reflection of father Jacob. This neither appears to be common in the OT, nor is it developed in the NT, but Jeremiah 9 refers to the deceiver to indict the nation. How can Israel progress to God's deliverance when they have regressed to being Jacob?

Limping, Bethlehem Ephrathah, and Migdal Eder in the Prophecy of Micah

Where Hosea dwells on Jacob's inconsistency, Micah presents God's consistency in keeping his promises. Perhaps the richest collection of references to Jacob's life can be found here. I say "perhaps" because I know of no one who develops these connections. The following suggests that Micah consciously employs the Jacob story to both accuse and provide hope for Jacob's children.

Micah 5:2–5a is one of Scriptures great messianic passages:

> But you, Bethlehem Ephrathah, though you are small among the clans of Judah, out of you will come for me one who will be ruler over Israel, whose origins are from of old, from ancient times.
>
> Therefore Israel will be abandoned until the time when she who is in labor bears a son, and the rest of his brothers return to join the Israelites.
>
> He will stand and shepherd his flock in the strength of the LORD, in the majesty of the name of the LORD his God. And they will live securely, for then his greatness will reach to the ends of the earth. And he will be our peace.

The agony of childbirth becomes the launching point for messianic fulfilment. Echoes of Rachel's travail are clear enough: connecting Bethlehem Ephrathah with labor, as in Genesis 35:19, forces recall of that earlier calamity.

We must concede, however, that Rachel's agony in giving birth to Benjamin, alluded to in 5:3 (and more extensively in 4:9–10) becomes a stock image of waiting for the Messiah.[54] Thus the presence of such imagery doesn't necessarily penetrate the surface of the Jacob story. But Micah offers additional links to Genesis.

54. Sailhamer, "Genesis," 219.

First, the oracle begins, "But you, Bethlehem Ephrathah." With these words, Micah goes beyond stereotyped expressions of labor yielding the coming one. He places the Messiah in the very place that Genesis 35 associates with Rachel's labor. "Small," moreover, is the same term God used when he promised, "the older will serve the younger" (Gen 25:23).

Second, 5:2 indicates that the "origins" of the coming ruler are "from of old, from ancient times." This could relate to the tribe of Judah, or more likely to the Davidic antitype who emerges from Judah.[55] Here though, it probably serves to connect Jacob with David as forerunners of the Messiah. The same phrase, "from of old," appears as the final word of Micah, where it is translated, "in days long ago." What is from "days long ago" in Micah 7:20? The answer is explicit: promises made to Jacob and Abraham. The temporal phrase's link to the patriarchs in 7:20 at minimum invites us to ask if the twice-stated antiquity of the ruler's origins in 5:2 similarly attaches to the patriarchal promises. If this is the proper referent for the ruler "whose origins are from of old," then the thought of 5:2 concerning the elevation of Bethlehem equates with: "Out of you will come for me one who will be ruler over Israel [in fulfilment of the ancient promises to Jacob and Abraham]."

Davidic hints permeate Micah's vision of restoration. But the extravagance of the words points to promises that precede David. Micah 5:7, with words reminiscent of Isaac's blessing in Genesis 27:28–29, promises Jacob "dew" and "showers on the grass." Moreover, 5:8's prophecy of Jacob as a lion imitates three blessings: Jacob's elevation of Judah in Genesis 49:9, and Balaam's oracles in Numbers 23 and 24.[56] Micah looks to David and then behind him to reiterate God's as yet unfulfilled oaths.

Third, Micah is filled with place-names. But Bethlehem and Ephrathah are not the only sites picked up from Genesis 35. In the verse immediately following Rachel's travails, "Israel" moves to Migdal Eder (35:21). This phrase in fact appears only once in the NIV, but twice in the Hebrew Bible. The exact form appears again in Micah 4:8.

Micah 4:6 begins with that great eschatological marker, "'In that day,' declares the LORD . . . ." Then the LORD specifies his agenda:

I will gather the lame . . . I will make the lame my remnant . . . .

As for you, watchtower of the flock, stronghold of Daughter Zion,

---

55. See the careful exegesis of Waltke (*Micah*, 275–77). He offers Amos 9:11 as a significant parallel.

56. Waltke, *Micah*, 318.

the former dominion will be restored to you; kingship will come
to Daughter Jerusalem.[57]

The "former dominion" of Migdal Eder (here rendered "watchtower of
the flock") "will be restored"—in parallel with the promise that "kingship
will come to Daughter Jerusalem." It is exactly at this point in Micah that
the first references to labor pains appear. Thus, at Migdal Eder in Genesis
35, the eldest son of Jacob is disqualified from kingship in the context of
childbirth, while at Migdal Eder in Micah another son—again in the context of childbirth—ascends to Jerusalem's throne.

Fourth, with respect to those same verses, observe the prophet's characterization of Israel. The previous verse reads: "All the nations may walk
in the name of their gods, but we will walk in the name of the LORD our
God" (4:5). Before this takes place, Israel will be crushed (3:12) until only
a dispirited, broken remnant survives (1:16). The walking of Micah 4:5 is
thus a post-apocalyptic reversal: "I will gather the lame . . . I will make
the lame my remnant" (4:6–7). In this context of walking with the LORD,
the prophet's description of Israel as "lame" is evocative. The term used in
Genesis 32:31[58] of Jacob at Peniel, "and he was limping because of his hip"
appears in only three other places. Two of them are Micah 4:6 and 7.[59] God
will "gather the limping" and "make the limping a remnant."

Sure Jacob is a scoundrel. Micah doesn't shrink from that fact. But
God in ancient times chose small Jacob and pronounced great things to and
through him. In David, another small one hears promises of great things. In
the same way, small Bethlehem of Judah, site of Rachel's death and David's
birth, will yield God's still greater king. Jacob's sin meant that he suffered
much in delayed fulfilment. Rachel becomes the emblem of longing for the
promised son. And now Israel, because of sin, will face the same pain of
delay. But just as Jacob one day limped home, and the hoped-for child arrived, so God will bring his rebellious people home.

God's promises passed from Abraham to Jacob to generate new hope
for Israel. So precise are these prophecies, so clearly indicative of the source
and nature of the coming king, that when Herod enquires concerning the
birthplace of the Christ, people reply with Micah 5:2 (Matt 2:4–6). This
baby from small Bethlehem will bring reconciliation in his hour of humiliation. He will answer the lingering question at the end of Micah: "Who is

57. Mic 4:6–8.
58. Gen 32:32 in MT.
59. The fourth use of the term is Zeph 3:19.

a God like you, who pardons sin and forgives the transgression of the remnant of his inheritance?"[60] The God of Jacob.

Obadiah and Jeremiah 49

Obadiah, quoted at length in Jeremiah 49, denounces Edom in terms from the birthright episode. God says,

> "See, I will make you small among the nations; you will be utterly despised. The pride of your heart has deceived you,[61] you who live in the clefts of the rocks and make your home on the heights, you who say to yourself,
> 'Who can bring me down to the ground?'
> Though you soar like the eagle and make your nest among the stars, from there I will bring you down," declares the LORD.[62]

Contact with Jacob's story may not be obvious, but verbal correspondences are impressive. God threatens to make Edom "small" with the word rendered "younger" throughout the Genesis narrative. It informs Jacob's conquest of Esau in Genesis 27:15[63] and 27:42.[64] As the plot repeats in Laban's deception of Jacob, the term again drives the narrative in Genesis 29.[65] The same word defines Jacob's desperate prayer in Genesis 32:10,[66] and then appears twelve times in Genesis 42 and 43 with reference to Jacob's youngest, Benjamin. In Obadiah, Esau the elder will be demoted.

Edom will not only forfeit his seniority, he will be "despised." This term explained Esau's foolish behavior in Genesis 25:34; "So Esau despised his birthright." The despiser will be despised.

60. Mic 7:18.

61. The term for "deceived" here is found in Gen 3:13 but not in the Jacob story.

62. Obad 2–4; see also Jer 49:15–16.

63. "Then Rebekah took the best clothes of Esau her older son . . . and put them on her younger son Jacob."

64. "When Rebekah was told what her older son Esau had said, she sent for her younger son Jacob."

65. Gen 29:16: "Now Laban had two daughters; the name of the older was Leah, and the name of the younger was Rachel." 29:18: "Jacob . . . said, 'I'll work for you . . . in return for your younger daughter Rachel.'"

66. Gen 32:11 in MT. "I am *unworthy* of all the kindness and faithfulness you have shown your servant." For the first time, the one who wanted to be big confesses his smallness. Fokkelman is one of a few who appreciate Genesis 32's artful manipulation of the word for small (*Narrative Art*, 203).

But now it is not Jacob who deceives Esau. "The pride of your heart [has] deceived you." The word for "pride" derives from a root found in forty OT verses, three of its occurrences being in Genesis 25:29 and 25:34. There, oddly enough, the root once means "cooking," and twice "stew." Obadiah doesn't say "the stew you loved has deceived you," but he comes close. Edom's downfall is linked with Esau's.

As Obadiah and Jeremiah draw this material into the eschaton, they take divergent paths. For Obadiah, the storyline of Genesis will finally be fulfilled in the "Day of the LORD" (v. 15), when "Jacob will possess his inheritance" (v. 17). This elevation of Jacob means the total annihilation of Esau, with Jacob himself being the fire that reduces Esau to stubble (v. 18).

Edom's destruction is just as complete in Jeremiah, and happens for the same reason. Nevertheless, Jeremiah alters our eschatological focus. Where Obadiah says that Jacob will be a destroying fire, Jeremiah says that God, like a lion, will "chase Edom from its land" (Jer 49:19). But then God himself asks the question that arises so naturally from the OT. The verse continues, "Who is the chosen one I will appoint for this?" Who indeed? Who is this lion-ish deliverer who destroys the enemies of God's people?[67]

Malachi

Within the Pentateuch, Jacob's story points to a king who fulfils God's promises. In the prophetic literature, as Israel faces annihilation, Jacob the deceiver recalls the nation's character and warns them to return to the LORD. Israel possesses these promises and warnings because God initiated a covenant.

Covenant, a future king, and threats converge in Malachi, announced with reference to Jacob. Malachi responds to a nation that replaces God with a veneer of religion. The prophet opens with protestations of divine love for Jacob over against a nation blind to evidence of divine fidelity. "Jacob I have loved." This love is not sentimentality, but God's recollection of his own covenant of love. Consider Deuteronomy 7:7–9:

---

67. Brueggemann speaks of "God and God's agent" but does not develop the thought (*Jeremiah*, 457). Concerning God's sword and Edom, see Isa 34:5–7: "My sword . . . descends in judgment on Edom, the people I have totally destroyed. The sword of the LORD is bathed in blood . . . . For the LORD has a sacrifice in Bozrah and a great slaughter in the land of Edom."

The LORD did not set his affection on you and choose you because you were more numerous than other peoples, for you were the fewest of all peoples. But it was because the LORD loved you and kept the oath he swore to your forefathers that he brought you out with a mighty hand and redeemed you from the land of slavery, from the power of Pharaoh king of Egypt. Know therefore that the LORD your God is God; he is the faithful God, keeping his covenant of love to a thousand generations of those who love him and keep his commands.

God loves Jacob by initiating a covenant with Israel. He "hates" the Esau who keeps losing his inheritance, meaning that he did not choose him (Mal 1:2–5).

Malachi then denounces the nation for breaking two inter-related covenants: they have rejected God and divorced their wives. So the LORD is returning, and when he does, he will refine, judge, and testify against (Mal 3:1–5). But threats are not the last word. He concludes:

> See, I will send the prophet Elijah to you before that great and dreadful day of the LORD comes. He will turn the hearts of the parents to their children, and the hearts of the children to their parents; or else I will come and strike the land with total destruction.[68]

And so the OT closes with a rekindling of the messianic flame. And the sum of its hope appears as words of reconciliation. But why, in a book that says so much about husband-and-wife relationships does Malachi switch so abruptly to fathers and sons, rendered here "parents" and "children"?[69] We saw that Isaiah 63 expanded on oracles concerning Jacob to describe the devastation heaped upon disobedient Edom. That chapter goes on to speak of Israel as a nation that knew God's favor, yet rebelled against him, grieving his Holy Spirit (63:10). As they faced the bitter consequences of sin, they remembered the glory days when Moses led them to freedom. They wander again, but claim God as Father. Indeed, they cling to this hope even though "Abraham does not know us or Israel acknowledge us" (63:16). That is to say, the recipients of the covenant, Abraham and Jacob, cannot recognize Israel in its present form. What is needed is for someone to turn Abraham and Jacob, the bearers of the covenant, back to their children. This will not happen until the children turn back to the covenant given to the fathers. And that turning is envisaged by Malachi: "He will turn the hearts of the children

68. Mal 4:5–6.
69. So NIV11.

to their parents."[70] Turn to the LORD. Inherit the covenant blessings. Or fall under the curse of those who reject his covenant.

Malachi 4:6 is quoted in Luke 1:17 to describe John the Baptist. The Angel of the Lord reveals to Zechariah that "he will go on before the Lord, in the spirit and power of Elijah, to turn the hearts of the parents to their children and the disobedient to the wisdom of the righteous—to make ready a people prepared for the Lord."

This finds further expression in Zechariah's song. Linking the fathers still more closely to the covenant, he specifies the purpose of God's "rais[ing] up a horn of salvation."[71] He does this "to show mercy to our [fathers], and to remember his holy covenant, the oath he swore to our father Abraham."[72] That is, God saves at least in part because of his character and because of his covenant with the fathers.

As the Baptist's ministry unfolds, the complexity of this covenantal relationship moves to the fore. The only father he mentions is Abraham, with John warning Israel *not* to claim Abraham as father. Indeed, God can "out of these stones . . . raise up children for Abraham."[73]

Here we see that Malachi's appropriation of Jacob—and Luke's appropriation of Malachi—are thoroughly covenantal. Malachi and the Baptist explore the benefits of election. But rather than the false security offered by false prophets, their ministry results in a warning to those who presume upon grace while awaiting the Lord's appearance. *Return to the fathers.* And with this warning, they create a context in which God can pour out his love upon his children: his covenant love upon his covenant children. For such is the privilege of the elect.

---

70. Verhoef, *Haggai and Malachi*, 342.
71. Luke 1:69.
72. Luke 1:72–73.
73. Luke 3:8; see also Matt 3:9.

Chapter 13

Jacob's Legacy

THE DECEIVING BROTHER, THE prodigal who returns, the source of kings, the one chosen because loved: Jacob's career, while remarkable, fits within the often bizarre events of Genesis. And as we have seen repeatedly, his story—consistent again with the surrounding material—raises questions without answers. Why was Abel's sacrifice accepted but not Cain's? How godly is Abraham if he lies to kings? Is Jacob more righteous than Esau, or does he simply have different priorities? Judah's sons die because they sin against Tamar, but Judah himself, unwittingly, impregnates her. Are his sins less than those of his sons?

God Chooses

In the end, we are forced to say that Genesis provides, occasionally—maybe—the rationale for the disqualification of some, but we can never move beyond the notion that God has chosen. Penultimately this extends to the nation itself, chosen not because of their righteousness but because of divine love (Deut 7:6–8; 9:4–6).[1] And ultimately it extends to us. Where is the righteousness that secures God's favor? It is all because God, against our character, has chosen us and reconciled us to himself in his unfailing love.

The seeds of the gospel are sown here, but the Bible's story unfolds slowly. Jacob's part in the larger drama teaches that God can place him where he wants him, richly blessed and in a relationship. It further teaches that God

1. McKeown, *Genesis*, 284–85.

can work with flawed material. Many, both ancient Jewish writers and modern Christians, attempt to rehabilitate Jacob, but the text offers them little support. The best we can say of Jacob is that he advances from stealing blessing to receiving it to giving it. His failings nevertheless elevate the grace of the God, who blesses and achieves divine ends through him.

If this is true with respect to Jacob, then his story suggests that God can also keep us where he wants us and bless us with a relationship. Further, it suggests that God can save and use even material like us to realize his purposes. Perhaps in our moments of suffering and hardship, when we wonder where God is, he is present and wrestling with us to accomplish something beyond our understanding. Nothing suggests this is normal or to be expected. But this perspective on life's challenges is consistent with Scripture. Who knows what form God's dealings will take in one's own life?

Once again we find some answers, but just as often uncover more questions. How could it be otherwise given the nature of our subject? Importantly, the answers we find often relate one way or another to Jesus and the gospel of the crucified savior. Here again we are drawn to one who is simultaneously chosen yet rejected, to the one who produces a family that God will call his own—but who far surpasses Jacob in his revealing of the divine. The Bible teaches that the story here begun will continue, and that its outcome rests on firm promises.

The Jacob narrative draws us forward into the life of Israel and the drama of salvation. Accordingly, the twelve sons of Jacob so define the nation that when it is reconstituted, twelve apostles become the obvious and unexplained counterpoint to the twelve tribes.[2] This typology runs through the Gospels, valid even when the apostles show their true colors, revealing that they too were not chosen because of superior character or insight.

An at-first-glance different but ultimately similar development of the story informs the oracles of judgment against Edom. These borrow material from Genesis and again build on Jacob's character, including his status as the deceiver and as the chosen one. This application only works because the choice of Jacob was presented not as a result of moral superiority but God's grace. If this were not so, one could scarcely indict Edom for mistreating Israel when Jacob so thoroughly exploits Esau.

---

2. Evans, "Typology," 865.

God Overturns All Things

Fraternal interactions provide the template for the larger biblical drama: turning things upside down never ends. If elevation and demotion begins with individuals—Jacob and Esau—it quickly develops into the story of Israel and Edom and from there stretches outward to the nations. But the nations are not enough: divine reordering transcends international concerns until ultimately drawing all humanity into the story of Scripture and the purpose of Jesus' work: "He has brought down rulers from their thrones but has lifted up the humble. He has filled the hungry with good things but has sent the rich away empty."[3]

God chooses the means. He also chooses the time. We have seen that at least since Balaam, the story of Jacob invites people of faith to peer through a long telescope. Centuries roll by before David claims the throne of Israel. Millennia pass before the Christ appears. Genesis, Hosea, Micah, Jeremiah, Obadiah, Malachi, and others would read Jacob's story positively and negatively, finding in it worries for today and hope for tomorrow. John and Paul rejoice that a particular tomorrow has finally arrived, but they also teach that followers of Jesus, like Israelites of old, continue to wait, wrestling against fatigue, clinging to hope that their Messiah will one day appear. Descendants of Jacob in the Old Testament and New have this in common.

Scripture harkens back to Jacob to present Israel as a deceiver with only a loose grip on grace and faith, someone who opposes God as much as aligns with him, and whose sins continue in his sons. So why did God choose Jacob? Why does he choose us? "What if he did this to make the riches of his glory known to the objects of his mercy, whom he prepared in advance for glory—even us?"[4] Continuing in Romans, "Christ has become a servant of the Jews on behalf of God's truth, so that *the promises made to the patriarchs* might be confirmed and, moreover, that the Gentiles might glorify God for his mercy."[5]

To us, in Christ, God reveals his glory. To us falls the privilege of making his mercy known. To do so is to participate in Jacob's story.

3. Luke 1:52–53; see also 1 Pet 5:6.
4. Rom 9:23–24.
5. Rom 15:8–9.

Appendix

Food and Feasts in the Bible

GIVEN THE CENTRALITY OF meals in Jacob's deception of Esau and Isaac to obtain the blessing and birthright, and later in Laban's duplicity, there may be value in exploring the significance of food and feasts more broadly in the Scriptures.

Meals and Relationships

Eating together in the ancient Near East declares solidarity, providing a "symbol and confirmation of fellowship and mutual social obligations." In eating, "participants are tied to one another by a bond of friendship. Indeed they become kinsmen, for only kinsmen eat together."[1] Because meals are a primary household activity, an invitation represents an expression of kinship, complete with the accompanying hospitality and protection offered within the family. An invitation implies not equality but acceptance. As such, meals play an important role in the biblical account of the relationship between people and, in application, between people and God.

Meals mark social life, including such events as the arrival of important visitors (Gen 19:3; 2 Sam 3:20), Isaac's weaning (Gen 21:8), forming a treaty or covenant (Gen 26:30; 1 Kgs 3:14–15), weddings (Gen 29:22; Judg 14:10), Pharaoh's birthday (Gen 40:20), commissioning (e.g., Judg 6:21 [of Gideon]; 1 Sam 9:12–24 [of Saul]), and recollection of God's deliverance (Exod 12:14, 17; 13:6). Some feast for its own sake (1 Sam 25:36; Job 1:4).

1. So Kalluveettil, *Declaration and Covenant*, 11; see also Ross, "Meals," 315.

Already in Genesis 2–3, food defines relationships between God and humanity. Wine features in the Noah narrative (Gen 9:20–27). In Genesis 14:18, Melchizedek feeds Abraham. Abraham honors three guests with a lavish meal after which two proceed to Lot's home. There they receive similar offers of hospitality and then hostility. Patriarchal residence is often dictated by food and water: famine in the land sends them to Egypt (Gen 12:10), among the Philistines (26:1), and to Egypt again (42:1–2; 43:1–2). For Joseph in Egypt, a cupbearer and a baker feature prominently (40:1–23), along with highly revealing meals (43:32–34). Coinciding with the exodus, the nation is inaugurated around the Passover meal (Exod 12:3–11).

If eating leads to curse in Genesis 3, it often provides the backdrop to blessing as well, going back to the aforementioned Melchizedek and his bread and wine in Genesis 14. When King David invites the crippled Mephibosheth to dine at his table (2 Sam 9:7), his promises express a profound and moving solidarity born of his loyalty to Jonathan, a blessing that extends beyond material benefits. Many of the numerous OT meals relate to treaties and covenants. Typical in the patriarchal period is the feast shared by Isaac and Abimelech, king of Gerar, as they enter into a non-aggression pact (Gen 26:30). This is repeated in the pact-forming meal eaten by Jacob and Laban (Gen 31:45–54, esp v. 54).

With reference to a meal, Moses asks Pharaoh to release his people (Exod 5:1; 10:9). Following the consumption of the Passover, the nation departs, instructed to commemorate events with an annual feast.[2] God's covenant with his people at Sinai, not surprisingly then, included a meal as well. Exodus 24, in recounting events immediately prior to the receipt of the ten commandments, reveals that Moses and Aaron, Nadab and Abihu, and the seventy elders of Israel "saw God, and they ate and drank" (Exod 24:11). Though God does not eat and drink, he nevertheless is "fully present," the unquestionable intent of the twofold reference to seeing God (Exod 24:10, 11). He thus participates in the feast, which marks a covenant between himself and Israel.[3] Hugenberger in this context summarizes thus: "The sacrifices of communion effect a union between God and people; the blood sprinkled on the altar and people expresses the reality that Yahweh and his people share

---

2. McFall, "Sacred Meals," 750.

3. Fretheim, *Exodus*, 260; McFall, "Sacred Meals," 750. Meals function similarly in Gen 31:46, 54, and Exod 18:12. For the view that the meal does not mark the covenant so directly, see Nicholson, *People*, 126–27.

the same blood and are members of the family."[4] While the blood speaks of more than kinship, it does not speak of less.

In 1 Kings these symbols highlight divine success against the backdrop of rebellion. Chapter 8 recounts Solomon's feast at the dedication of the temple. It lasts fourteen days and celebrates a single people, united under a single king, declaring allegiance to the true and living God.[5] In chapter 13, a prophet denounces Jeroboam. The king responds by inviting the man of God to "come home with me for a meal, and I will give you a gift." To this royal pressure to compromise, the prophet offers a sharp retort: You could offer me half your net worth and I still wouldn't go with you, "nor would I eat bread or drink water here. For I was commanded by the word of the Lord: 'You must not eat bread or drink water or return by the way you came'" (13:7–9). When another prophet deceives him into eating, a lion kills him—though, curiously, does not eat him. Chapter 18, in which Elijah and Ahab clash, in order to indicate the nature of their opposition to God, describes the 450 prophets of Baal and four hundred prophets of Asherah as those "who eat at Jezebel's table" (1 Kgs 18:19). As events unfold, God himself feeds Elijah, who rejects the queen's table, through a raven (17:1–6), a foreign widow who serves miraculous fare (17:14–16), and food hidden in the desert (19:6–8). In 1 Kings, to ask, who feeds you? is to ask, to whom do you give allegiance?[6]

The sacrificial system speaks by including or excluding the one who brings the offering from eating it. The most commonly offered sacrifice in early Israel, the final one in biblical lists of sacrifices, was the peace offering. The main alternatives in translating its Hebrew name are two: "a sacrifice of peace,"[7] which has the virtue of maintaining *shalom*; and "a communion sacrifice," "fellowship offering," or "shared-offering."[8] The second set of translations captures well the notion that God, the priest, the presenter, and those with whom he chooses to dine consume the offering. The occasion of this sacrifice-meal ranges from moments of familial joy

4. Hugenberger, *Marriage*, 210.

5. House, *1 & 2 Kings*, 150.

6. In Isa 36:16–17, capitulation to the Assyrians will mean that "each of you will eat fruit from his own vine and fig tree and drink water from his own cistern, until I [i.e. the king of Assyria] come and take you to a land like your own—a land of grain and new wine, a land of bread and vineyards."

7. So RSV. This intersects with the LXX, which renders it θυσία σωτηρίου (*thysia sōtēriou*). Hartley (*Leviticus*, 38) translates it with "an offering of well-being."

8. So JB, NIV, and NEB respectively.

to great events in the life of the nation such as the ratification of the Sinai covenant (Exod 24), Saul's accession to the throne (1 Sam 11:15), David's restoration of the Ark (2 Sam 6:17–18), and the dedication of the temple (1 Kgs 8:64).[9] Sacrifices that propitiate are not shared by the one whose sin is being covered (so that even those typically consumed by the priest are not eaten if the priest is identified with the sin), suggesting that they are preliminary to a relationship, i.e., they point to the restoration of fellowship, not fellowship itself. The peace offering, however, symbolizes a gathering at which God and his friends dine together.

Food and Drink in Jesus' Teaching

Once we recognize the social value of meals, elements of Jesus' ministry come into focus. The one harassed for eating with the wrong crowd feeds multitudes and teaches that those who hunger and thirst for righteousness are blessed (Matt 5:6). The Synoptics place the feeding of the five thousand (Matt 14:13–21//Mark 6:32–44//Luke 9:10–17) immediately after reference to Herod as the killer of John the Baptist. In Jesus, born in Bethlehem (i.e. "house of bread"), a new king has arrived who brings not death but life, whose feasts are not murderous but sustain the soul. While John omits Herod and John the Baptist from his feeding account, he too depicts the audience as responding to Jesus' activity in terms of a kingly event (John 6:15). Jesus generates a (short-lived) unity around a banquet that clearly echoes, yet surpasses, the exodus. Tragically, like Israel of old in the wilderness, so this group grumbles concerning food. Once again the nation is willingly fed by the Lord, but withholds its allegiance.

In John 6, Jesus offers a discourse concerning food that "endures to eternal life which the Son of Man will give you" (6:27). And further, "the bread of God is the bread that comes down from heaven and gives life to the world" (6:33). When asked for such bread, Jesus answers: "I am the bread of life. Whoever comes to me will never go hungry, and whoever believes in me will never be thirsty" (6:35). This analogy is then explained in v. 40 with the words, "For my Father's will is that everyone who looks to the Son and believes in him shall have eternal life, and I will raise them up at the last day" (6:40). Over the next several verses, and in response to the multitude murmuring in the wilderness concerning divinely given food, Jesus explains further that he is the life-giving gift provided by the Father

9. Hartley, *Leviticus*, 38.

(6:43–51). The very center of this paragraph repeats the notion that the one who believes will live forever (6:47). But the audience, like so many within John's Gospel, fails to move from analogy to spiritual truth and so misunderstands Jesus' offer. At this point, Jesus, feeling the antagonism of the crowd, enlists metaphor more fully:

> Unless you eat the flesh of the Son of Man and drink his blood, you have no life in you. Whoever eats my flesh and drinks my blood has eternal life, and I will raise them up at the last day. For my flesh is real food and my blood is real drink. Whoever eats my flesh and drinks my blood remains in me, and I in them.[10]

The dividing lines having been drawn, and, having described faith metaphorically as eating and drinking, Jesus once more explains every-thing: "*The words I have spoken* to you—they are full of the spirit and life" (6:63).[11] Believe his words.

This ties into Jesus' warning in Matthew 16: "be on your guard against the yeast of the Pharisees and Sadducees." The disciples think Jesus says this because they forgot to bring bread (Matt 16:6–7), but in 16:8–11 he sets his own feeding miracles alongside the false "bread" of the Pharisees and Sad-ducees. 16:12 then explains that Jesus refers to the teaching of the Pharisees and Sadducees. These words employ the language of table fellowship to speak of allegiances, theological structures, and ultimately life and death. They envisage fellowship with Jesus as the outworking of his teaching in the believer's life even as they warn against fraternizing with the enemy by partaking of their bread. Do not sit at table with those who teach falsely, for divided loyalties are deadly.

10. John 6:53–56.

11. A similar movement from metaphor to straightforward expression is found in John 3, where having confused Nicodemus by asserting that one cannot "see the kingdom of God" without a new birth (3:3) and cannot "enter the kingdom of God" without being "born of water and the Spirit" (3:5), in 3:15 Jesus says that "everyone who believes may have eternal life in him" and in 3:18 that "whoever believes in him is not condemned." Surely seeing and entering the kingdom point to overlapping realities, as do, at least in this context, having eternal life and not being condemned. In John 4 the imagery changes, so that everyone who "drinks the water I will give them will never thirst. Indeed, the water I give them will become in them a spring of water, welling up to eternal life" (4:14). Further examples of metaphors for faith abound.

Meals as Early Christian Fellowship

Acts repeatedly shows fellowship, inclusion and divine acceptance by means of meals. The church breaks bread together after Pentecost (2:42, 46). In chapter 9, the blinded Saul takes no food for three days (9:9), but after Ananias visits him, he eats. While the aftermath of Peter's preaching at Cornelius' house does not refer directly to food, close fellowship is nevertheless intended, and meals implied, by the words, "they asked Peter to stay with them for a few days" (10:48). After all, the central imagery of the chapter is formerly unclean food and people. Thus Peter eats with foreigners, but only after God drags him to the table. Lydia (16:16) and the Philippian jailer, following their conversion, host Paul and his party. 16:34 specifically relates that the jailer "set a meal before them." By means of these "fellowship meals," Luke shows that God extends his hospitality to foreigners, even former enemies.

If meals indicate solidarity, the offence implied in Acts 6 is great: the "Hellenistic Jews among them complained against the Hebraic Jews because their widows were being overlooked in the daily distribution of food" (6:1). Exclusion from fellowship, appropriately, is met with swift action as the apostles move to restore harmony. Paul is equally resolute in Antioch in the face of Peter's withdrawal from meals with gentiles, for that which has social implications elsewhere has theological ones in the church (Gal 2:11–21).

Uneaten Meals

Given these cultural resonances, refusing a dinner invitation is problematic, understood as disassociation or, as when David fails to appear before Saul (1 Sam 20), rebellion.[12] When Daniel rejects food, his motivation is not scruples about meat and wine (10:3 implies that such things form his normal diet).[13] He rejects food *from the king* (1:5, 8, 13, 15, 16).[14] Daniel 1:7 twice states that the chief official "determined" with respect to names. But in Daniel 1:8, with the same verb, Daniel "determines" that he will "not defile himself" with the king's food.[15] At least since Calvin it has been

12. Blomberg, *Contagious*, 43. See esp. Sharon, "When Fathers Refuse to Eat," 135–48.
13. Collins, *Daniel*, 143.
14. Seow, *Daniel*, 26.
15. Seow, *Daniel*, 26.

suggested that eating such things would erode his Jewish identity.[16] Given the biblical use of names to define the person, it is astonishing that Daniel adopts a new name and language, but draws a line at food. This sets him apart from Jehoiachin (2 Kgs 25:30), who, in partaking of the king's table, arguably enacts the complete subjugation of the house of David.[17] Daniel declares solidarity with the Lord and with the depravations of his people rather than with the conquering king.[18]

Not surprisingly, Jesus employs the metaphor of rejected invitations. His parable of the wedding banquet denounces invitees who refuse meals (Matt 22:1–14//Luke 14:16–24). Matthew 22:5–6 informs that prospective guests "paid no attention and went off—one to his field, another to his business. The rest seized his servants, mistreated them and killed them." Luke, without reference to abusing the servants, portrays a host who rejects those who refuse his hospitality: "I tell you, not one of those who were invited will get a taste of my banquet" (Luke 14:24).

Meals and Betrayal

Worse than rejecting an invitation is the hypocrisy of dining (thus embracing kinship) and then betraying one's host.[19] Meals provide the backdrop to Amnon's rape of Tamar (2 Sam 13:7–10) and Absalom's vengeance on Amnon (2 Sam 13:23–29). David in Psalm 41:9 writes, "Even my close friend, someone I trusted, one who shared my bread, has turned against me."[20] Just as unsettling as Judas' kiss is his betrayal of Jesus on the night they shared a meal—indeed, a covenantal meal. That the apostles join in, denying and abandoning Jesus, is comprehensible only to those who know the weakness of fearful humanity. That Jesus restores the apostles with a meal (John 21:12–13) is grace beyond comprehension.

16. Calvin, *Daniel*, 9:96–99.

17. Seow, *Daniel*, 26.

18. Collins (*Daniel*, 142–3) cites several figures from intertestamental literature who eschew such food.

19. Hugenberger, *Marriage*, 206.

20. This translation obscures the referent to the heel and possibly to Jacob. David charges, "he has lifted his heel against me," using a form that resembles Jacob's name (*'aqeb*).

Meals and Judgment

Food, especially during the divided monarchy, becomes God's vehicle of judgment on idolatry and apostasy. When Israel rejects him, God sends famine, implying that if Israel wants to eat with foreign gods,[21] the Lord will not eat with Israel. The prophets extend this food imagery, speaking no longer of famine but of invading armies that consume what Judah has worked for.[22] This connection of food and judgment flows into eschatological pronouncements. The prophets speak of two sorts of banquets: horrific meals of judgment and feasts of blessing.

In banquets of judgment, the guilty comprise the main course. The Major Prophets combine meal imagery with the language of sacrifice— this time God's deadly sacrifice—to indict those who oppose the Lord and his people.

Isaiah employs such imagery to describe the annihilation of Esau.

> My sword has drunk its fill in the heavens; see it descends in judgment on Edom, the people I have totally destroyed. The sword of the LORD is bathed in blood, it is covered with fat—the blood of lambs and goats, fat from the kidneys of the rams. For the LORD has a sacrifice in Bozrah and a great slaughter in Edom.[23]

Jeremiah, sharing Isaiah's sentiments, writes of sacrifice. Where in Isaiah the Lord wields the sword, here the sword itself is hungry and thirsty.

> But that day belongs to the LORD, the LORD Almighty—a day of vengeance, for vengeance on his foes. The sword will devour till it is satisfied, till it has quenched its thirst with blood. For the LORD, the LORD Almighty, will offer sacrifice in the land of the north by the River Euphrates.[24]

Ezekiel speaks not of a devouring sword but of nature itself participating in the sacrificial meal offered up by the Lord.

---

21. "The children gather wood, the fathers light the fire, and the women knead the dough and make cakes of bread for the Queen of Heaven. They pour out drink offerings to other gods to provoke me to anger" (Jer 7:18).

22. "I will take away their harvest declares the LORD. There will be no grapes on the vine. There will be no figs on the tree and their leaves will wither. What I have given them will be taken from them" (Jer 8:13; see also 5:17; Isa 32:12–13; 56:9).

23. Isa 34:5–6.

24. Jer 46:10.

Son of man, this is what the Sovereign LORD says: Call out to every kind of bird and all the wild animals: "Assemble and come together from all around to the sacrifice I am preparing for you, the great sacrifice on the mountains of Israel. There you will eat flesh and drink blood. You will eat the flesh of mighty men and drink the blood of the princes of the earth as if they were rams and lambs, goats and bulls—all of them fattened animals from Bashan. At the sacrifice I am preparing for you, you will eat fat till you are glutted and drink blood till you are drunk. At my table you will eat your fill of horses and riders, mighty men and soldiers of every kind," declares the Sovereign LORD.[25]

Those who refuse to acknowledge God are served up cold, a painful and literal lesson for Herod, who is eaten by worms (Acts 12:23). God thereby expresses his evaluation of this divine pretender. The king who undergoes decay before death is doubtless to be contrasted with King Jesus, who despite death will not see decay—which forms the text and subject of both Peter and Paul's first sermon in Acts (see Acts 2:27–31 and 13:34–35 respectively, citing Ps 16:10).

Another type of judgment meal envisages not the guilty as the meal, but as partakers of a menu provided by the Lord, "This is what the LORD, the God of Israel, said to me: 'Take from my hand this cup filled with the wine of my wrath and make all the nations to whom I send you drink it.'"[26]

Judgment meals culminate in Revelation 19:17–18, where an angel calls to the birds, "Come, gather together for the great supper of God, so that you may eat the flesh of kings, generals, and the mighty, of horses and their riders, and the flesh of all people, free and slave, great and small."[27]

Meals and Hope

But the prophetic vision does not end with meals of judgment. Isaiah's food oracles discriminate, and in so doing engender hope for those who believe. Addressing those who "forsake the LORD," he says:

25. Ezek 39:17–20.

26. Jer 25:15. See also Jer 9:15: "See, I will make this people eat bitter food and drink poisoned water"; Ezek 23:32–34; Zech 12:2.

27. Similarly Ezek 29:5, "I will give you as food to the beasts of the earth and the birds of the sky."

Therefore this is what the Sovereign LORD says: "My servants will eat, but you will go hungry; my servants will drink, but you will go thirsty; my servants will rejoice, but you will be put to shame. My servants will sing out of the joy of their hearts, but you will cry out from anguish of heart and wail in brokenness of spirit. You will leave your name to my chosen to use in their curses; the Sovereign LORD will put you to death, but to his servants he will give another name."[28]

The three tenses of meals as metaphor appear sequentially in Isaiah 32, moving from denunciation to judgment to blessing. Fools are condemned because they "practice ungodliness and spread error concerning the LORD." The shape of their sin is that "the hungry they leave empty and from the thirsty they withhold water" (32:6). God repays in kind. Because of this and other injustice, "the grape harvest will fail, and the harvest of fruit will not come. . . . Beat your breasts for the pleasant fields, for the fruitful vines and for the land of my people, a land overgrown with thorns and briers" (32:10, 12–13). But this will last only "till the Spirit is poured out upon us from on high, and the desert becomes a fertile field, and the fertile field seems like a forest. . . . [H]ow blessed you will be, sowing your seed by every stream, and letting your cattle and donkeys range free."[29]

The riches of the eschaton cannot, however, be contained by the imagery of feasts:

See, I will create new heavens and a new earth. The former things will not be remembered, nor will they come to mind. But be glad and rejoice forever in what I will create, for I will create Jerusalem to be a delight and its people a joy.[30]

God's overturning of the present order so impacts the cosmos that the prophet portrays the wolf as feeding not *on* but *with* the lamb, while lions will eat straw.[31] Revelation 7 picks up the language of Isaiah 55 to speak of the multitude from all nations: "Never again will they hunger; never again will they thirst. The sun will not beat down on them, nor any scorching

---

28. Isa 65:13–15.

29. Isa 32:15, 20. See also 30:23–24, and 51:17, 22–23, where God passes the cup of wrath which makes Israel stagger to the nations (so also Ezek 25:4–5), and 62:8, where the Lord swears to never again give Israel's grain and wine to the enemy.

30. Isa 65:17–18.

31. Isa 65:25; this recapitulates much of 11:6–7.

heat. For the Lamb at the center of the throne will be their shepherd; he will lead them to springs of living water" (Rev 7:16–17).

Christians taste this grace in the Lord's Supper, proclaiming with bread and wine solidarity with each other and the Lord who died for them. The breadth of this fellowship informs Hebrews 12:22–24, which describes the gathering thus:

> But you have come to Mount Zion, the city of the living God, the heavenly Jerusalem. You have come to thousands upon thousands of angels in joyful assembly, to the church of the firstborn, whose names are written in heaven. You have come to God, the Judge of all, to the spirits of the righteous made perfect, to Jesus the mediator of a new covenant, and to the sprinkled blood that speaks a better word than the blood of Abel.

With extravagant imagery Hebrews mixes welcome and warning, and exhorts the reader not to refuse this invitation (Heb 10:25).

Bibliography

Alexander, T. Desmond. *From Paradise to the Promised Land: An Introduction to the Main Themes of the Pentateuch.* Carlisle, UK: Paternoster, 1995.

Alter, Robert. *The Art of Biblical Narrative.* New York: Basic, 1981.

———. *Genesis.* New York: Norton, 1996.

Andersen, Francis I., and David Noel Freedman. *Hosea: A New Translation with Introduction and Commentary.* Anchor Bible 24. New York: Doubleday, 1980.

Ararat, Nissan. "Reading according to the 'Seder' in Biblical Narrative: To Balance the Reading of the Dinah Episode." *Hasifruit* 27 (1978) 15–34.

Arnold, Bill T. *Genesis.* New Cambridge Bible Commentary. Cambridge: Cambridge University Press, 2009.

Bar-Efrat, Shimon. *Narrative Art in the Bible.* Journal for the Study of the Old Testament Supplement Series 70. Sheffield, UK: Almond, 1989.

Bartholomew, Craig G., and Michael W. Gohee. *The Drama of Scripture: Finding Our Place in the Biblical Story.* Grand Rapids: Baker, 2004.

Bechtel, Lyn M. "What If Dinah Is Not Raped? (Genesis 34)." *Journal for the Study of the Old Testament* 62.1 (1994) 19–36.

Benjamin, Don C., and Victor H. Matthews. *Social World of Ancient Israel: 1250–587 BCE.* Peabody, MA: Hendrickson, 1993.

Berg, W. "Der Sündenfall Abrahams Und Saras Nach Gen 16:1–6." *Biblische Notizen* 19 (1982) 7–14.

Blomberg, Craig. *Contagious Holiness: Jesus' Meals with Sinners.* Downers Grove, IL: IVP, 2005.

Boling, Robert G., and G. Ernest Wright. *Joshua.* Anchor Bible 6. Garden City, NY: Doubleday, 1982.

Brant, Jo-Ann A. "Husband Hunting: Characterization and Narrative Art in the Gospel of John." *Biblical Interpretation* 4.2 (1996) 205–23.

Brett, Mark G. *Genesis: Procreation and the Politics of Identity.* Old Testament Readings. London: Routledge, 2000.

———. "The Politics of Marriage in Genesis." In *Making a Difference: Essays on the Bible and Judaism in Honor of Tamara Cohn Eskenazi*, edited by David J. A. Clines, Kent Harold Richards, Jacob L. Wright, 49–59. Sheffield, UK: Sheffield Phoenix, 2012.

Brueggemann, Walter. *A Commentary on Jeremiah: Exile and Homecoming.* Grand Rapids: Eerdmans, 1998.

———. *Genesis.* Interpretation. Atlanta: John Knox, 1982.

Bush, Frederic W. *Ruth, Esther.* Word Biblical Commentary 9. Nashville: Thomas Nelson, 1996.

Calvin, John. *Commentaries on the Book of the Prophet Daniel, Volume First.* Translated by Thomas Myers. Calvin's Commentaries, volume 9. Reprint, Grand Rapids: Baker, 1989.

———. *Commentaries on the First Book of Moses Called Genesis, Volume Second.* Translated by John King. Calvin's Commentaries, volume 2. Reprint, Grand Rapids: Baker, 1989.

Campbell, John K. *Honour, Family and Patronage: A Study of Institutions and Moral Values in a Greek Mountain Community.* Oxford: Oxford University Press, 1973.

Carroll, M. Daniel. "Hosea." In *Daniel–Malachi.* Expositor's Bible Commentary: Revised Edition, edited by Tremper Longman III, 8:213–305. Grand Rapids: Zondervan, 2008.

Cartledge, Tony W. *Vows in the Hebrew Bible and the Ancient Near East.* Journal for the Study of the Old Testament Supplement Series 147. Sheffield, UK: JSOT, 1992.

Cole, Dennis R. Numbers. *New American Commentary.* Nashville: Broadman & Holman, 2000.

Clines, David J. A. *The Theme of the Pentateuch.* Journal for the Study of the Old Testament Supplement Series 10. Sheffield, UK: JSOT, 1978.

Clowney, Edmund. "A Biblical Theology of Prayer." In *Teach Us to Pray: Prayer in the Bible and the World*, edited by D. A. Carson, 136–73. Grand Rapids: Baker, 1990.

Coats, George W. *Forms of Old Testament Literature: Genesis, with an Introduction to Narrative Literature.* Grand Rapids: Eerdmans, 1983.

Cohen, Chaim. *Biblical Hapax Legomena in the Light of Akkadian and Ugaritic.* Missoula, MT: Scholars, 1978.

Collins, John Joseph. *Daniel.* Hermeneia. Minneapolis: Fortress, 1993.

Couffignal, Robert. "Le Songe de Jacob: Approches Nouvelles de Genèse 28,10–22." *Biblica* 58 (1977) 342–60.

Daniels, Dwight R. *Hosea and Salvation History: The Early Traditions of Israel in the Prophecy of Hosea.* Berlin: de Gruyter, 1990.

Diamond, James Arthur. "The Deception of Jacob: A New Perspective on an Ancient Solution to the Problem." *Vetus Testamentum* 34.2 (1984) 211.

Dickemann, Mildred. "Women, Class, and Dowry." *American Anthropologist*, New Series, 93.4 (1991) 944–46.

Dodd, C. H. *The Interpretation of the Fourth Gospel.* Cambridge: Cambridge University Press, 1968.

Drazin, Israel. *Targum Onkelos to Numbers: An English Translation of the Text with Analysis and Commentary: Based on the A. Sperber and A. Berliner Edition.* Brooklyn: Ktav, 1998.

Driver, S. R. *The Book of Genesis.* 8th ed. London: Methuen, 1911.

Duguid, Iain M. *Living in the Grip of Relentless Grace: The Gospel in the Lives of Isaac & Jacob.* Phillipsburg, NJ: P&R, 2002.

Dumbrell, William J. *Covenant and Creation: An Old Testament Covenantal Theology.* Exeter, UK: Paternoster, 1984.

———. *The Search for Order: Biblical Eschatology in Focus.* Grand Rapids: Baker, 1994.

Eslinger, Lyle, "The Wooing of the Women at the Well: Jesus, the Reader and Reader Response Criticism." *Journal of Literature and Theology* 1.2 (1987) 167–83.

Evans, Craig A. "Typology." In *Dictionary of Jesus and the Gospels*, 862–66. Downers Grove, IL: IVP, 1992.

Fewell, Danna Nolan, and David M. Gunn. "Tipping the Balance: Sternberg's Reader and the Rape of Dinah." *Journal of Biblical Literature* 110.2 (1991) 193–211.

Finkelstein, Jacob J. "An Old Babylonian Herding Contract and Genesis 31:38f." *Journal of the American Oriental Society* 88.1 (1968) 30–36.

Firmage, Edwin. "Zoology." In *Anchor Bible Dictionary*, edited by David Noel Freedman, 6:1109–67. New York: Doubleday, 1992.

Fitzmyer, Joseph A. *The One Who Is to Come.* Grand Rapids: Eerdmans, 2007.

Fleishman, Joseph. "Why Did Simeon and Levi Rebuke Their Father in Genesis 34:31?" *Journal of Northwest Semitic Languages* 26.2 (2000) 101–16.

Fokkelman, Jan. P. *Narrative Art in Genesis: Specimens of Stylistic and Structural Analysis.* Assen: Van Gorcum, 1975.

Fretheim, Terence E. "The Book of Genesis: Introduction, Commentary, and Reflections." In *New Interpreter's Bible*, edited by Leander Keck, 1:319–674. Nashville: Abingdon, 1994.

———. *Exodus.* Interpretation. Louisville: John Knox, 1991.

Frymer-Kensky, Tikva. *In the Wake of the Goddesses: Women, Culture and the Biblical Transformation of Pagan Myth.* New York: Ballantine, 1993.

———. "Virginity." In *Gender and Law in the Hebrew Bible and the Ancient Near East*, edited by Tikva Frymer-Kensky, Bernard Levinson, and Victor H. Matthews, 79–98. Edinburgh: T. & T. Clark, 2004.

Glueck, Nelson. *Hesed in the Bible.* Translated by Alfred Gottschalk. Cincinnati: Hebrew Union College Press, 1967.

Goody, Jack. *Production and Reproduction: A Comparative Study of the Domestic Domain.* Cambridge: Cambridge University Press, 1976.

Graetz, Naomi. *Unlocking the Garden: A Feminist Jewish Look at the Bible, Midrash, and God.* Piscataway, NJ: Gorgias Press, 2004.

Greidanus, Sidney. *Preaching Christ from Genesis: Foundations for Expository Sermons.* Grand Rapids: Eerdmans, 2007.

Griffith, John G. "The Celestial Ladder and the Gate of Heaven [Genesis Xxviii 12, 17]." *Expository Times* 76 (1964) 229–30.

Gruber, Mayer I. "Review of Away from the Father's House: The Social Location of Naar and Naarah in Ancient Israel by Carolyn S Leeb." *Jewish Quarterly Review* 93.3 (2003) 612.

Gunkel, Hermann. *Genesis.* Macon, GA: Mercer University Press, 1997.

Hamilton, Victor P. *The Book of Genesis Chapters 18–50.* 2nd ed. New International Commentary on the Old Testament. Grand Rapids: Eerdmans, 1995.

———. "Šhl." In *New International Dictionary of Old Testament Theology and Exegesis*, edited by Willem A. VanGemeren, 4:106. Grand Rapids: Zondervan, 1997.

Hankore, Daniel. *The Abduction of Dinah: Reading Genesis 28:10—35:15 as a Votive Narrative.* Eugene, OR: Wipf & Stock, 2013.

Hari, Johann. "Kidnapped. Raped. Married. The Extraordinary Rebellion of Ethiopia's Abducted Wives." *The Independent*, Wednesday, March 17, 2010. http://www.independent.co.uk/news/world/africa/kidnapped-raped-married-the-extraordinary-rebellion-of-ethiopias-abducted-wives-1922263.html.

Hartley, John E. *Leviticus*. Word Biblical Commentary 4. Dallas: Word, 1992.

Hayashi, Noriko. "Grab and Run: Kyrgyzstan's Bride Kidnappings." *Newsweek*, November 4, 2013. http://www.newsweek.com/grab-and-run-1634.

Hepper, F. Nigel. *Baker Encyclopedia of Bible Plants: Flowers and Trees, Fruits and Vegetables, Ecology*. Grand Rapids: Baker, 1993.

Himmelfarb, Martha. *A Kingdom of Priests: Ancestry and Merit in Ancient Judaism*. Philadelphia: University of Pennsylvania Press, 2006.

House, Paul R. *1 & 2 Kings*. New American Commentary 8. Nashville: Broadman & Holman, 1995.

Houtman, C. "What Did Jacob See in His Dream at Bethel? Some Remarks on Genesis 28:10–22." *Vetus Testamentum* 27 (1977) 337–52.

Hugenberger, Gordon P. *Marriage as a Covenant: A Study of Biblical Law and Ethics Governing Marriage, Developed from the Perspective of Malachi*. Supplements to Vetus Testamentum, 52. Leiden: Brill, 1994.

Humphreys, W. Lee. *The Character of God in the Book of Genesis: A Narrative Appraisal*. Louisville: John Knox, 2001.

Jacobs, Mignon R. *Gender, Power, and Persuasion: The Genesis Narratives and Contemporary Portraits*. Grand Rapids: Baker, 2007.

Kaiser, Walter C. *Toward an Old Testament Theology*. Grand Rapids: Zondervan, 1978.

Kalluveettil, Paul. *Declaration and Covenant: A Comprehensive Review of Covenant Formulae from the Old Testament and the Ancient Near East*. Analecta Biblica 88. Rome: Biblical Institute, 1982.

Kaminsky, Joel S. *Yet I Loved Jacob: Reclaiming the Biblical Concept of Election*. Nashville: Abingdon, 2007.

Kidner, Derek, Genesis. *Tyndale Old Testament Commentaries*. Downers Grove, IL: IVP, 2008.

Kunin, Seth Daniel. *The Logic of Incest: A Structuralist Analysis of Hebrew Mythology*. Sheffield, UK: Sheffield Academic Press, 1995.

Landy, Francis. *Hosea*. Readings: A New Biblical Commentary. Sheffield, UK: Sheffield Academic Press, 1995.

Leeb, Carolyn S. *Away from the Father's House: The Social Location of Na'ar and Na'arah in Ancient Israel*. Journal for the Study of the Old Testament Supplement Series 301. Sheffield, UK: Sheffield Academic Press, 2000.

Lipton, Diana. *Revisions of the Night: Politics and Promises in the Patriarchal Dreams of Genesis*. Journal for the Study of the Old Testament Supplement Series 288. Sheffield, UK: Sheffield Academic Press, 1999.

Longman, Tremper, III. *How to Read Genesis*. Downers Grove, IL: IVP, 2005.

Maher, Michael, *Targum Pseudo-Jonathan: Genesis: Translated with Introduction and Notes*. The Aramaic Bible: The Targums, Volume 1B. Edinburgh: T. & T. Clark, 1992.

Mathews, Kenneth A. *Genesis 11:27—50:26*. New American Commentary. Nashville: Broadman & Holman, 2005.

McFall, L. "Sacred Meals." In *New Dictionary of Biblical Theology*, edited by T. Desmond Alexander and Brian S. Rosner, 750–53. Downers Grove, IL: IVP, 2000.

McKay, Heather A. "Making a Difference, Then and Now: The Very Different Lives and Afterlives of Dinah and Rizpah." In *Making a Difference: Essays on the Bible and Judaism in Honor of Tamara Cohn Eskenazi*, 224–41. Sheffield, UK: Sheffield Phoenix, 2012.

McKenzie, Brian Alexander. "Jacob's Blessing on Pharaoh: An Interpretation of Gen 46:31—47:26." *Westminster Theological Journal* 45 (1983) 386–99.

Mckenzie, Steven L. "The Jacob Tradition in Hosea XII 4–5." *Vetus Testamentum* 36.3 (1986) 311–22.

McKeown, James. *Genesis.* Two Horizons Old Testament Commentary. Grand Rapids: Eerdmans, 2008.

Meek, Theophile J. *Hebrew Origins.* First Harper Torchbook Edition. Gloucester, MA: Peter Smith, 1960.

Merrill, Eugene H. *Kingdom of Priests: A History of Old Testament Israel.* Grand Rapids: Baker, 1987.

Millard, Alan R. "The Celestial Ladder and the Gate of Heaven [Genesis Xxviii 12,17]." *Expository Times* 78 (1966) 86–87.

Mitchell, Christopher Wright. *The Meaning of Brk "to Bless" in the Old Testament.* Society of Biblical Literature Dissertation Series 95. Atlanta: Scholars, 1987.

Moberly, R. Walter. *Genesis 12–50.* Old Testament Guides. Sheffield, UK: Sheffield Academic Press, 1992.

Motyer, Alec. *The Prophecy Of Isaiah.* Downers Grove, IL: IVP, 1993.

Neusner, Jacob. *Genesis Rabbah: The Judaic Commentary on the Book of Genesis: A New American Translation: Volume III: Parashiyyot 68 through 100 on Genesis 28:10 to 50:26.* Brown Judaic Studies 106. Atlanta: Scholars, 1985.

Noble, Paul. "A 'Balanced' Reading of the Rape of Dinah: Some Exegetical and Methodological Observations." *Biblical Interpretation* 4.2 (1996) 174–204.

Nicholson, Ernest W. *God and His People: Covenant and Theology in the Old Testament.* Oxford: Clarendon, 1986.

Osborne, Grant R., *Revelation*, Baker Exegetical Commentary on the New Testament. Grand Rapids: Baker, 2002.

Pao, David W., and Eckhard J. Schnabel. "Luke." In *Commentary on the New Testament Use of the Old Testament*, edited by G. K. Beale and D. A. Carson, 251–414. Grand Rapids: Baker, 2007.

Parry, Robin. "Feminist Hermeneutics and Evangelical Concerns: The Rape of Dinah as a Case Study." In *Tamar's Tears: Evangelical Engagements with Feminist Old Testament Hermeneutics*, edited by Andrew Sloane, 30–64. Eugene: Pickwick, 2012.

———. *Old Testament Story and Christian Ethics: The Rape of Dinah as a Case Study.* Milton Keynes, UK: Paternoster, 2004.

Peleg, Yitzhak (Itzik). *Going Up and Going Down: A Key to Interpreting Jacob's Dream (Gen. 28:10–22).* Translated by Betty Rozen. Library of Hebrew Bible/Old Testament Studies 609. London: Bloomsbury T. & T. Clark, 2015.

Pitt-Rivers, Julian. *The Fate of Shechem, or the Politics of Sex: Essays in the Anthropology of the Mediterranean.* Cambridge Studies in Social Anthropology 19. Cambridge: Cambridge University Press, 1977.

Pressler, Carolyn. *The View of Women Found in the Deuteronomic Family Laws.* Berlin: de Gruyter, 1993.

Rad, Gerhard von. *Genesis: A Commentary.* Rev. ed. Old Testament Library. London: SCM, 1972.

Ross, Allen P. *Creation and Blessing: A Guide to the Study and Exposition of Genesis*. Grand Rapids: Baker, 1996.

Ross, J. F. "Meals." In *Interpreter's Dictionary of the Bible*, edited by Keith R. Crim and George A. Buttrick, 3:315–18. Nashville: Abingdon, 1976.

Ryken, Leland, Jim Wilhoit, Tremper Longman, Colin Duriez, Douglas Penney, and Daniel G. Reid, eds. "Stew." In *Dictionary of Biblical Imagery*, 814. Downers Grove, IL: IVP, 1998.

Sailhamer, John H. "Genesis." In *Genesis-Numbers. Expositor's Bible Commentary*, 2:3–284. Grand Rapids: Zondervan, 1990.

———. *The Meaning of the Pentateuch: Revelation, Composition, and Interpretation*. Downers Grove, IL: IVP, 2009.

———. *The Pentateuch as Narrative: A Biblical-Theological Commentary*. Library of Biblical Interpretation. Grand Rapids: Zondervan, 1992.

Sarna, Nahum M. *Genesis: The Traditional Hebrew Text with New JPS Translation/ Commentary*. The JPS Torah Commentary. Philadelphia: Jewish Publication Society, 1989.

Scharbert, J. "Brk." In *Theological Dictionary of the Old Testament*, edited by G. Johannes Botterweck and Helmer Ringgren; translated by Geoffrey W. Bromiley et al., 2:281–308. Grand Rapids: Eerdmans, 2004.

Schlegel, Alice. "Status, Property, and the Value of Virginity." *American Ethnologist* 18.4 (1991) 719–34.

Schneider, Tammi J. *Mothers of Promise: Women in the Book of Genesis*. Grand Rapids: Baker, 2008.

Scholz, Susanne. *Rape Plots: A Feminist Cultural Study of Genesis 34*. Studies in Biblical Literature 13. New York: Lang, 2000.

Schreiner, Thomas R. *Romans*. Baker Exegetical Commentary on the New Testament 6. Grand Rapids: Baker, 1998.

Seow, Choon Leong. *Daniel*. Westminster Bible Companion. Louisville: Westminster John Knox, 2003.

Sharon, Diane M. "When Fathers Refuse to Eat: The Trope of Rejecting Food and Drink in Biblical Narrative." *Semeia* 86 (1999) 135–48.

Sheres, Ita. *Dinah's Rebellion: A Biblical Parable for Our Time*. New York: Crossroad, 1990.

Staley, Jeffrey Lloyd. *The Print's First Kiss: A Rhetorical Investigation of the Implied Reader in the Fourth Gospel*. Society of Biblical Literature Dissertation Series 82. Atlanta: Scholars, 1988.

Sternberg, Meir. *The Poetics of Biblical Narrative: Ideological Literature and the Drama of Reading*. Reprint ed. Bloomington, IN: Indiana University Press, 1987.

Stiebert, Johanna. *Fathers and Daughters in the Hebrew Bible*. Oxford: Oxford University Press, 2013.

Stuart, Douglas K. *Hosea–Jonah*. Word Biblical Commentary 31. Fort Worth, TX: Word, 1987.

Syrén, Roger. *The Forsaken First-Born: A Study of a Recurrent Motif in the Patriarchal Narratives*. Journal for the Study of the Old Testament Supplement Series 133. Sheffield, UK: JSOT, 1993.

Thiessen, Matthew. "Protecting the Holy Race and Holy Space: Judith's Reenactment of the Slaughter of Shechem." *Journal for the Study of Judaism* 49 (2018) 165–88.

Turner, Laurence A. *Announcements of Plot in Genesis*. Journal for the Study of the Old Testament Supplement Series 96. Sheffield, UK: JSOT, 1990.

———. *Genesis*. Readings, a New Biblical Commentary. Sheffield, UK: Sheffield Academic Press, 2000.

Verhoef, Pieter A. *The Books of Haggai and Malachi*. Grand Rapids: Eerdmans, 1987.

Vos, Geerhardus. *Biblical Theology: Old and New Testaments*. Grand Rapids: Eerdmans, 1948.

Vrolijk, Paul D. *Jacob's Wealth: An Examination into the Nature and Role of Material Possessions in the Jacob-Cycle (Gen 25:19—35:29)*. Leiden: Brill, 2011.

Waltke, Bruce K. *A Commentary on Micah*. Grand Rapids: Eerdmans, 2007.

———. *Genesis: A Commentary*. Grand Rapids: Zondervan, 2001.

Walton, John H. *Ancient Near Eastern Thought and the Old Testament: Introducing the Conceptual World of the Hebrew Bible*. Grand Rapids: Baker, 2006.

———. *Genesis: From Biblical Text to Contemporary Life*. NIV Application Commentary. Grand Rapids: Zondervan, 2001.

Walton, Kevin. *Thou Traveller Unknown: The Presence and Absence of God in the Jacob Narrative*. Carlisle, UK: Paternoster, 2003.

Webb, Barry G. "Heaven on Earth: The Significance of the Tabernacle in Its Literary and Theological Context." In *Exploring Exodus: Literary, Theological and Contemporary Approaches*, edited by Brian S. Rosner and Paul R. Williamson, 154–76. Nottingham, UK: Apollos, 2008.

———. *The Message of Isaiah: On Eagles' Wings*. The Bible Speaks Today. Downers Grove, IL: IVP, 1996.

Wenham, Gordon J. *Exploring the Old Testament: A Guide to the Pentateuch*. Downers Grove, IL: IVP, 2003.

———. *Genesis 16–50*. Word Biblical Commentary 2. Dallas: Word, 1994.

———. *Story as Torah: Reading the Old Testament Ethically*. London: A & C Black, 2004.

Van Wolde, Ellen. "Does 'innâ Denote Rape? A Semantic Analysis of a Controversial Word." *Vetus Testamentum* 52.4 (2002) 528–44.

Westermann, Claus. *The Promises to the Fathers: Studies on the Patriarchal Narratives*. Translated by David Green. Philadelphia: Fortress, 1980.

Williams, Jenni. "Adding Insult to Injury? The Family Laws of Deuteronomy." In *Tamar's Tears: Evangelical Engagements with Feminist Old Testament Hermeneutics*, edited by Andrew Sloane, 84–111. Eugene, OR: Pickwick, 2012.

Wright, Christopher J. H. *The Mission of God: Unlocking the Bible's Grand Narrative*. Downers Grove, IL: IVP, 2006.

Youngblood, Ronald F. *The Book of Genesis: An Introductory Commentary*. 2nd ed. Grand Rapids: Baker, 1991.

Zakovitch, Yair. "A Survey of the Literary Study of the Bible in Israel." *Newsletter of the World Association for Jewish Studies* 20 (1982) 19–38.

Zlotnick, Helena. *Dinah's Daughters: Gender and Judaism from the Hebrew Bible to Late Antiquity*. Philadelphia: University of Pennsylvania Press, 2002.

Zucker, David J., and Moshe Reiss. *The Matriarchs of Genesis: Seven Women, Five Views*. Eugene, OR: Wipf and Stock, 2015.

Author Index

Schnabel, Eckhard J., 127n19, 128n22

Schneider, Tammi J., 103n12, 111n50, 114n67, 115nn70–72

Scholz, Susanne, 103n12, 103n17, 115n70

Schreiner, Thomas R., 60n39

Seow, Choon Leong, 160nn14–15, 161n17

Sharon, Diane M., 160n12

Sheres, Ita, 102n11, 117nn81–82, 118n83

Staley, Jeffrey Lloyd, 39n10

Sternberg, Meir, 104n22, 109n47

Stiebert, Johanna, 102n10, 107n40, 112nn61–62, 113n63

Stuart, Douglas K., 139n43

Syrén, Roger, 4n12

Thiessen, Matthew, 117n79

Turner, Laurence A., 22n1, 28n22, 33n48, 34n57, 38n9, 41n19, 43n24, 43n27, 44n29, 49n2, 54n20, 57n27, 70n19, 85n20, 96nn4–5, 97nn8–9, 124n11, 129n29

Van Wolde, Ellen, 106n29

Verhoef, Pieter A., 151n70

Vos, Gerhardus, xiii, 27n18, 34nn52–53

Vrolijk, Paul D., 102n7, 103n14, 115n68

Waltke, Bruce K., 13n18, 20n34, 23n3, 26n13, 29n27, 29n28, 32n42, 33nn45–47, 36n1, 40n13, 43n23, 52n6, 52n8, 52n10, 52n13, 54n19, 55n23, 57n30, 65n4, 66n6, 67n11, 69n17, 80n5, 86, 91n39, 101n3, 101n4, 102n8, 111n49,

112n60, 116n74, 119n91, 120n93, 146nn55–56

Walton, John, 4n11, 12n10, 19, 20, 26nn13–14, 27, 29n28, 34n55, 41n16, 42n20, 43n23, 52n6, 64n2, 67n10, 67n11, 67n12, 73n7, 74n14, 74n16, 76nn25–26, 80n3, 88n28, 120n95, 132n8

Walton, Kevin, 3n4, 3n7, 5n13, 8nn2–3, 28n21, 28n23, 30n30, 30n33, 47n33, 57n30, 67n14, 69n18, 72n2, 72n5, 89nn31–33, 91n37, 92n42, 93n45, 93nn47–48, 118n87

Webb, Barry G., 31n35, 133n16

Wenham, Gordon J., 3n4, 9n6, 29n24, 29n25, 30n32, 32n44, 33n49, 34n51, 38n7, 41n17, 43n23, 45n32, 51n4, 52n11, 67n11, 69n17, 74n17, 75nn20–21, 76n24, 77n27, 80n6, 86n24, 91n37, 92n43, 101n1, 102n8, 102n9, 103n15, 119n90, 120n93, 137n34

Westermann, Claus, 14n20, 97n8

Williams, Jenni, 105n24, 107n38, 107nn35–37

Wright, Christopher J. H., 122n4

Wright, G. Ernest, 116n75

Youngblood, Ronald F., 23n2

Zakovitch, Yair, 104n22

Zlotnick, Helena, 112n61

Zucker, David J., 41n16, 73n12, 107n39

Subject Index

abductive marriage, 103–4, 110
Abraham
  failures, 45–46, 50, 116
  faith, 7, 26, 29
  journeys, 26, 99, 101
  kingly descendant, 122, 125, 147
  promises to, 1, 11, 19, 25, 28, 55, 80,
    124, 125, 131, 131–32, 146, 151
Abraham's servant, 38, 40, 81
Amalek, 23
Amnon, 105
angels, 27, 79–80, 90
Asher, 53, 56
atonement, 86–87

Babel, 29
Balaam, 131, 135–37, 138, 146
bargaining, 4, 33–34, 41–42, 66–67,
  109–10, 113–14
Benjamin, 126–27
Bethel, 30, 79, 123–24, 140–41
Bethlehem, 126–27, 145–47
Bilhah, 50–52, 128
birthright, 1–6, 14, 132n8, 148
blessing
  to Abraham, 81
  in Christ, 83–84
  to Esau, 96–97

to Jacob, 7–21, 25, 42, 65–66, 72, 76,
  84, 90–94, 96, 124, 132, 146
to Jacob's sons, 119–20, 128, 131, 137
to Judah, 132, 137–38, 146
and meals, 156
to the nations, 28, 118, 128
to Pharaoh, xii
see also promises
Bozrah, 133–34
bride price, 42
brothers, in Genesis, 2, 17, 18, 107–8, 144

Cain, 18
Canaan, 99–100, 129
childbirth, 126, 145, 147
church, the, 6, 17, 31, 160
clothing, 9–10, 15n21, 124, 133, 134
covenant, 33, 81–83, 149–51, 156
see also promises
curse, 9, 11–12, 16–17, 19, 22, 119, 128

Dan, 52, 56
Daniel, 136–37, 160–61
David, 82–83, 108, 146
Davidic King, 61
Deborah, 124, 129
deception, 8n3, 148–49
see also Jacob, as deceiver
descendants, 28, 58

179

Laban, 37, 40–42, 43, 44, 65–68, 72–76, 107
land, 18, 25, 28, 99–100, 125–26,
Leah, 41, 42–43, 46–47, 48–50, 52–57, 72–73
Levi, 49, 50, 115, 116, 119
limping, 147
lion/lioness, 132, 135, 157, 164
Lord's Supper, 165

magic, 69–70
Mahanaim, 79
marriage, 107–9
see also abductive marriage; Esau, marriages; Jacob, marriages
meals, 5, 155–65
Messiah, 61–62, 127–28, 130–31, 133, 135, 138, 145–46, 150, 154
Migdal Eder, 146–47
Moses, 38, 82, 143

Naphtali, 52, 56
nations, 11, 28, 118, 125, 128

Pentateuch, xii, 130–38
Pharaoh, xi, 20–21
pillars, 30, 32–33, 77
prayer, 80–81, 84–85
pride, 149
promises, xii–xiv, 16, 28–29, 80–81, 120, 143
see also Abraham, promises to; blessing
prophets, 142–43

Rachel, 37–38, 40, 41, 46–47, 48–52, 53–57, 64, 72–73, 126–27, 129
Ramah, 126
rape, 111–12, 118
Rebekah, xii, 2, 4, 8–10, 11–12, 14, 22–23, 24, 50, 127
reconciliation, 1–2, 86–87
red, 3, 4, 69, 125, 133–34
relationship, 1, 155–58
remembering, 56–57
Reuben, 49–50, 56–57, 119, 128

sacrifice, 86, 87, 157–58, 162–63
Sarah, 45
Saul, 108
shame, 111–12, 113
Shechem/Shechemites, 103–6, 110, 111–16
Simeon, 49, 50, 110–11, 115, 116, 119
slavery, 65, 76, 142

Tamar, 105, 131
temple, 31–32
toledot, 122–23, 129, 130

warrior, 133–34
weakness, 92–93
wrestling, 88–92, 93–94

Zebulun, 55
Zilpah, 52–53

Ancient Document Index

Genesis (continued)

Made in the USA
Middletown, DE
13 December 2021